IMAGES
of America

NORTHERN CAMBRIA

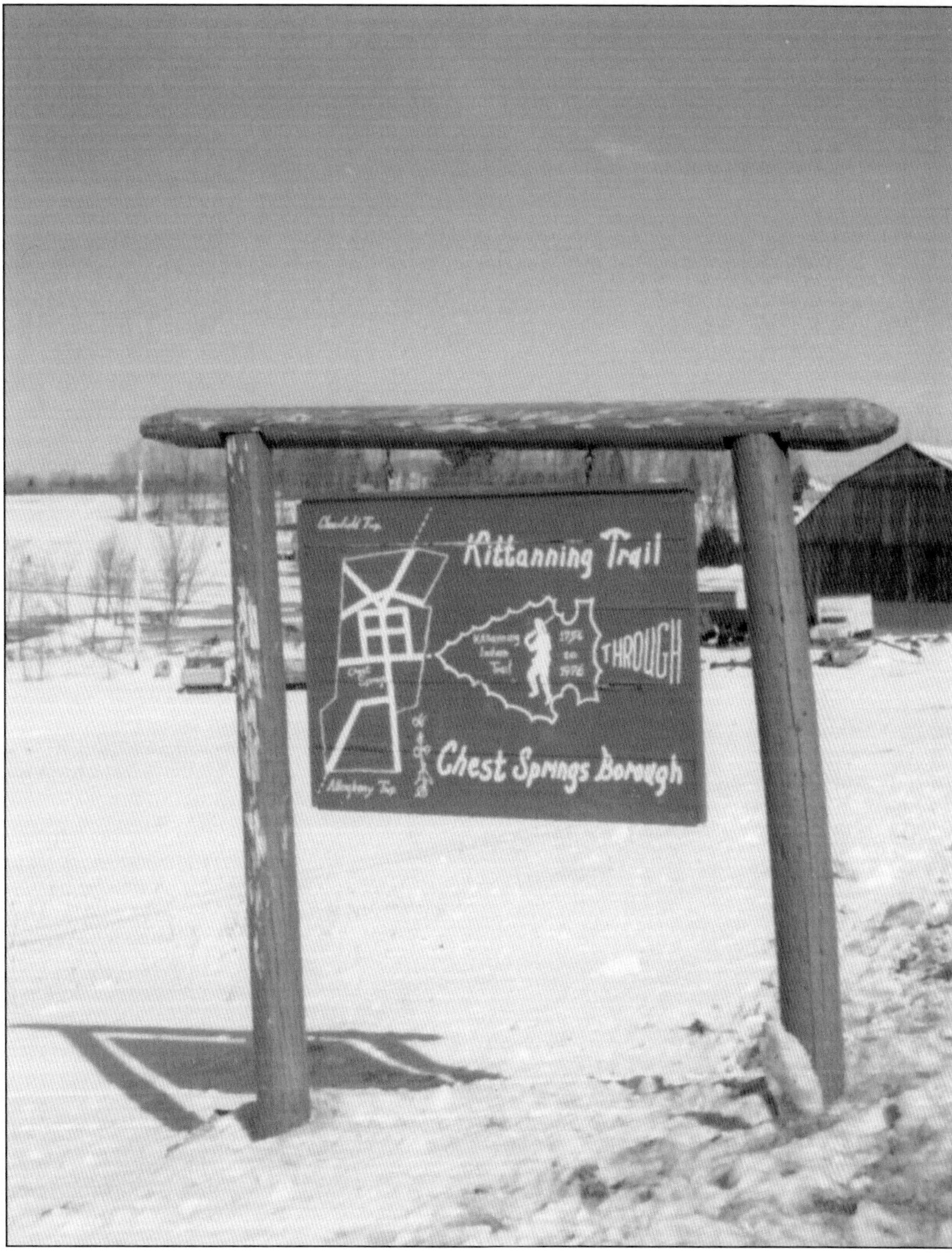

The Kittaning Trail crossed Cambria County in an east–west course through Ashville, Chest Springs, Carrolltown, Patton, Hastings, and Cherry Tree. The 23-mile trail offered the best route over the mountain from the Valley of Altoona in the east to the Valley of Kittanning in the west. Encampments were established along the trail. Mountain streams provided an abundant supply of water.

IMAGES
of America

NORTHERN CAMBRIA

Sr. Anne Frances Pulling

ARCADIA
PUBLISHING

ISBN 978-0-7385-0415-5

Published by Arcadia Publishing
Charleston, South Carolina

Printed in the United States of America

Library of Congress Catalog Card Number: applied for

For all general information contact Arcadia Publishing at:
Telephone 843-853-2070
Fax 843-853-0044
E-mail sales@arcadiapublishing.com
For customer service and orders:
Toll-Free 1-888-313-2665

Visit us on the Internet at www.arcadiapublishing.com

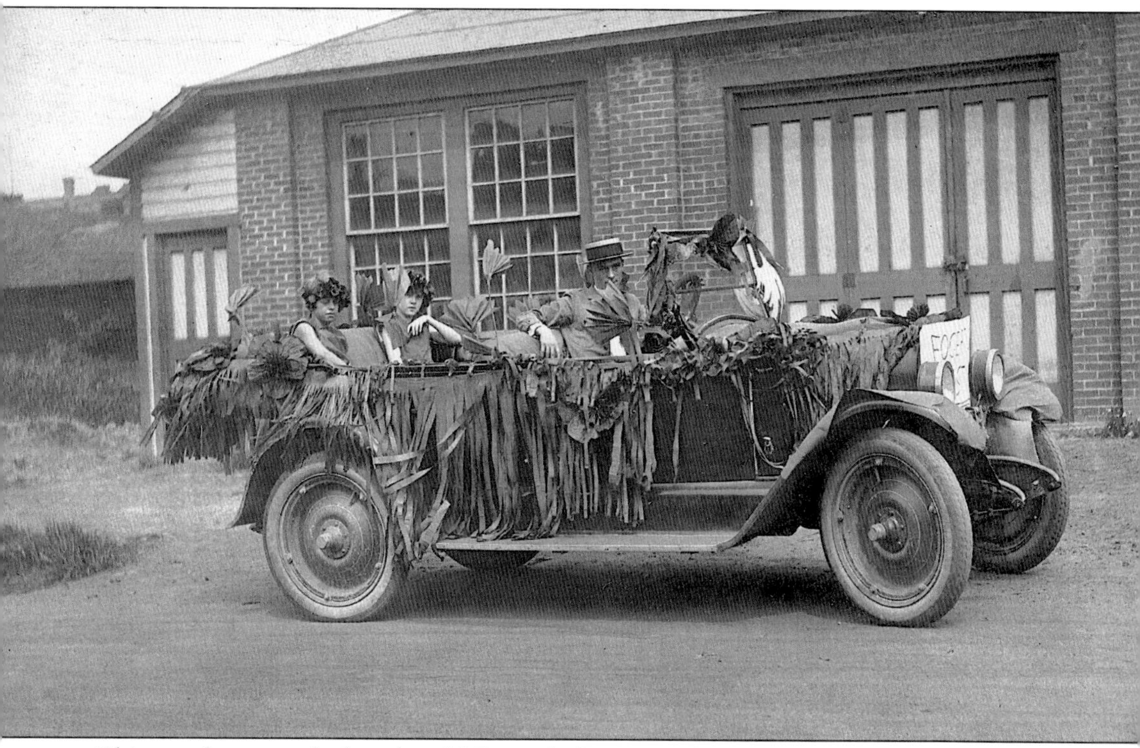

This parade car, parked at the old Dietrick Garage on Lang Avenue in Patton, is ready for action. Early in the second decade of the 20th century, parades featured the new innovation of open-air cars. Note the driver's flat straw hat and the flowered hats of his passengers. This mode of transportation became commonplace during the Roaring Twenties. The car is waiting to join an Independence Day parade through Patton.

Contents

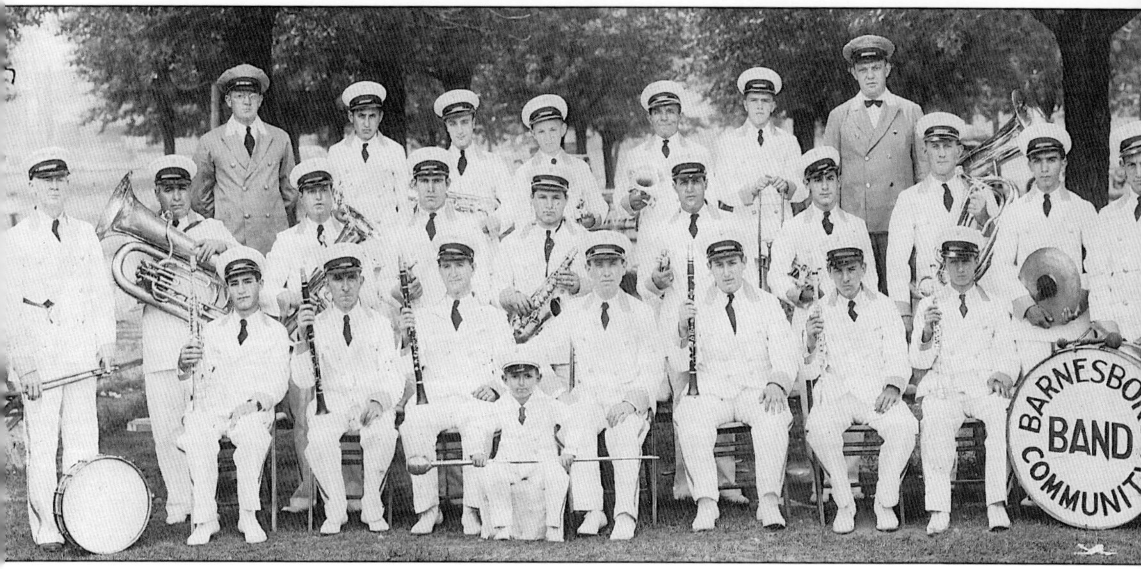

The members of the Barnesboro Band were performers as well as musicians. In the decade preceding the Great Depression, Barnesboro enjoyed a period of well-earned success. The mines brought a steady payroll and the town was bustling with achievement. Businesses were springing up, and Northern Cambria residents looked to Barnesboro for necessities as well as entertainment and diversion. In that era, several marching bands entertained the population at parades and concerts.

ACKNOWLEDGMENTS

This publication is based on research, records, periodicals, documents, newspapers, and interviews with townsfolk knowledgeable on local history, many of whom supplied information and offered constructive suggestions. A special thank-you goes to Helen and Richard Paige for sharing many photographs, a wealth of knowledge, and the initial thrust this project needed.

A word of gratitude goes to the Cambria County Historical Society, Fred Nastasi of the Boro Office, Alice and Charles Krug for the Heritage wagon trains, Herman and Rosemary Lieb, William Martin, Anne Kokus, Anne and George Stoyka for his expertise on the coalmines, Dolores Yeckley, David Huber, Rose Funare of Colver, Sharon Killen of the Co-generation plant, John Smylniky, Arthur Julian, John Paul and David E. Thompson of the *Mountaineer Herald*, and Daniel Connell—all of whom were most helpful supplying information and photographs. A special thank-you goes to the first mayor of Northern Cambria, Gennaro Cantalupo, and to Ben Root, who first recognized the value of merging municipalities. Gratitude goes to Fr. Owen Gallagher for his phrase "Tilling Field and Delving Mine."

A prayerful gratitude goes to all who assisted in any way by supplying photographs, constructive suggestions, assistance with captions, proofreading, et cetera. I am especially grateful to my own religious community, the Sisters of Mercy of the Dallas Regional Community, for their support and encouragement in this project.

INTRODUCTION

Northern Cambria is a new millennium entity. It is comprised of Barnesboro and Spangler, two century-old independent communities that have recently merged into one municipality known as Northern Cambria. This name has long been applied to all those towns and villages that lie north of the county seat, Ebensburg. Cambria County is shaped like an uneven parallelogram. Its eastern boundary follows the crest of the Allegheny Mountains, and the county contains a continental divide known as Dividing Ridge. The county was formed on March 26, 1804, consisting of 695 square miles of dense forest.

The land held an abundance of virgin forests of oak, white pine, hemlock, cherry, poplar, chestnut, beech, and birch trees. This dense acreage led to the development of numerous sawmills. Ideal conditions for timber production in the Alleghenies created choice wood. Trees were felled and logs were floated on rafts down the Chest Creek to the Susquehanna and on to Williamsport, the lumbering capital of the world, where the wood was sorted and identified.

Logging was prominent because of the county's huge acreage of vital timber. Between 1850 and 1890, 15 billion feet of lumber were floated down to the Susquehanna on rafts. The last raft left Cambria County in 1896. Logging created a need for agricultural pursuits. Scenic farmland was cleared and cultivated. Railroad lines spread across the county, and manufacturing plants drew immigrants. Lumbering and farming were the prominent sources of income for the earliest settlers.

In the late 19th century, veins of rich bituminous coal were discovered beneath the picturesque rolling hills high in the Allegheny Mountains. Millions of years ago, most of Pennsylvania was a heavily vegetated swampland. Plant debris sank, and shifting tides added additional debris. Erosion and landslides added intense pressure. Heat forced the gas and moisture out of the decayed matter, resulting in coal. In 1841, a geological society was formed to obtain information on mineral resources in the state of Pennsylvania. The group discovered bituminous coal beds in Cambria County. Once word of this natural resource was circulated, interest in opening new railroad lines to the coalfields became paramount. The coal industry picked up with the coming of the railroad.

Bituminous coal, common to Cambria County, creates dust and burns longer, but is not as hot or hard as anthracite coal, which is plentiful in eastern Pennsylvania. Anthracite coal creates less dust and burns hotter, but for less time than bituminous coal. The extraction of coal from deep within the earth became the life of the Northern Cambria community. Coalmines became numerous amid the spectacular marvels of nature. Black diamonds, as coal was dubbed, were extracted in thousands of tons and provided not only heat, but also a means of support for many immigrants. Man had learned to delve into the earth and remove this commodity that would change the face of Northern Cambria. The immense tonnage of coal found in the region led to a thriving steel production. Coal had become king.

A miner prepared for his subterranean venture in the engine house. In the very early days of mining, carbide lamps with open flames were used. Later, battery-operated lamps guided the miner to his work. The distance from the entrance to the miner's workplace was often many miles. The miner left boundless space and weather changes behind him for a stark, prehistoric fossil world. Limited mobility was obvious as he rode to his dark destination. The miner was faced with a sense of restriction in an austere milieu. Miners worked on the buddy system; however, a buddy existed only as a helmet light or the noise of a shovel. There was no verbal communication.

The golden era of coalmining gradually declined. A diminishing demand for coal created layoffs in 1980. Former miners left the area to seek employment elsewhere. Others returned to school to be retrained in new careers. Mount Aloysius College in Cresson trained many former miners in diverse pursuits. Today, the mines are sealed and abandoned. They stand in silent tribute to those thousands of immigrants who came to forge an existence in the new world. Strip mines, where machines do the digging, continue to function.

Ebensburg came into existence more than seven years before the county was formed. Welsh immigrants made their way from Philadelphia to the Allegheny Plateau in the fall of 1796. They were led by the Reverend Rees Lloyd. During the first winter, Lloyd was quick to recognize the needs of his community. His little band patiently created a permanent settlement with dwellings and sawmills. He ensured the survival of the community by his constant presence and leadership. Lloyd donated land for the first courthouse on March 5, 1805. He named the county for his homeland of Wales. *Cymru* in Welsh is *Cambria* in Latin.

In the spring of 1797, a second group of Welsh immigrants bypassed Lloyd's community and settled one mile west in the vicinity of present-day Revloc. Led by the Reverend Morgan John Rhys, the tiny settlement was called Beulah. Cabins were constructed and Rhys advertised along the east coast the availability of land for purchase in the mountains. Among those who bought land in Beulah were Joseph Priestly, the discoverer of oxygen. Rhys returned to Philadelphia and left his band of settlers to face the harsh mountain winters. The decline of Beulah was precipitated by settlers in search of warmer climates. The settlement rapidly phased into history.

Lloyd built the first house of worship in the settlement in 1798 and named it the Ebenezer Chapel. He had been ordained in the Ebenezer Church in Wales. Ebenezer was written into an old Welsh hymn that evolved into an appropriate name for the new county seat, Ebensburg.

One

A Millennium Borough

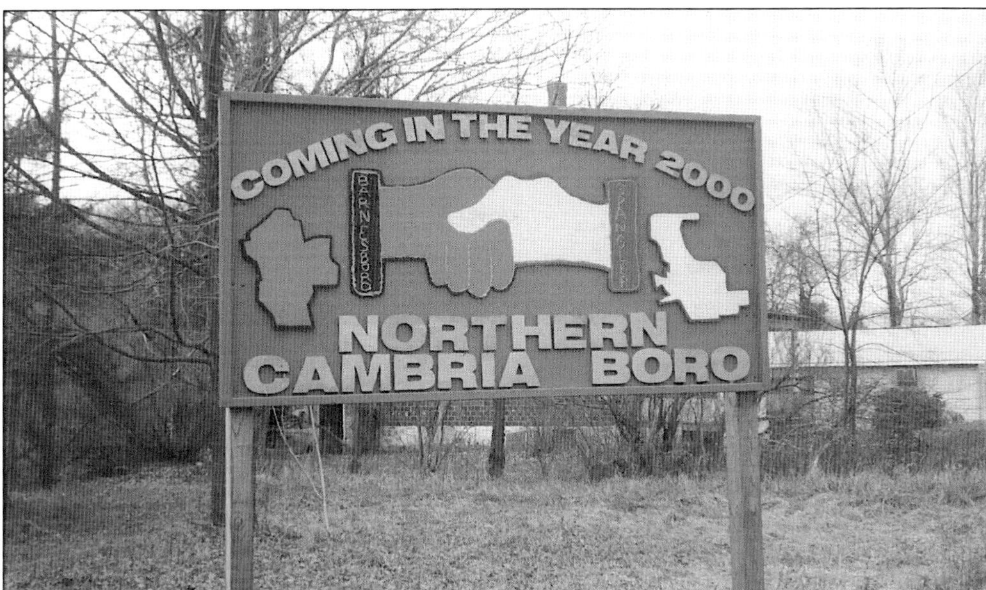

Northern Cambria is a new millennium entity. Comprised of Barnesboro and Spangler, both century-old independent communities, the two have merged into one municipality known as Northern Cambria. This title has long been applied to all the hamlets north of the county seat, Ebensburg. Cambria County was formed on March 26, 1804. It comprised 695 square miles of dense forest. Welsh immigrants had settled in the area; hence, it was named Cambria, the Welsh name for Wales. Rich bituminous coal veins were discovered beneath the picturesque rolling hills of Cambria County.

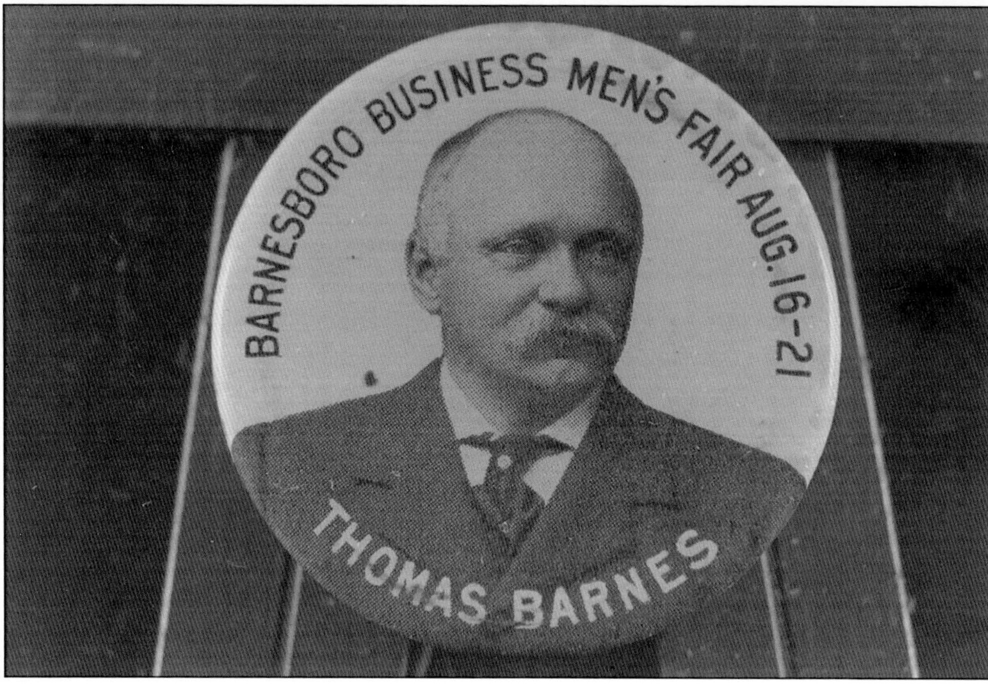

Thomas Barnes, for whom Barnesboro was originally named, was born in 1843 in England. Two brothers preceded him to Philipsburg. Once Barnes owned and operated his own mines, he sent for his fiancée, Ann Ashcroft. The couple was married in 1864. She was an asset to his mining business. Barnes became president of the Moshannon Bank in Philipsburg. In 1899, he became interested in the virgin coalfields of Cambria County. The family relocated and built a home in North Barnesboro called Hillcrest.

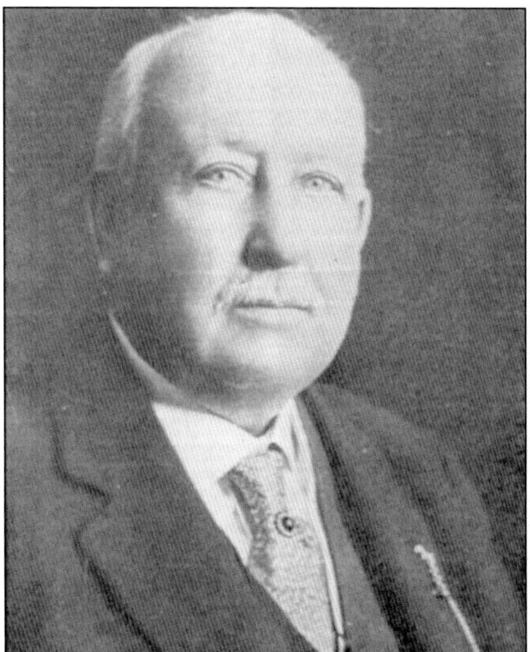

Jackson Levi Spangler was born September 27, 1849 in Snyder County. The family relocated in 1860. He attended Dickinson Seminary and studied law. Admitted to the bar in 1874, he formed the Spangler & Hewes law firm. Spangler became interested in the coalfields of the area while retaining an interest in politics. Colonel Spangler bought 12,000 acres of coal lands and developed the Bluebaker Coal Company. He was also general manager of the Sterling Coal Company.

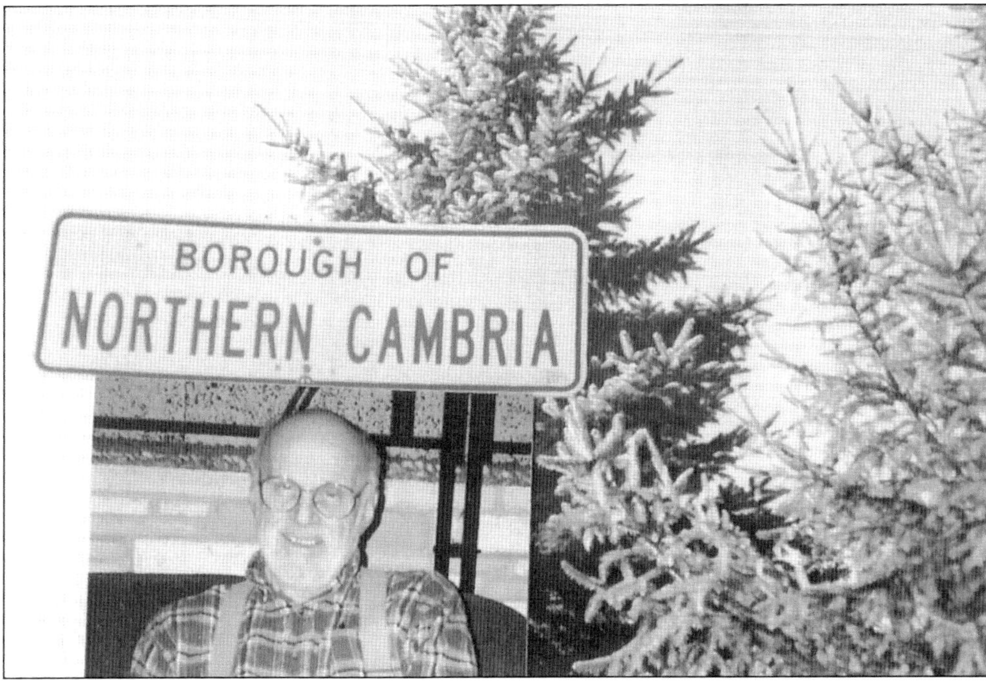

Ben Root was chairman of the consolidation project, the guiding force behind merging Barnesboro and Spangler. He graduated from North Carolina State University and has resided in Northern Cambria for the past half century. The combined population of 4,600 qualifies the merged town to "entitlement community" status. This grants the new borough $122,000 per year for revitalization projects, streets, or recreational facilities.

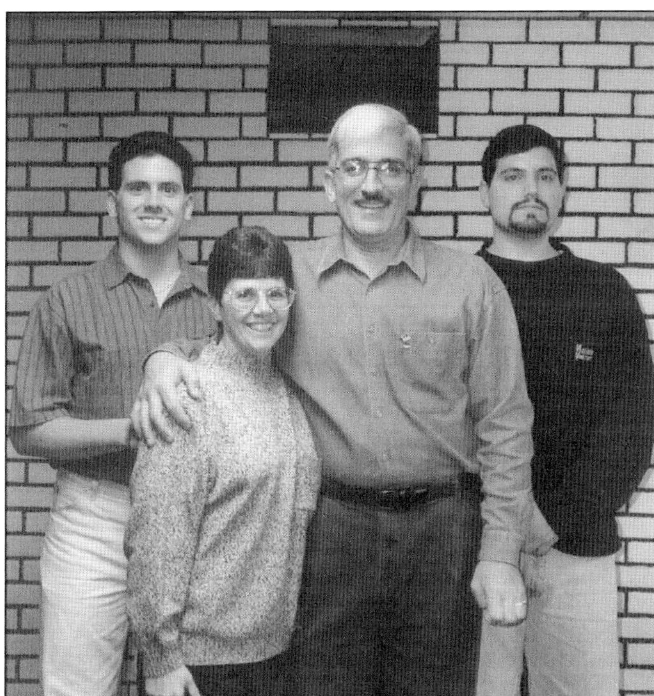

Mayor Gennaro Cantalupo with his wife, Maria, and his sons, Paul and David, has taken on an historic challenge. He was elected the first mayor of Northern Cambria Borough, a consolidation of the municipalities of Barnesboro and Spangler. Cantalupo will initiate unification and lead the new borough into revitalization and stability. A graduate of Lock Haven University and the University of Pittsburgh, he is librarian at North Cambria High School.

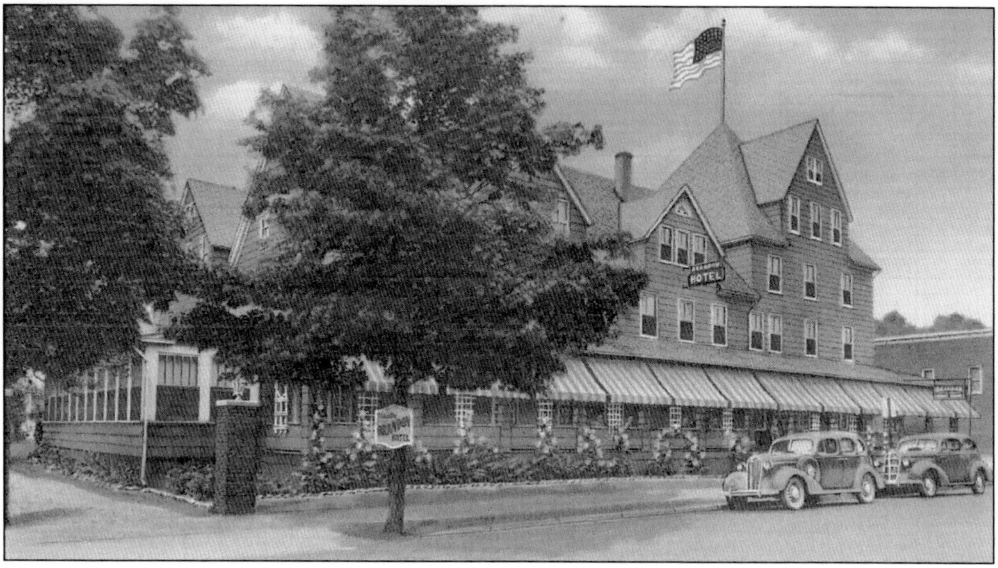

The Brandon Hotel in Spangler was built on the corner of Bigler Avenue and Fourth Street in 1893. This three-story hotel was built in colonial style and accommodated 60 patrons. The Brandon's proximity to the railroad and its reputation of clean, comfortable lodging made it quite popular. Summer band concerts were held on its veranda. The Brandon was renowned for its Sunday dinners. Hotels were a necessity in the early days, but they declined with the advent of the automobile.

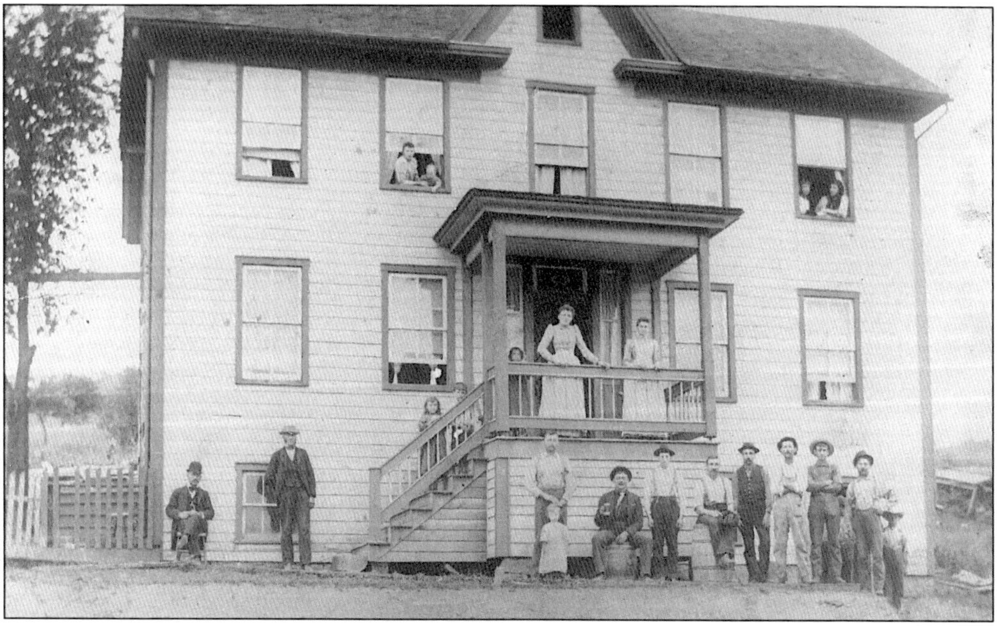

The Franklyn Hotel was part of the Spangler landscape early in the 20th century. Constructed in 1892 on Bigler Avenue in Susquehanna Township, it was later owned by Mr. Gordon. Those in the photograph are as follows: Frank H. Bearer and his little son Earl stand beneath the porch; Rose Bearer Luther with her son Clair are at the left window; Edith and Ralph Bearer are the children on the porch steps. Others are patrons of the Franklyn Hotel. The population grew faster than housing, creating a thriving hotel business.

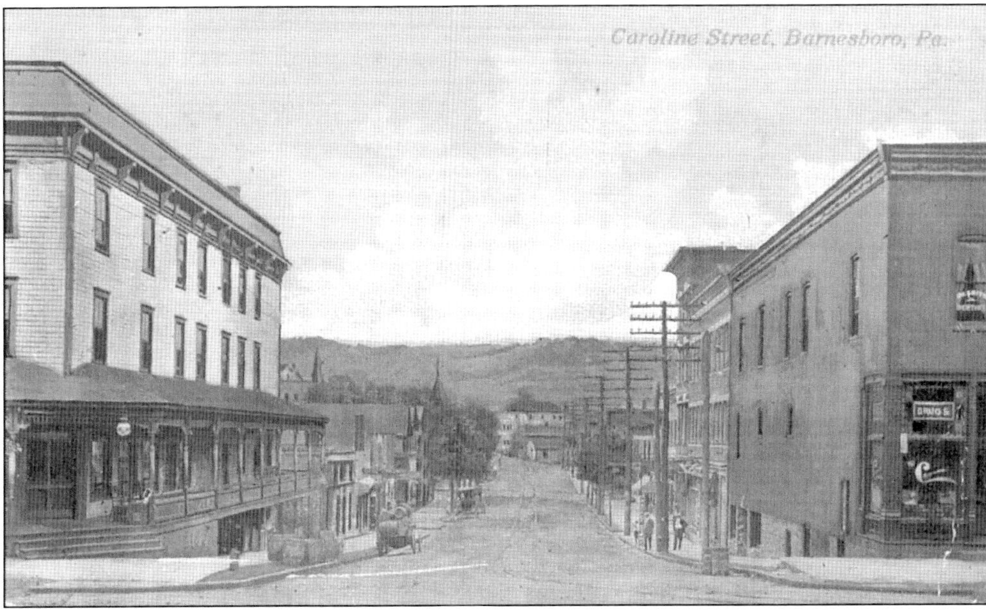

This 1908 image features the Commercial Hotel on the left, at the corner of Barnesboro's Caroline Street and Philadelphia Avenue. Tenth Street was then Caroline Street and Philadelphia Avenue was Pine Street. Trolleys necessitated that Philadelphia Avenue be graded from the square to the north end, where tracks were laid. When trolley operations ceased in 1926, the tracks were removed and the main street through town was rerouted into Route 219. Note the tracks extending from the right down Caroline Street.

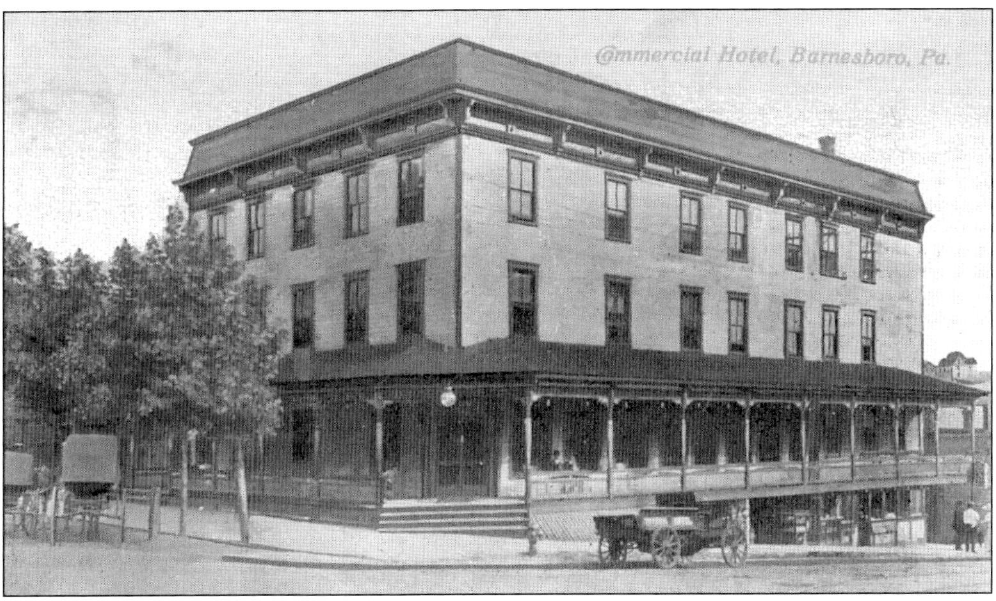

In its original setting, the Commercial Hotel was constructed on the corner of Philadelphia Avenue and Tenth Street in 1908. Its elaborate porch was an attractive luxury for early settlers. In May 1923, it took two weeks to move the huge structure one block with one mule. The Barnesboro of the 1920s was a thriving business community. Families resided in hotels for months and sometimes longer while waiting to move into their newly constructed homes.

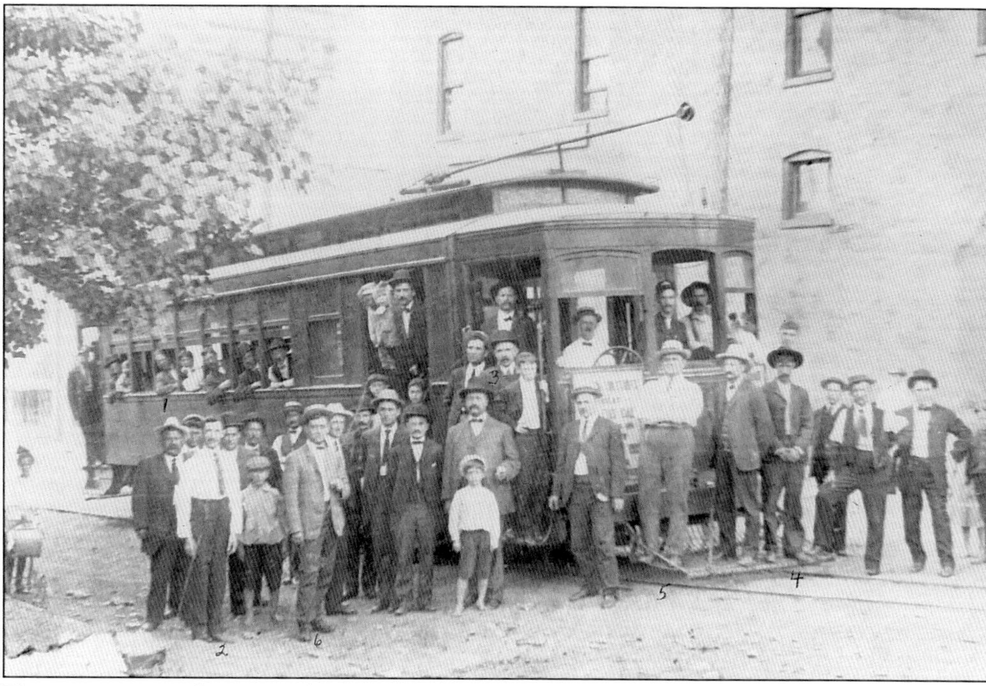

The streetcar made its maiden run in 1902. Pausing on the corner of Tenth Street and Philadelphia Avenue in Barnesboro, it made hourly stops through Northern Cambria. The goal was to establish transportation from Patton to Barnesboro with a spur line to Carrolltown. Lawrence Kline is the motorman. The others are, from left to right, John McCormick, Henry Friedman, William Delinger, Abe Dougher, Frank McAnulty, and Frank Wood. The last run was made on March 13, 1926.

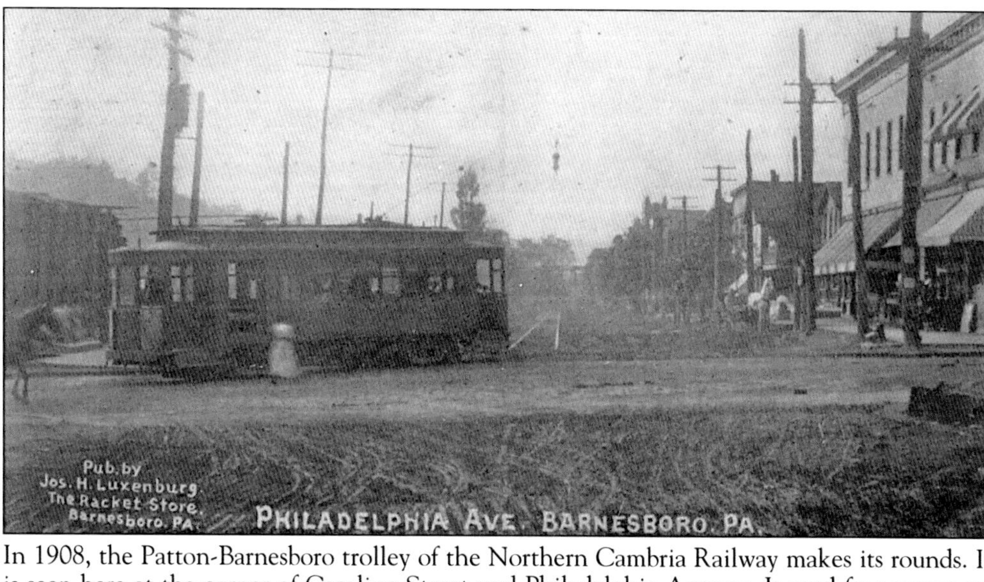

In 1908, the Patton-Barnesboro trolley of the Northern Cambria Railway makes its rounds. It is seen here at the corner of Caroline Street and Philadelphia Avenue. It used four passenger cars with baggage compartments. When it reached the end of the line at 25th Street near the Barnesboro Cemetery, the motorman turned the trolley pole around, moved to the opposite end of the car and headed back in the opposite direction. Note the horse behind the trolley.

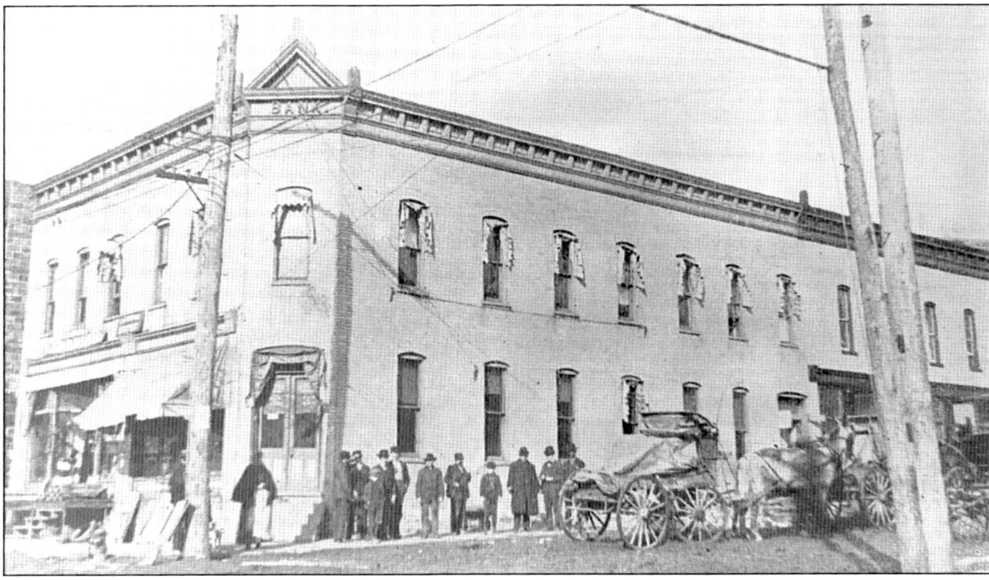

The Barnesboro Bank was the first bank in what is now Northern Cambria. Population and businesses were on the rise. The area's golden age of coal had dawned. The business section of town was already thriving when it shifted from the hilltop to the crossroads. The crossroads would later be called the square. The town was bustling with commerce when the bank was constructed on the square. The new enterprise accommodated miners, farmers, and merchants alike.

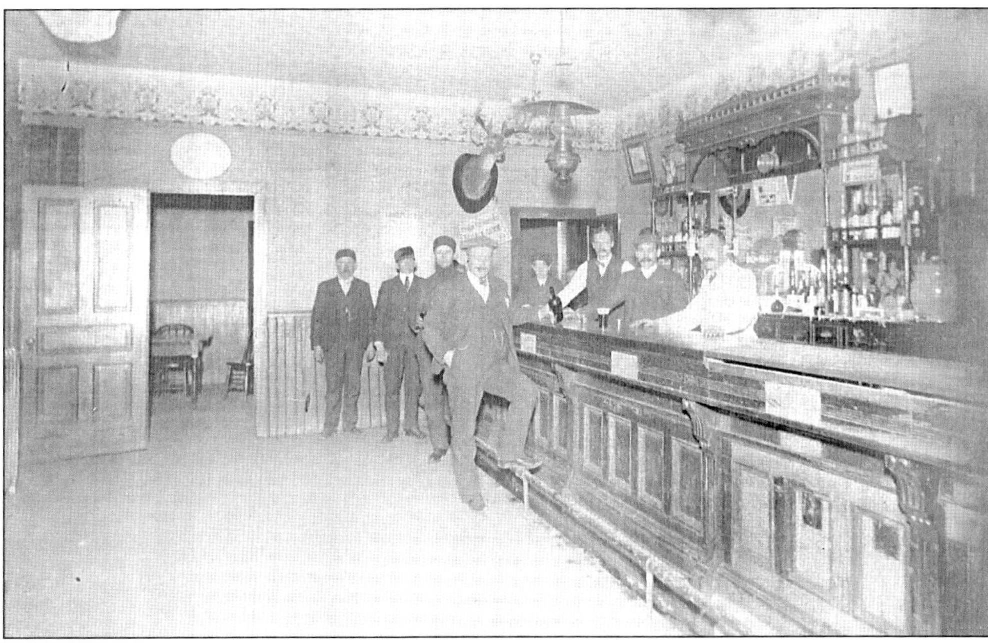

In the barroom of the Antler Hotel, formerly the Eureka Hotel, there were innovative cuspidors for tobacco-chewing gentlemen. A trough was installed along the floor that encircled the bar with running water. Debris was quickly carried away as a clean stream of water flowed continuously. The Antler Hotel was located on the corner of Maple Street and Tenth Avenue, where the PNC bank now stands. Hotel lobbies often set the stage for business meetings.

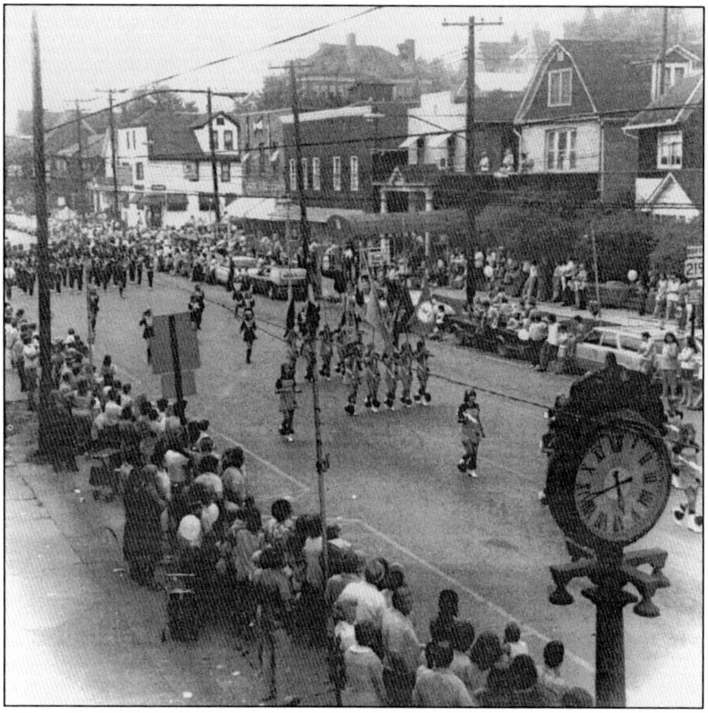

Parades drew thousands of spectators to Barnesboro early in the 20th century and this Firemen's Convention parade of 1902 was no exception. The town clock was bought by Louis Luxenberg, a merchant and one-time mayor. He placed the 15-foot cast-iron clock in front of his store on Philadelphia Avenue in 1915. It became a landmark and many referred to it as "Louie's clock." In 1992, it was refurbished and donated to the borough.

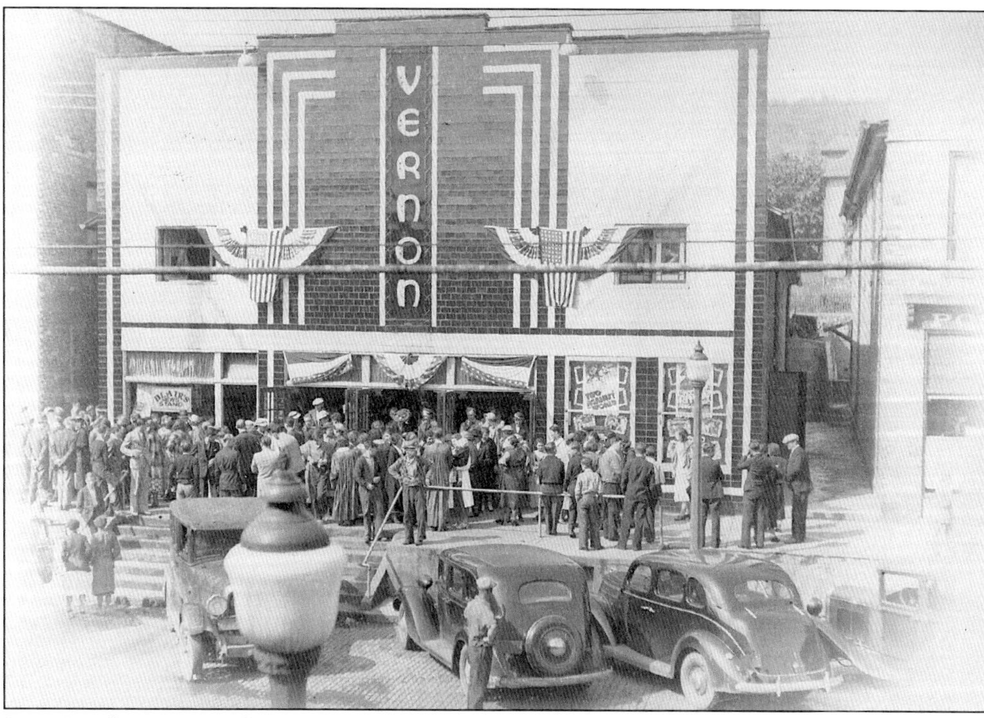

In 1939, the Vernon theater sponsored Barnesboro's high school graduation. Located in the area of Friedman Park on Philadelphia Avenue, it was the last theater in town. Blair's News Stand is on the left. A few graduates can be seen greeting their parents and relatives. The Vernon theater was consumed by fire in 1975.

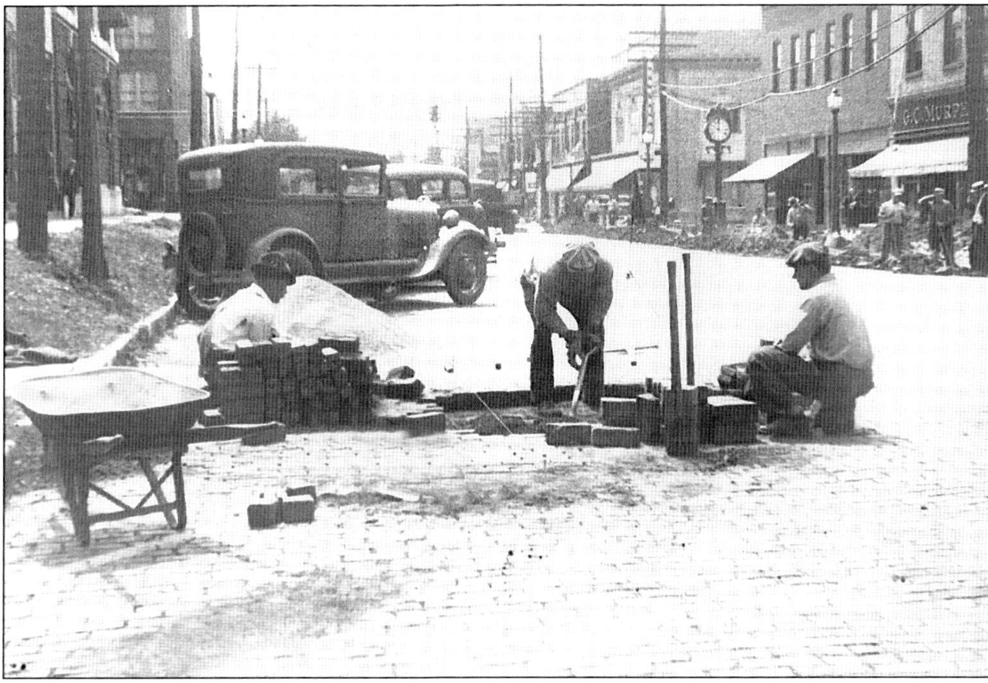

In June 1906, Philadelphia Avenue was paved. Three years later, Ninth, Eleventh, and Mary Streets were paved along with Maple Avenue. Paver bricks that were manufactured at Patton Clay Works were used. During this time, the town spent $34,000 paving streets. Most of the work was done by hand, brick by brick.

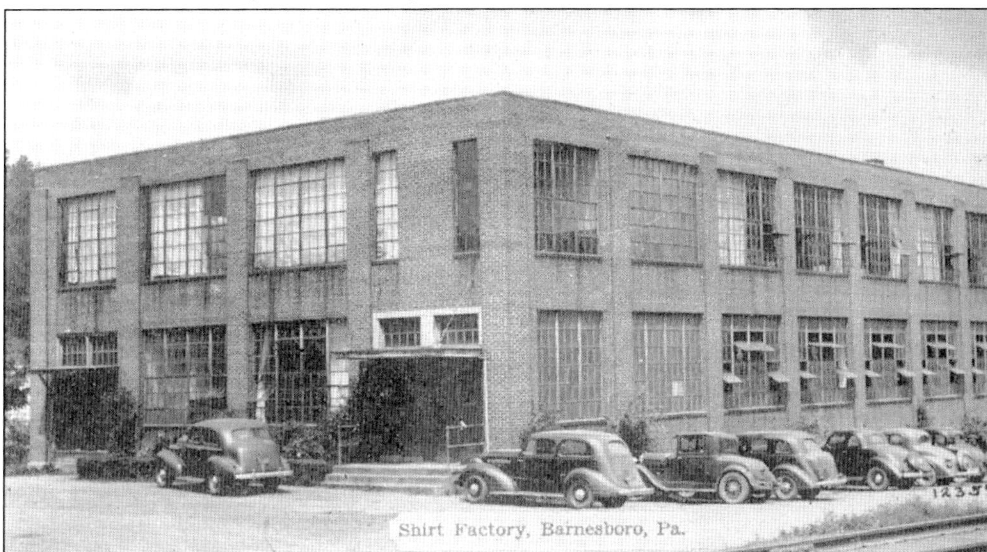

The shirt factory was established by the Phillips-Jones Corporation in 1930. It was built through community funds. The production of shirts and clothing provided employment for hundreds of townsfolk. In 1976, Yale Shanfield bought the plant and operated it under the name Barnesboro Shirt Company. The workforce consisted of 100 full-time employees who were all members of the United Garment Workers. In later years, the shirt factory operated under the name Van Heusen. It was the town's largest employer.

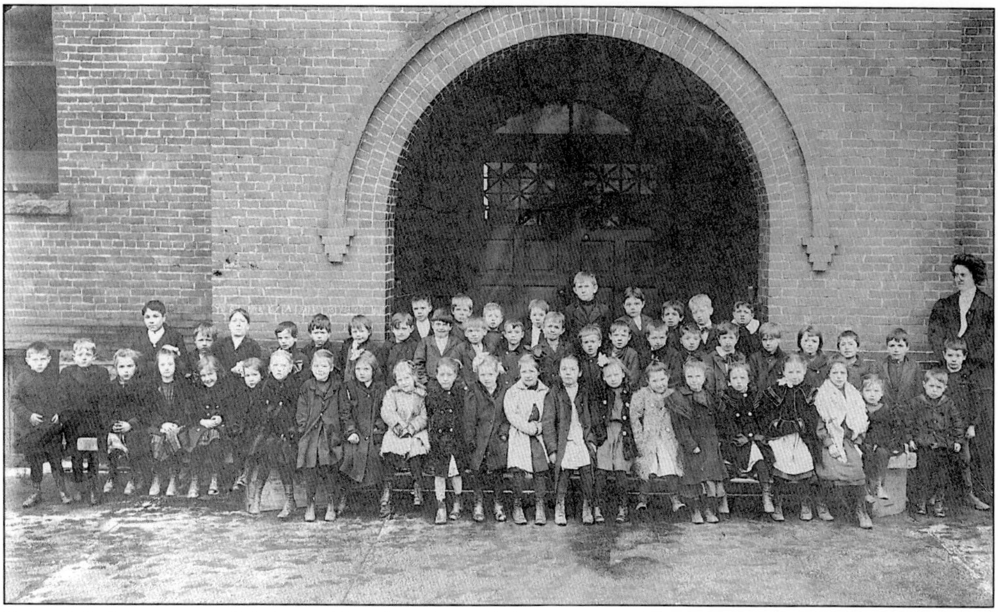

Schoolchildren assembled on October 11, 1895 in one of the early schools. Education in Barnesboro goes back to 1840, when a one-room schoolhouse was opened on Chestnut Street. This building also served as a church. The earliest schools were owned by local people, and the teacher was usually a native of the area. Population expansion necessitated the establishment of public schools.

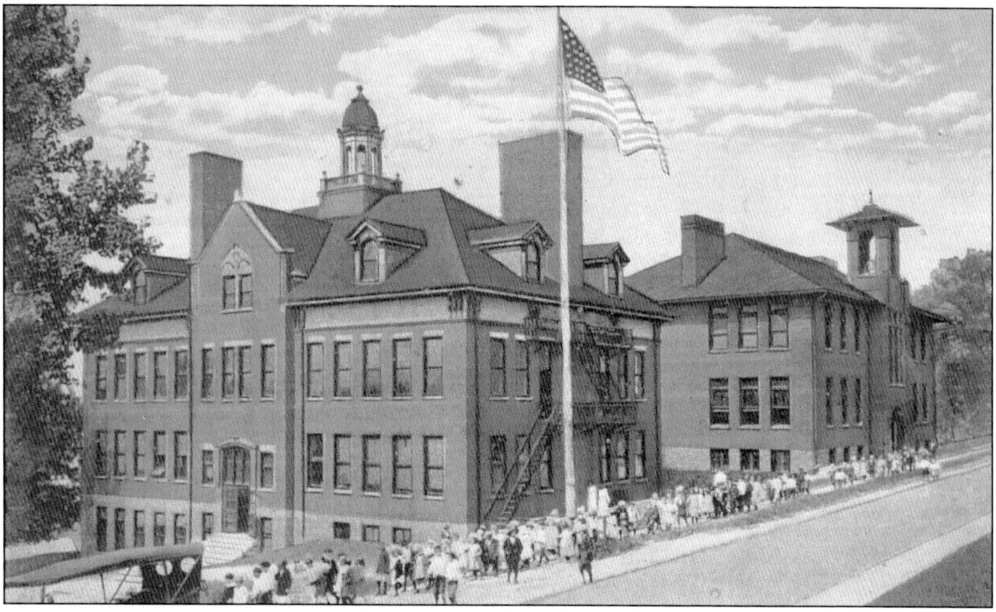

In 1894, a two-story frame building with four classrooms was built on Chestnut Street. The rapid enrollment in the area necessitated additional classroom space. Rooms were added to this structure in 1899. In 1904, the first brick building, known as the Washington Building, was erected adjacent to the wooden frame structure. In 1910, a brick school was constructed and became the Barnesboro High School. This functioned as a full, four-year high school until the last class graduated in 1962.

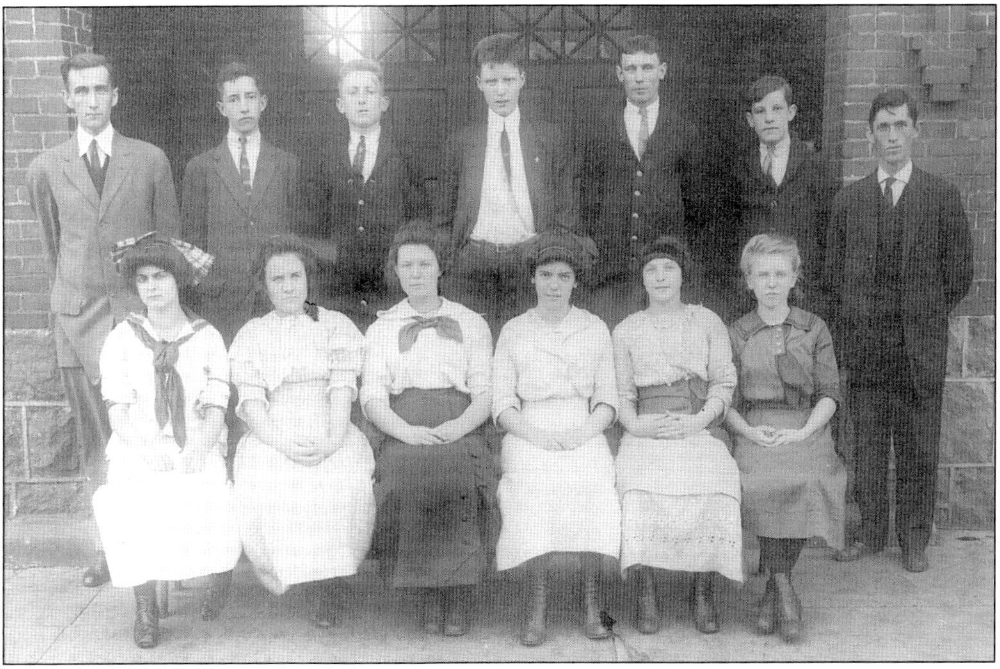

The freshmen of 1912 are assembled at Barnesboro High School in this photograph. The class, from left to right, consisted of the following: (front row) Edith Prosser, Clemens Ray, Sarah Scallon, Natlia Lowman, Amber Ward, Mary Wallasa; (second row) H.B. English (the instructor), Sam McMillane, Thomas Duka, John Scallon, Wilbur Swanboro, Eddie Binder, and the principal G.M. Stevens.

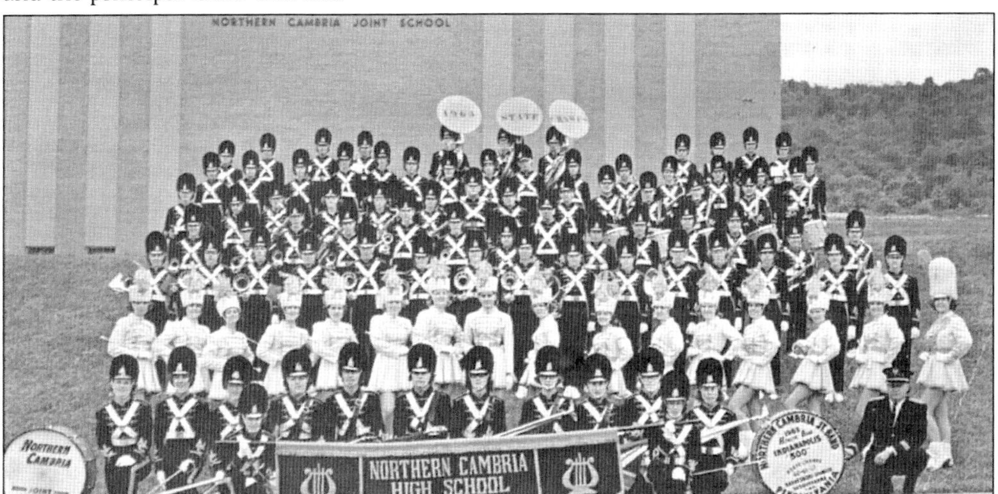

The members of the Northern Cambria High School varsity marching band were known as the "Twisting Tigers." The band won the state championships in 1960, 1961, and 1963. They performed at the 1964 World's Fair in New York and at the Cherry Blossom Festival in Washington. The band went on to Indiana and attended the Indianapolis 500 Speedway. They also achieved success in Pittsburgh and Philadelphia and were awarded numerous trophies and citations. The band director, John Woods, now works as the band director at Ohio State University.

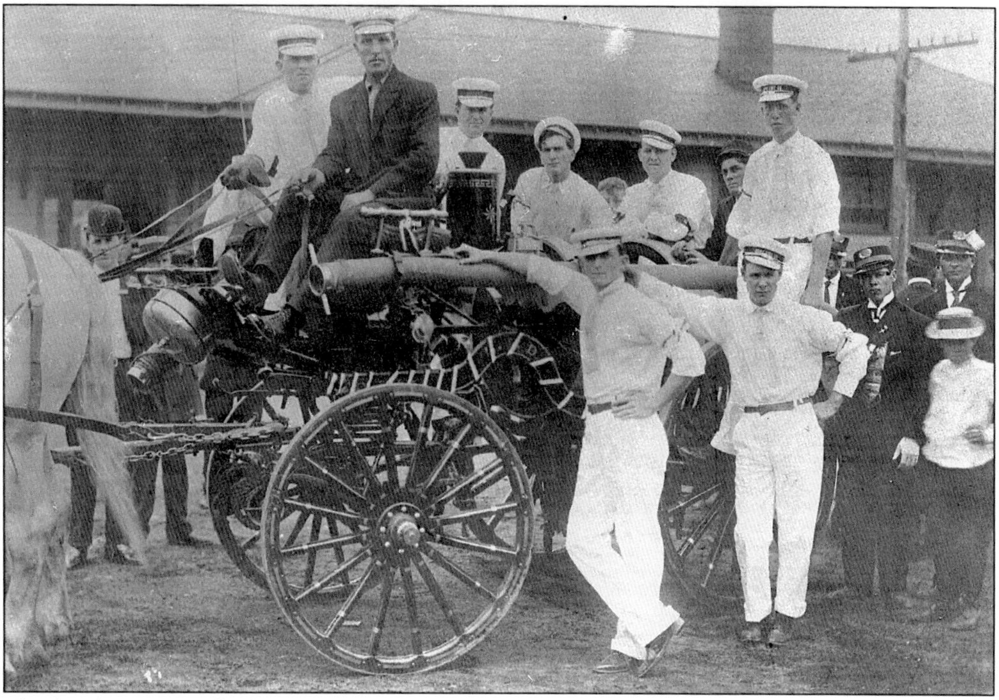

The fire department had an unique beginning. In 1899, J.D. Ritter owned a hotel in Barnesboro. In the hall of his hotel, he called a meeting to form a fire department. He organized Volunteer Fire Company No. 1. Hope Fire Company was organized in Miners Hall near Christ the King Rectory. Thomas Barnes donated a whistle from mine No. 17 when these two companies merged. A code was established to indicate the location of the fire. This horse-drawn pump was among the first apparatus used by the company.

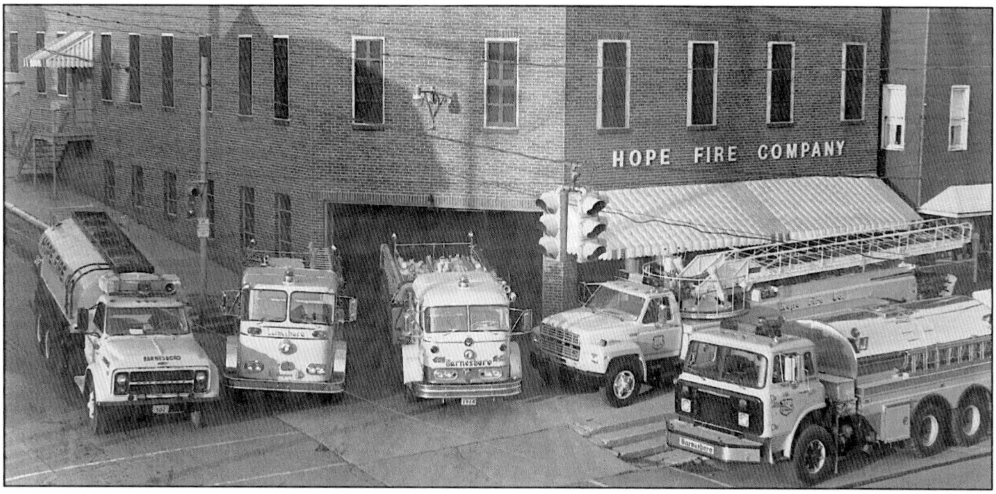

Hope Fire Company kept pace with the changing times. In 1923, the first gasoline-powered fire engine, a pumper truck, was put into service. Expansion and updated equipment followed in rapid succession. The company built a roller rink at Electric Park to raise funds for a fire hall. They obtained the Malta Building at the corner of Eleventh Street and Philadelphia Avenue in 1947. The building was razed and construction began on the present fire hall, which also doubles as a community center and municipal building.

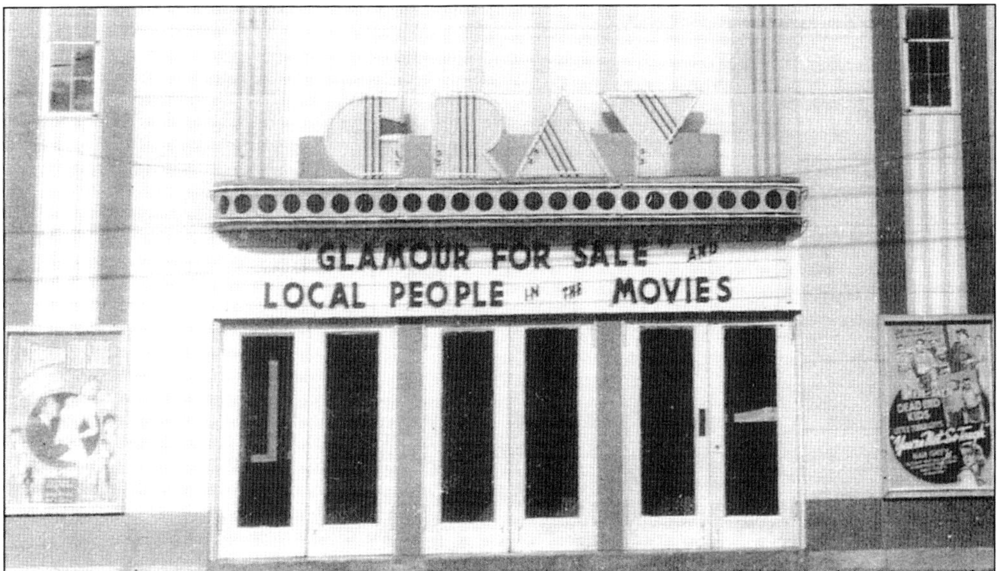

The Gray theater was part of the Honorable Joseph Gray's projects for Spangler. He was the only Spanglerite elected to the Pennsylvania state legislature, serving as a congressman from 1935 to 1939. His father, Joseph Gray Sr., had been elected sheriff and served at the democratic national convention in 1896. His grandfather was Philip. His great-grandfather, Caleb Gray, brought the family from Switzerland before the golden age of coalmining.

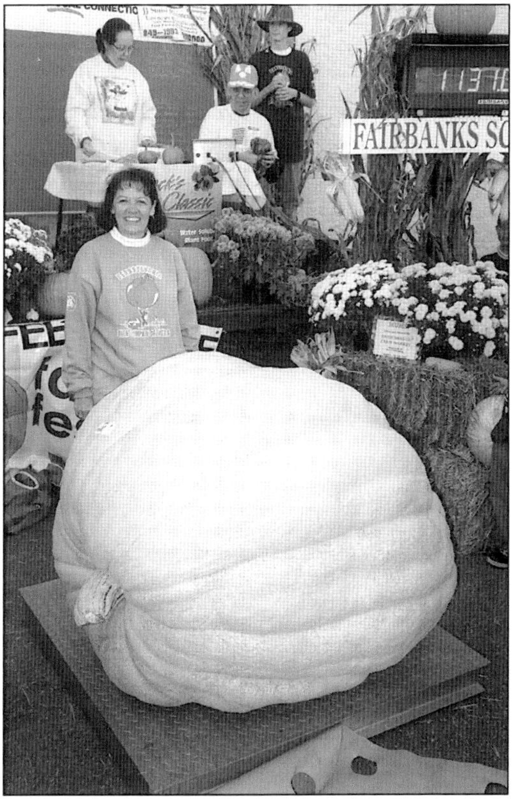

Gerry Checkon of Spangler grew the world's largest pumpkin in 1999. It weighed in at 1,131 pounds, which would be enough to bake 1.5 million pies. It was crated and taken by U-Haul to New York City, where it was featured on the David Letterman show. Later, a professional carved a face in the pumpkin and it was put on display. Gerry's husband, Larry Checkon, learned the art of growing large pumpkins from his father, George. The family lives in the homestead on Riverside Avenue in Spangler where the famous pumpkin was grown.

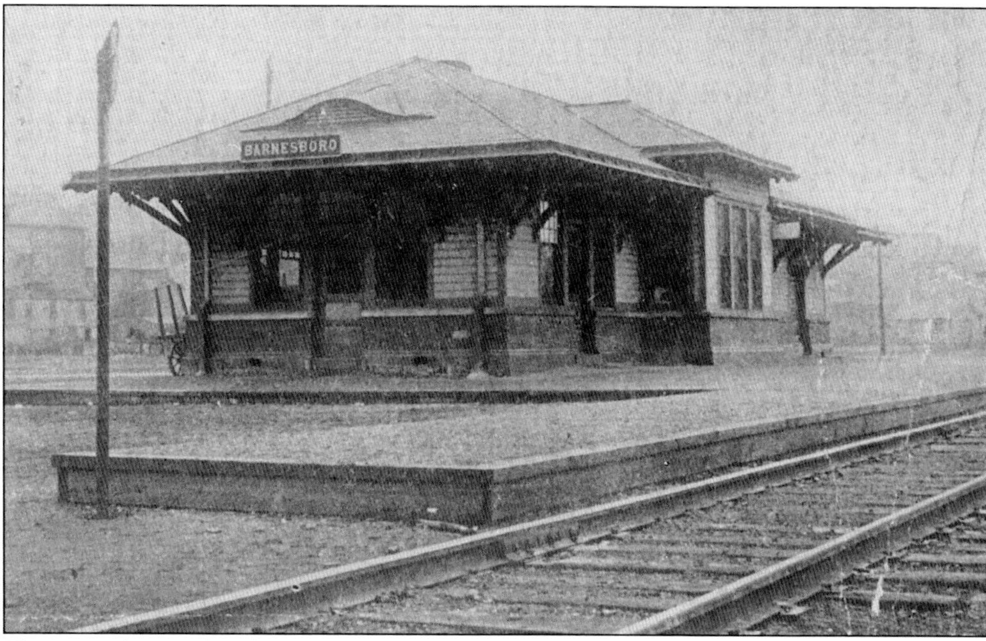

The Barnesboro railroad station stood where the Giant Eagle market is today. Built early in the century, it was an asset to the coalmines. The railroad served the coalmining business during the entire time of its existence. Passenger trains gave townsfolk mobility until the arrival of cars. Passenger trains were discontinued; the last run was on September 25, 1947. Conductor A.W. Brickley was known for his famous announcement as the train chugged into town: "Barnes-boor-oo, Barnes-boor-oo."

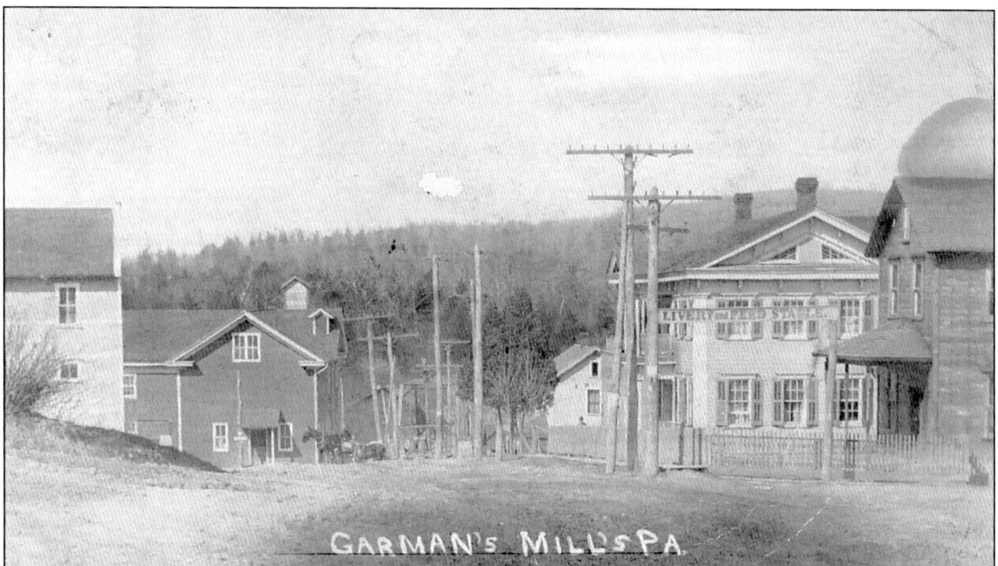

Garmans Mills was a little settlement with a multiplicity of post offices. Situated between Barnesboro and Cherry Tree, it had three different post offices as a result of different spellings. Garman's Mills, Garmantown, and Garman. Finally, it became Garmans Mills. John Garmans came from Blair County in 1840 and bought the Ralston Place. Here, he and sons established a sawmill. Much of his lumber was shipped to Indiana. This scene dates to 1908.

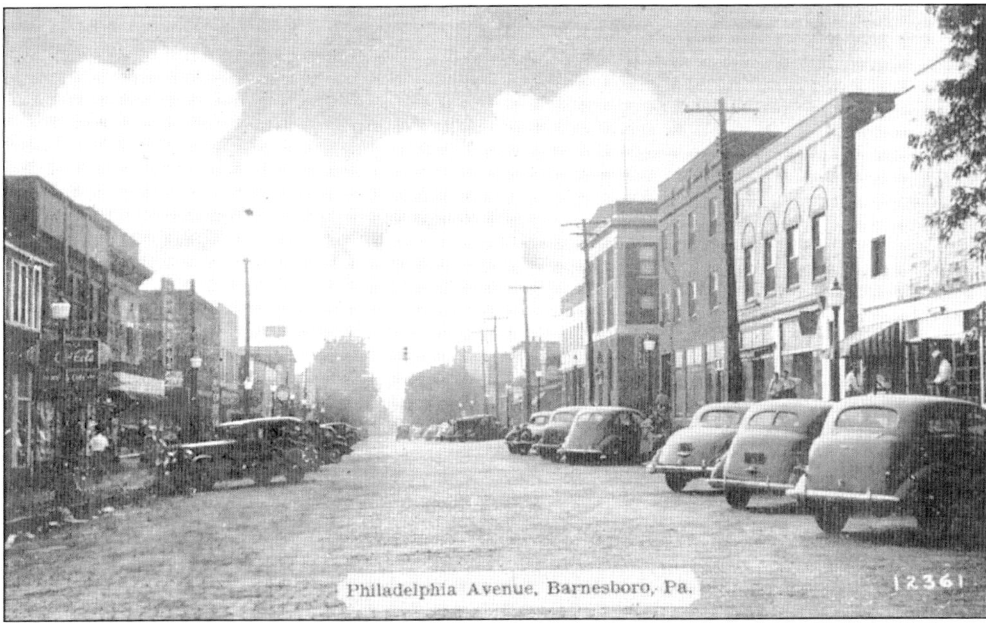

This view of Philadelphia Avenue was taken long after the trolley tracks were removed. The cars of 1946 can be seen parked at an angle. Note the newly installed streetlight. Electricity first came to Barnesboro in 1919. Before that, electric power was supplied by Elmer Schroth for the church, theater, and bank. This was one of the busiest streets in Barnesboro. The hamlet had become a central shopping center for the Northern Cambria region.

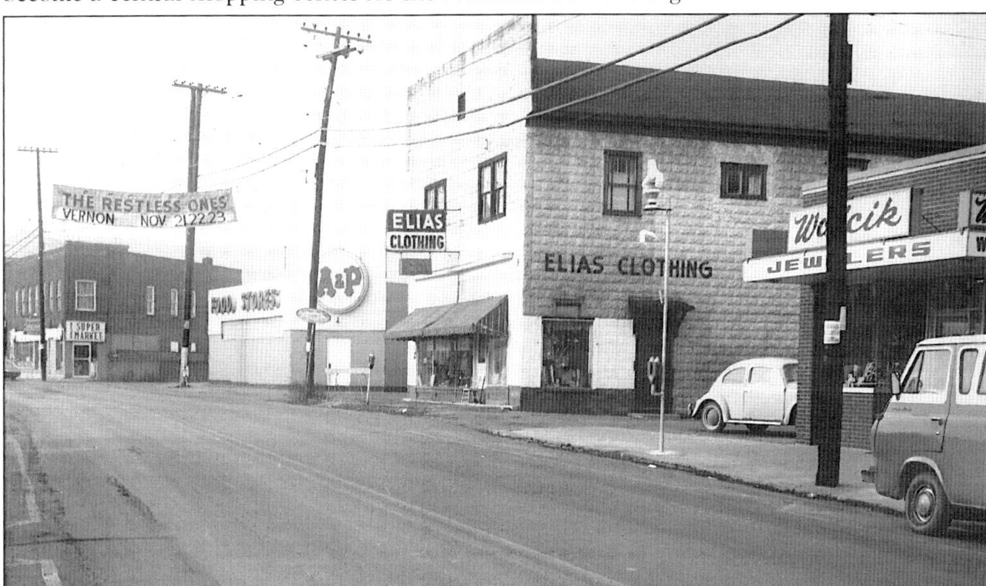

Looking south along Tenth Street *c.* mid-century, we see that *The Restless Ones* was playing at the Vernon theater. The supermarket on the extreme left was a new innovation in town. To the right of the advertisement stood the A&P supermarket, Elias Clothing, and Wojcik Jewelers. John Wojcik and family came to the area in 1902 and settled on Cabbage Hill. He had been apprenticed as a watchmaker and established a jewelry business upon arrival. John sold jewelry door to door until 1925, when he opened his jewelry store.

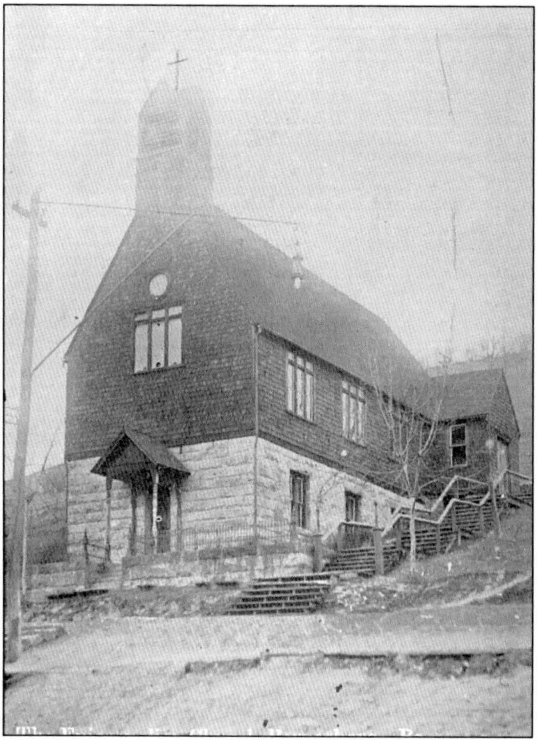

The St. Thomas Episcopal Church was established in Barnesboro in 1894, when the first services were conducted. Early residents requested the services of an Episcopal priest. Thomas Barnes donated the land for the church. The first service was held on February 10, 1895. The parish house was donated by Esther Barnes, c. 1921. It became a community center, a gym, and a social hall for local clubs and organizations.

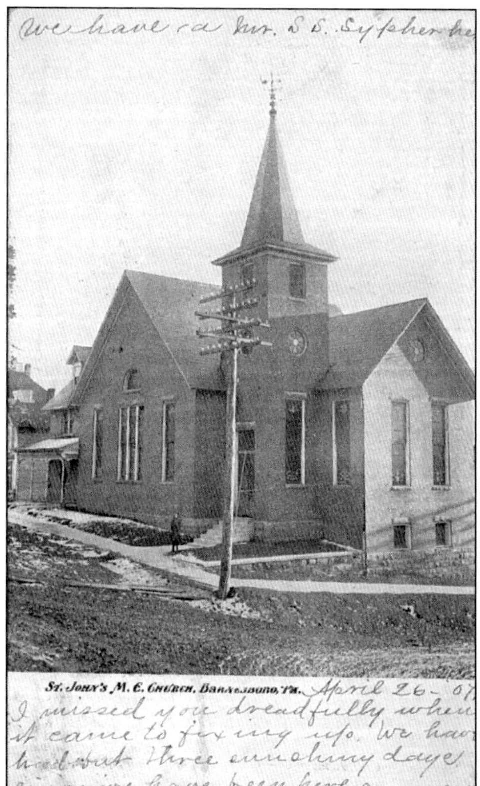

Held in Spice's Hall with seven members, St. John's Methodist Episcopal Church began as a Sunday school in June 1900. A new church was established on the corner of Chestnut and Caroline Streets in 1903. A 1920 addition was necessary to provide additional Sunday school facilities and increase the capacity for worship. Chimes and speakers were installed outside the edifice by the youth group. In 1968, the Methodist Church joined with the United Brethren Church and became the United Methodist Church

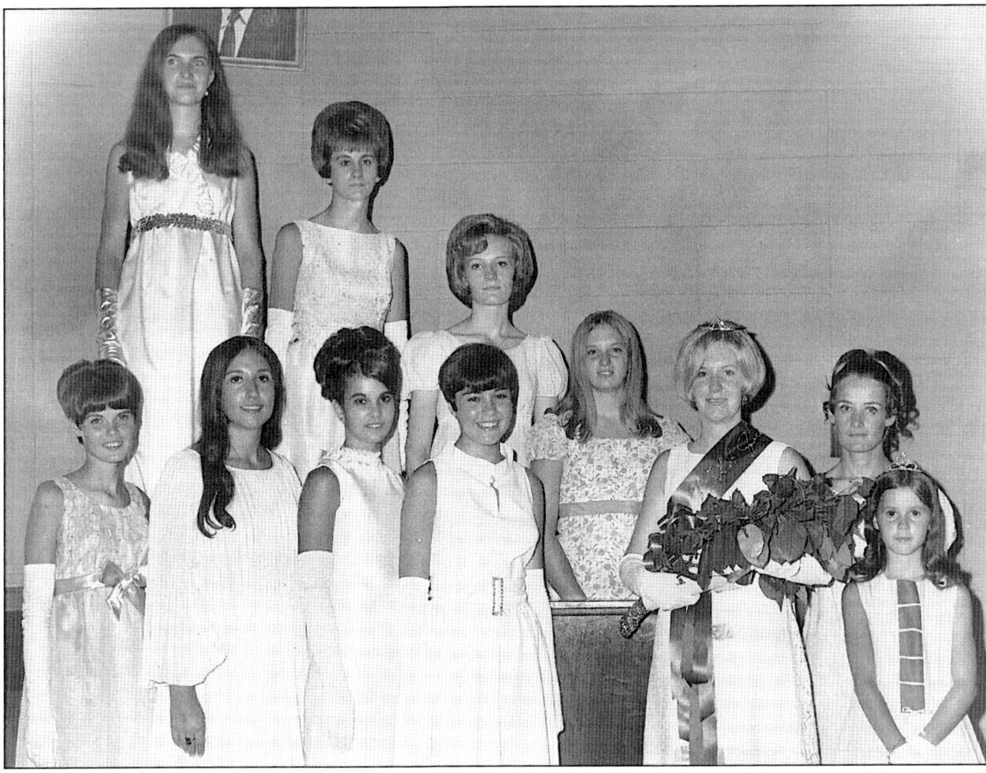

Barnesboro's Diamond Jubilee marked the 75th anniversary of the incorporation of the borough (1884–1969). It was celebrated, in part, by a contest to select a Jubilee Queen. The honor went to Lyn Davis, third from the right. Her court, from left to right, consisted of the following: (first row) Terry Lonegran, Toni Ann Previte, Debby Linden, Janice Wagner, Jeanette Daisley; (second row) Doris Radcliffe, Anne Mae Weakland, Mary Whited, Mary Jane Smith, and Kerry Lonegran.

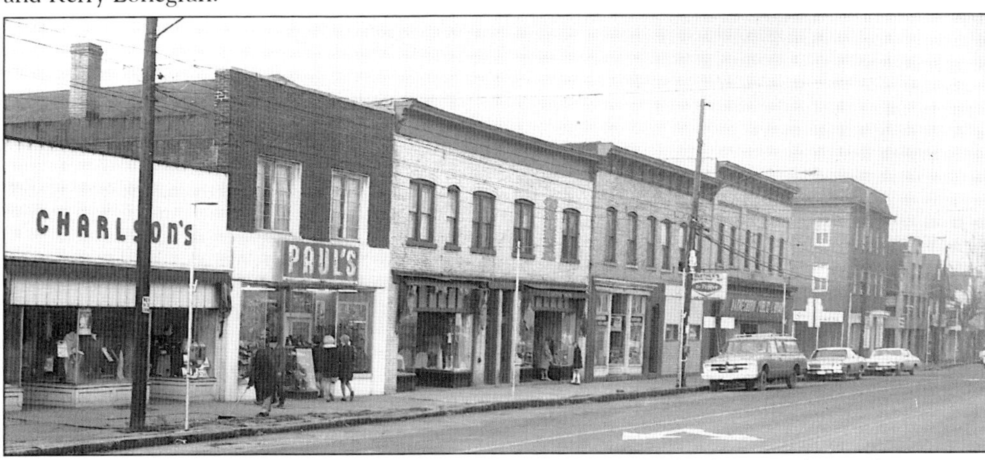

Charlson's furniture store goes back to the arrival of Wolf Charlston early in the century. Originally a peddler of household items, he and his brother rented a store on Caroline Street in Barnesboro, setting up a general store in 1904. The site was later occupied by McCrory's Five & Ten store. Other businesses along Philadelphia Avenue during the mid-century included Paul's shoe store, Friedman's ladies shop, and the Barnesboro Library.

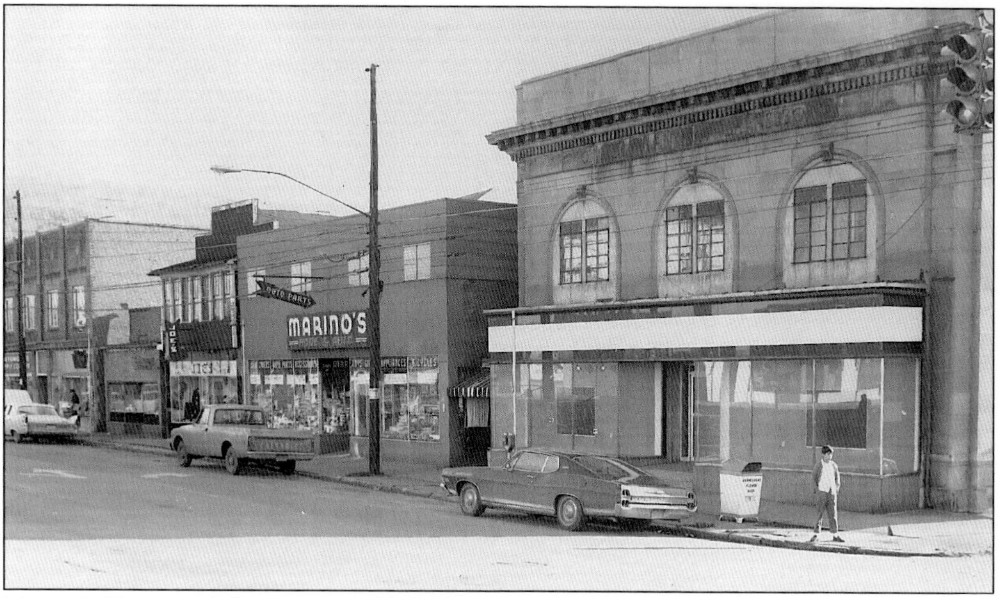

Marino's Home and Auto was established in 1939 when Anthony Marino opened a service station in North Barnesboro. Following a period of military service, he reopened his business in the Kemp building at the intersection of Philadelphia and Eleventh Streets. He relocated several times to larger buildings. In 1989, Marino's Home and Auto celebrated its 50th anniversary. Marino became an Ace Handyman dealer, selling auto parts and accessories, hardware, housewares, and sporting goods.

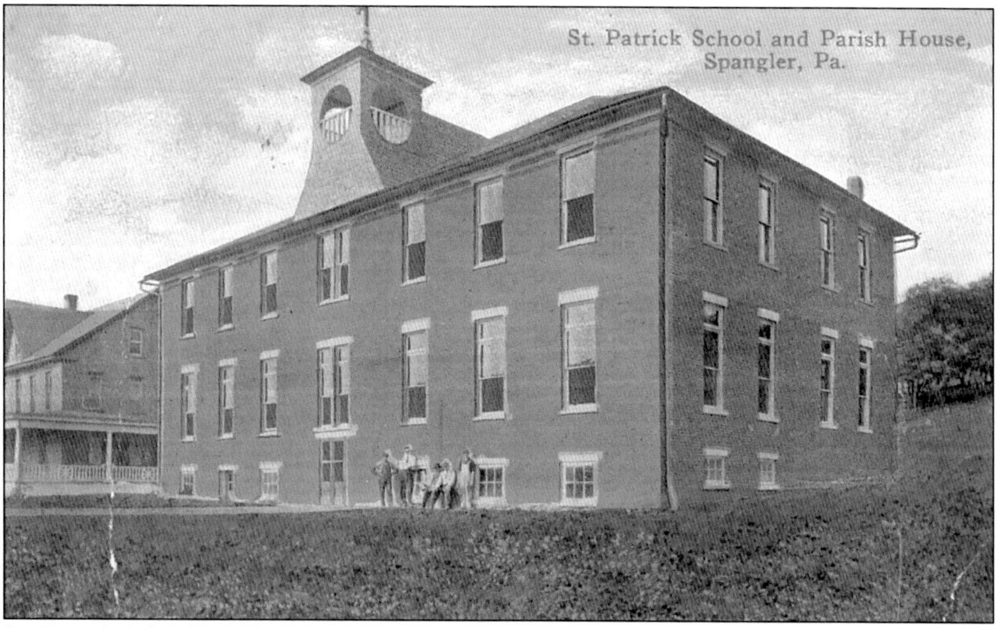

St. Patrick School was the first Catholic school in the area. Established in 1912, it included a high school that offered excellent training in business education and the classics. In 1927, the high school closed. The parish house is in the background. The Holy Cross School was opened in 1921 and staffed by the Sisters of Mercy. In 1971, both schools were consolidated with the St. Nicholas school in Nicktown to become the North Cambria Consolidation.

The Holy Cross Roman Catholic Church was built in 1896 to serve a growing catholic population. It is the oldest congregation in the area. St. Patrick's Roman Catholic Church, completed in 1893, was the original Holy Cross Church. The congregation rapidly outgrew the building due to the unexpected population expansion that resulted from the opening of the coalmines. The original building was idle until June 1902, when it was pressed into service and renamed St. Patrick's.

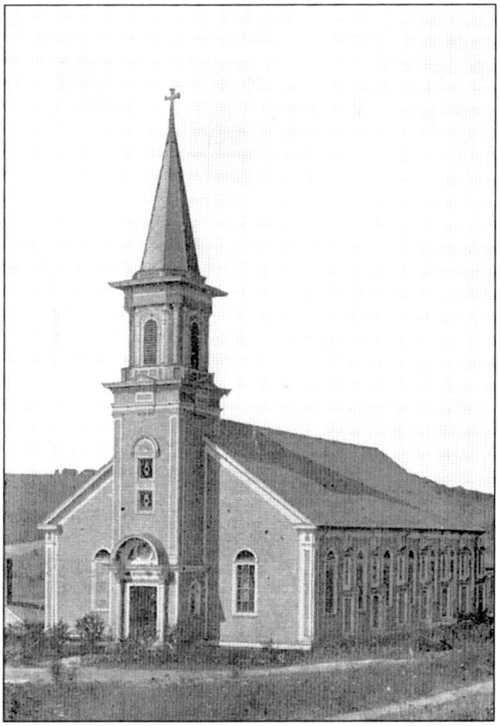

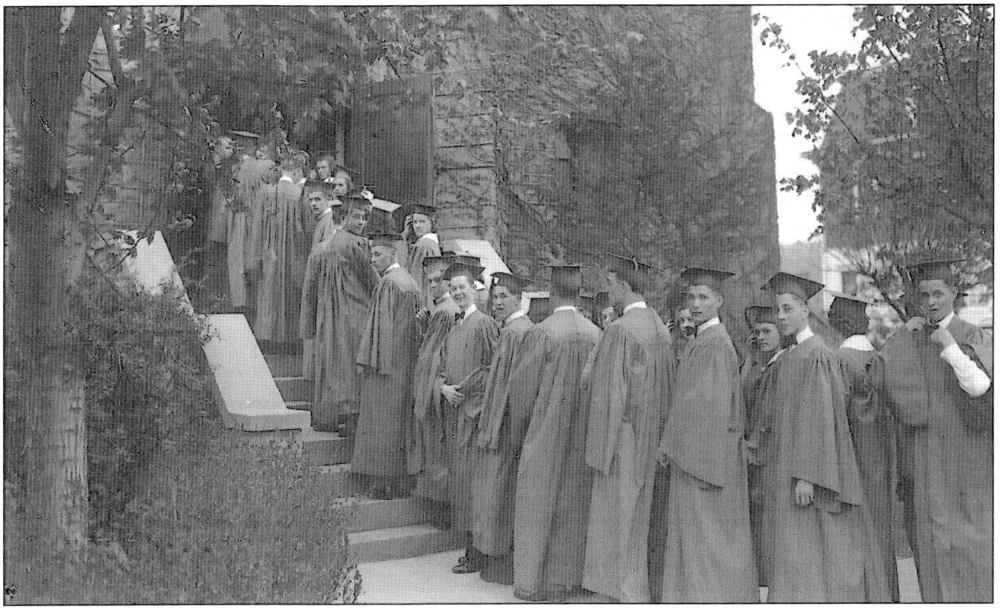

Graduates of 1937 enter St. Edward's Church for commencement exercises. There were five Roman Catholic ethnic parishes in Barnesboro: St. Edward's preached in English; St. Patrick's provided for the Irish population; Mount Carmel served the Italian population; St. Stanislaus attended to Polish immigrants; and St. John the Baptist served the Slovak congregation. In Spangler, there was the Holy Cross Parish. These six parishes are merging into fewer worship sites. On June 23, 1993, St. Edward's and the Most Precious Blood in Emeigh were united, assuming the name of Christ the King.

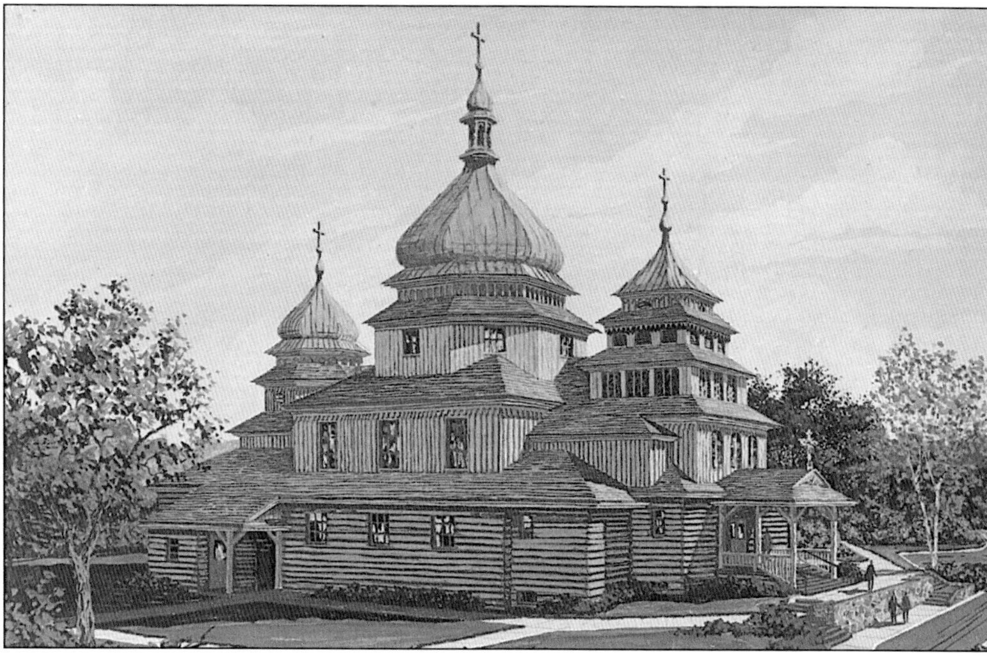

St. Mary's Ukrainian Catholic Church dominates the landscape on Campbell Hill overlooking Barnesboro. Founded in 1912 by Catholics of the Byzantine Rite, the original church served for many years. In 1968, the present building was completed. The unique design attracts tourists from far and wide; their names are collected in the church register. Beneath the triple-domed exterior, the body is built of California redwood. The windows are arranged on three levels and the ancient belfry contains the bells from the original church building.

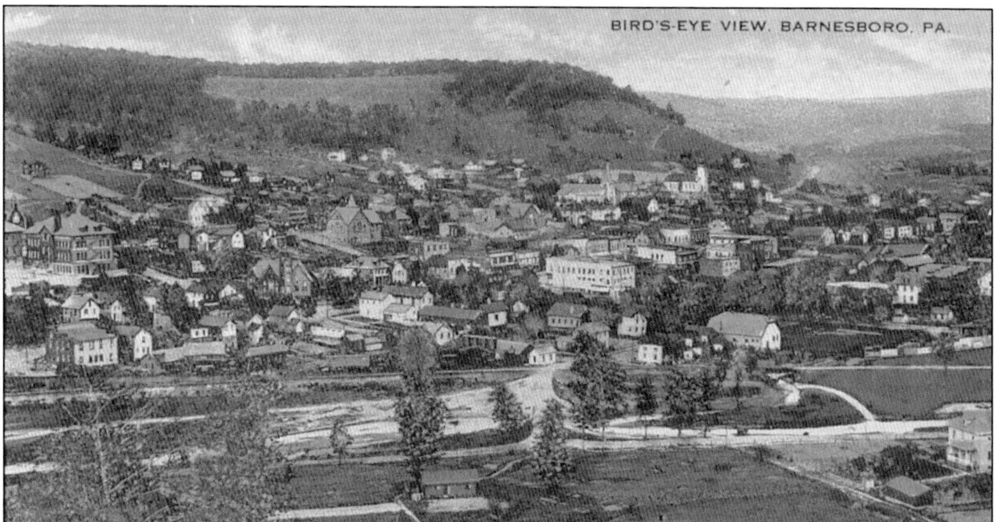

This bird's-eye view of Barnesboro was taken in 1944. The tract of land first graded by Edward C. Fisher a century earlier had become populated when coal beds were discovered and mines became operative. Among the first to develop land was David Raiston, who conducted a sawmill on what is now Philadelphia Avenue. His home stood on the site of Heilig Myers Furniture. From 1885 to 1900, coal companies that once operated in the vicinity of Houtzdale, Osceola Mills, and Philipsburg relocated to Northern Cambria.

Two

Tilling Field and Delving Mine

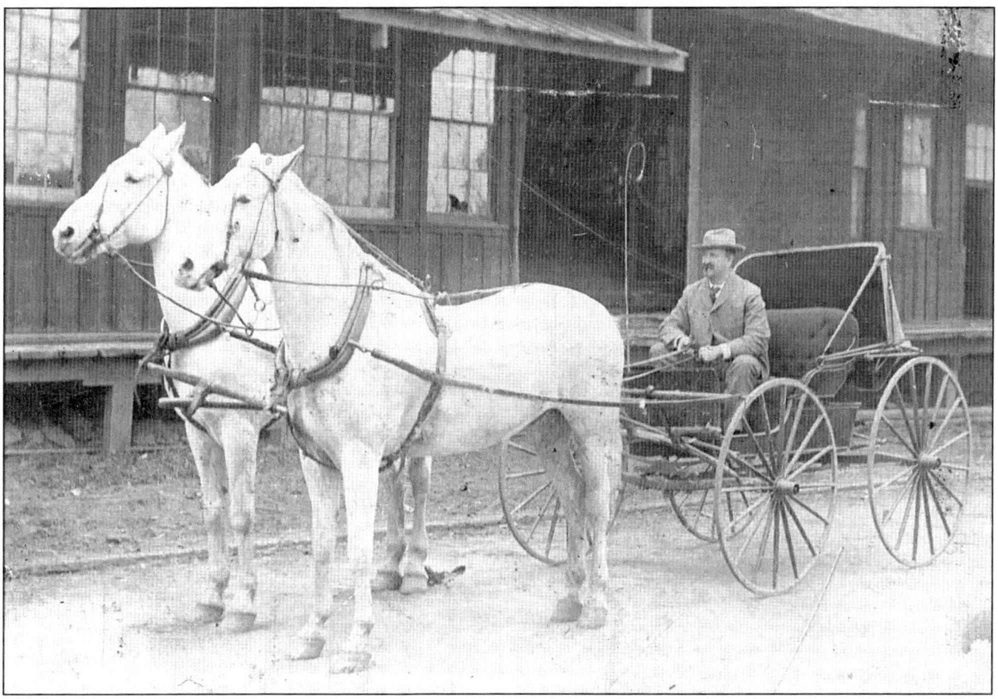

Thomas Barnes and his buckboard were once a common site around Barnesboro. He made daily rounds of both the village and his holdings. The wagon was pulled by chestnut-colored horses. Barnes delivered the payroll for the miners by horse and buggy. This entailed a trip of 50 miles over dusty, muddy roads to his bank in Philipsburg. The Whiporwill tract came into existence when Thomas Barnes purchased land in the area. His Barnesboro office was located on the site of Rebekah Manor.

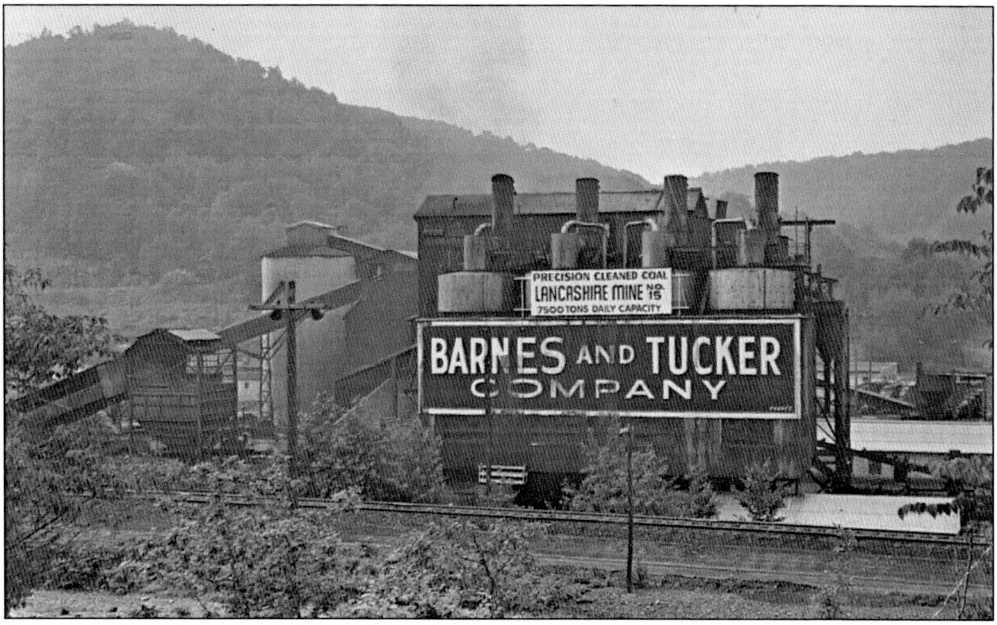

Barnes and Tucker Mine, located at the intersection of Thirteenth Street and Chestnut Avenue in Barnesboro, introduced electric haulage to the area in 1906. Barnes was associated with Alfred Tucker in the coalmining business in Philipsburg. On December 17, 1892, the picturesque hamlet of McAnulty, rich in black diamonds (as coal was called), was changed to Barnesboro in honor of Barnes. It was officially incorporated as a Cambria County borough in March 1894.

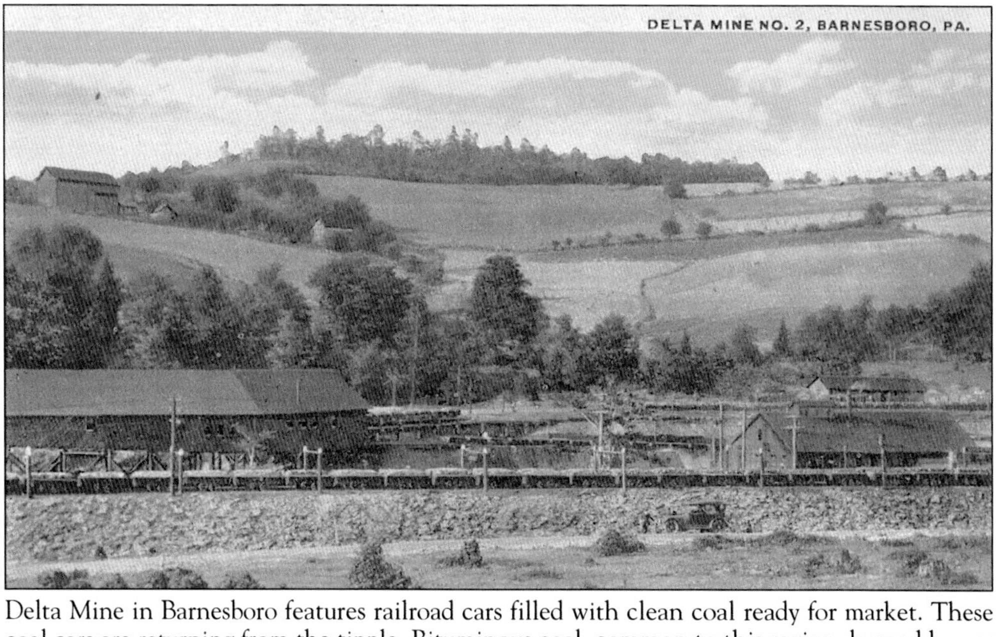

Delta Mine in Barnesboro features railroad cars filled with clean coal ready for market. These coal cars are returning from the tipple. Bituminous coal, common to this region, burned longer than anthracite (hard) coal and also created less dust. Anthracite coal, common to eastern Pennsylvania, burned hotter but not as long as bituminous coal. Note the mountains, farmland, and barns in the background.

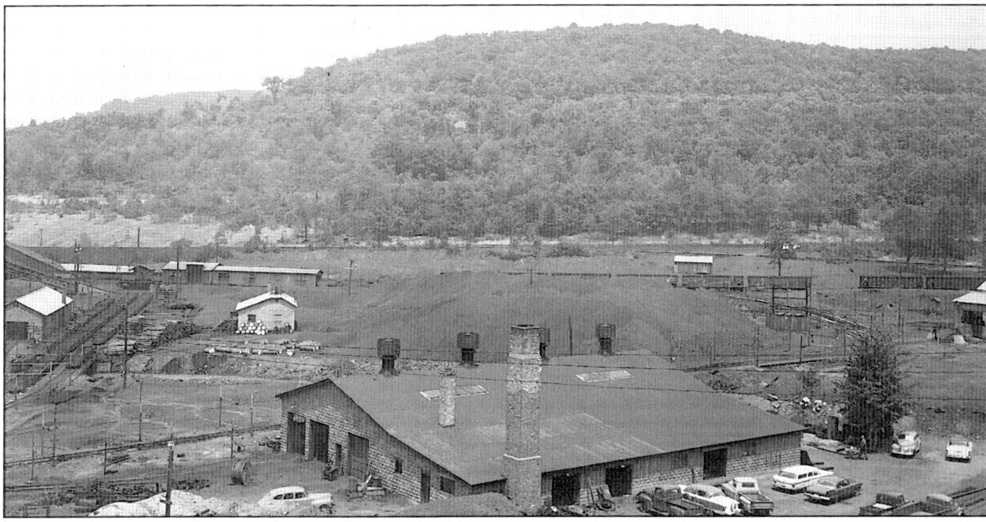

A huge mine is nestled below the picturesque mountains near Spangler. The entrance to the mine is on the extreme left. A large refuse pile rises on the right. A miner would prepare for his subterranean venture in the engine house: he would don his mining clothes and adjust the light on his helmet. Then, carrying his pick, shovel, and lunch bucket, he would head for the rail car that would take him to his workplace, which could be miles into the mine.

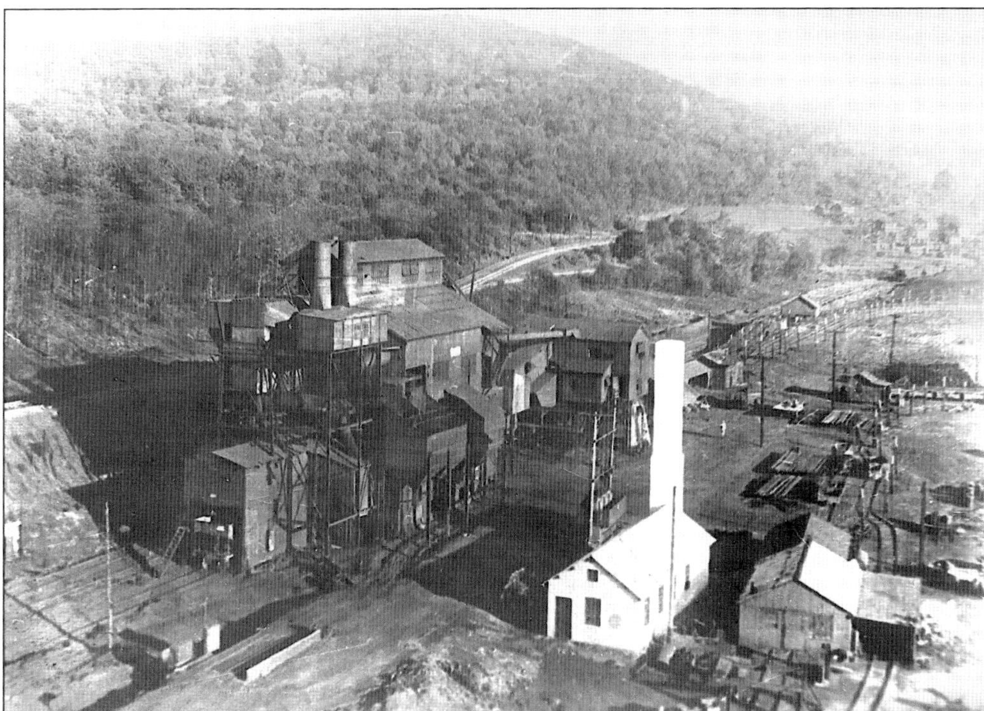

Reilly Mine was opened in 1893 when Joseph Reilly bought coal lands in Spangler. The operation of his mine was turned over to his brother John, who was designated the general manager. In 1893, Charles R. Jones opened the Reilly Mine company store in Spangler. Charles lived at the Brandon Hotel while his home was constructed. Tennessee Ernie Ford, the famous singer, described the store in his well-known song "Sixteen Tons."

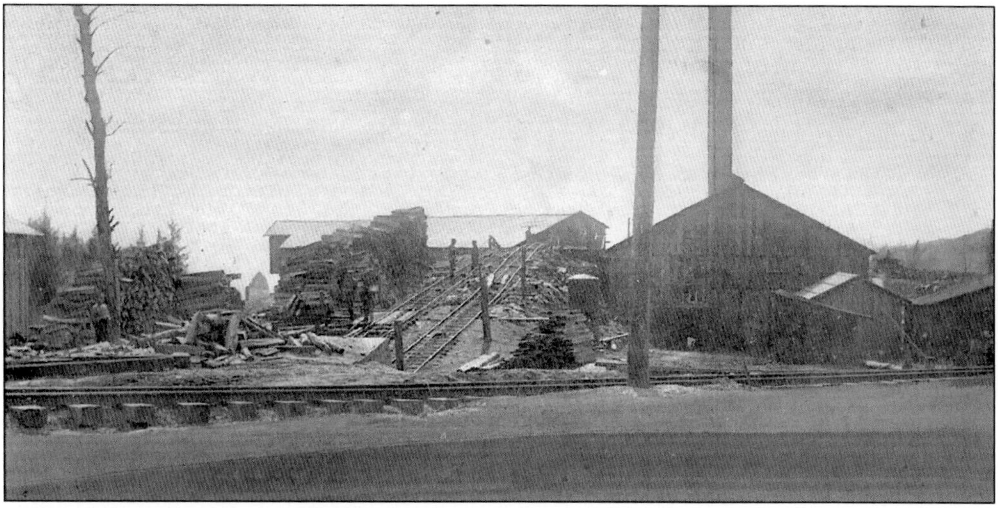

Reilly Mine Slope No. 9 exhibits the tracks where men rode down into the mine in cars provided for that purpose. This was called a man trap. Miners learned to recognize coal seams. A coal vein is located between two strata of horizontal, parallel rocks or slate. Coal is layered in seams designated by a letter. There are several types of bituminous coal in the region.

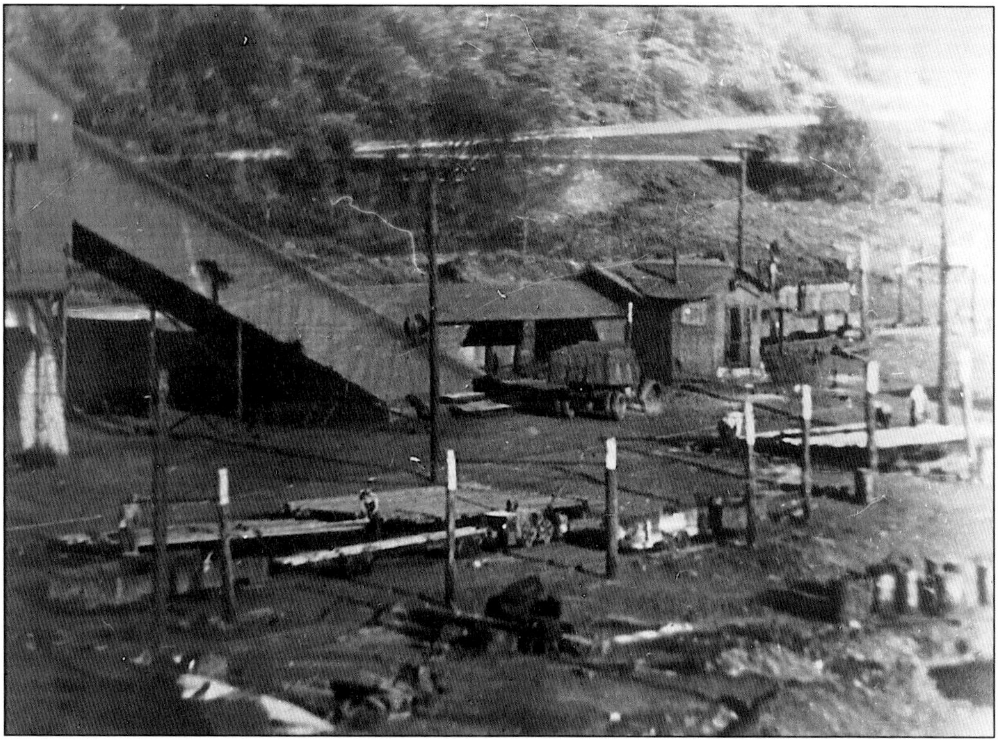

Reilly Mine Colliery No. 1 experienced a methane gas explosion on November 6, 1922 at 7:45 a.m., taking 77 lives. It occurred a mile inside the mine and shattered the fan house. Smoke and dust were thick as safety crews attempted to rescue those trapped. Nearly every home in Northern Cambria was touched by this disaster. Notes were later found in the mine from those who perished. A monument to the miners was erected in Spangler by the United Mine Workers of America (UMWA) and stands beside the bank on Bigler Avenue.

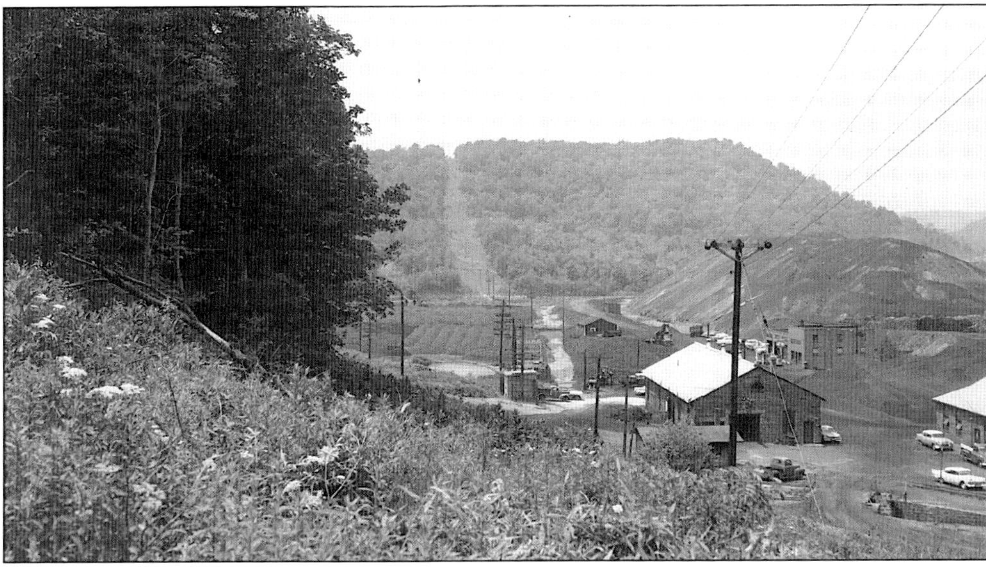

In Northern Cambria, the miner leaves behind not only daylight, but also magnificent mountains and exquisite vistas to enter a stark, prehistoric world. The draft mouth, or entrance, takes the miner into an austere environment where primeval vegetation has been converted into coal. In "dust college," as some called it, the miner quickly learns to recognize coal seams and judge their worth. Marketable coal forms vertically, while unsaleable coal appears in horizontal strata.

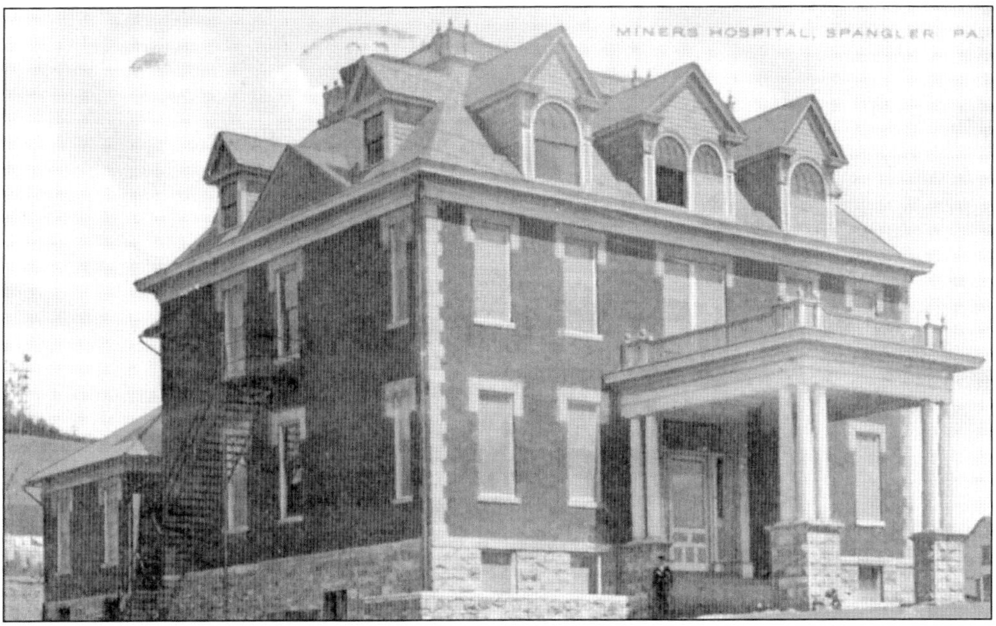

Dr. T. Orlando Helfrick called a meeting in his office on January 24, 1905 to discuss a Miners Hospital for the area. A site was donated on Crawford Avenue in Spangler in 1906. J.D. Rittner of Spangler began construction on a hospital building that would house 30 patients. Note the laundry on the line during the 1918 flu epidemic and the small house in back for incurable cases. The Miners Hospital was incorporated on October 20, 1908; the first patient, Daniel Campbell of Carrolltown, was admitted January 3, 1909.

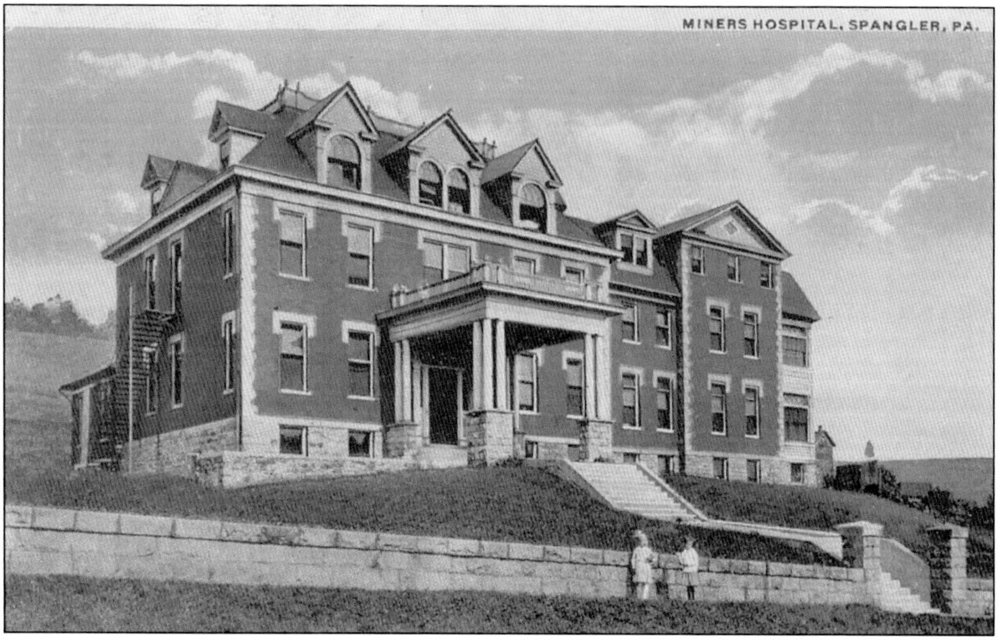

The patient population at Miners Hospital grew. The hospital met new trends through additional construction and renovation. A laundry and heating plant were installed in 1919, followed by an obstetrics department, a nurses home, the Holton and south wings, an intensive care unit, a coronary unit, and a new school of nursing. The buildings were connected by tunnels. Patient occupancy rose to a peak of 147 in 1970. In 1991, the Miners Hospital acquired equipment to accommodate nuclear medicine.

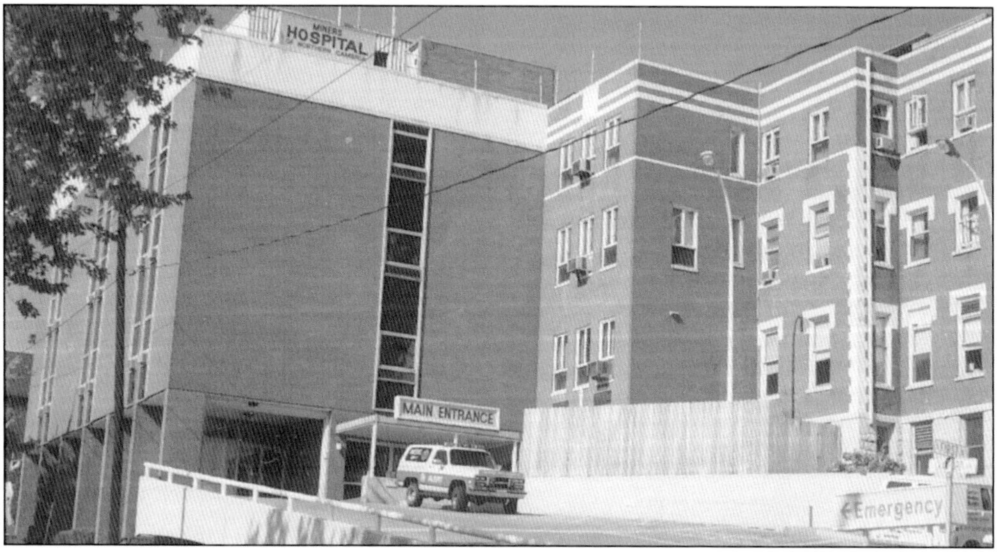

Initially, the Miners Hospital was established in response to the need for such a facility near the mines. In 1909, the hospital accommodated 30 patients. They were hospitalized an average of 16 days. By 1998, patient population had decreased to 49 because of new medical trends. The area for outpatient care, parking, and limited access became paramount. In September 1999, the entire facility left its Crawford Avenue site in Spangler and moved to a new building in Hastings.

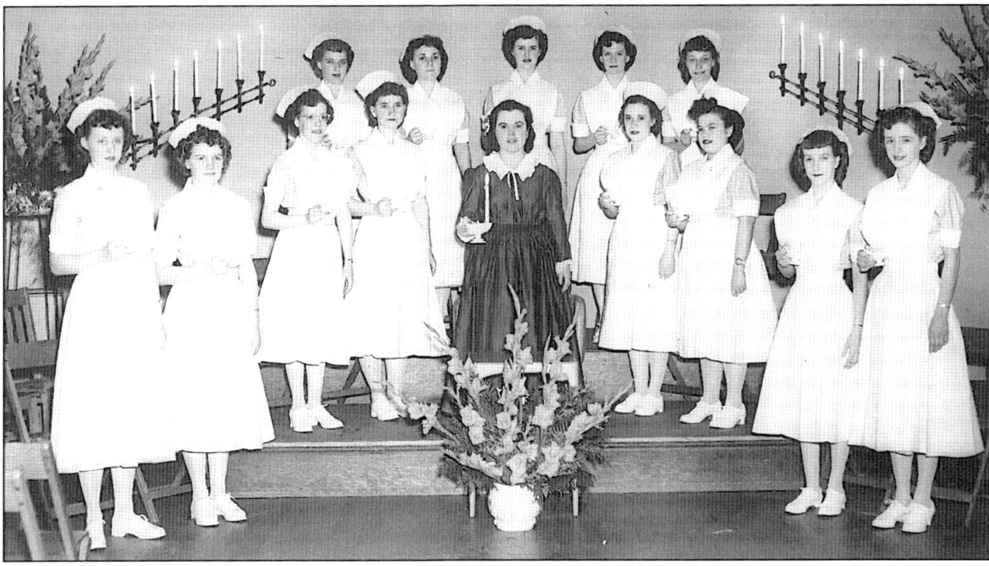

The Miners Hospital graduating class of 1951 included, from left to right, the following: (first row) Norma Stitt Abrams; Shirley Penn Dunchak; Mona Weakland Thomas; Louise Dobransky Yeager; Mrs. Frances Vogtho, instructor; Theresa Parrish Yeckley; Leona Carpinello Cipolla; Kathy Tocarchich Katy; Ruth Mehall Resco; (second row) Mary Jane Culver Mitchell, Jean Cronouer Mello, Phyllis Farabaugh Contres, Jean Kosic Bearer, and Florence Zieminski Dongilla. The School of Nursing was established in 1910. Nursing students were housed on the third floor of the main building until 1927, when the three-story Nurses Home was built. There were three graduates in its first class.

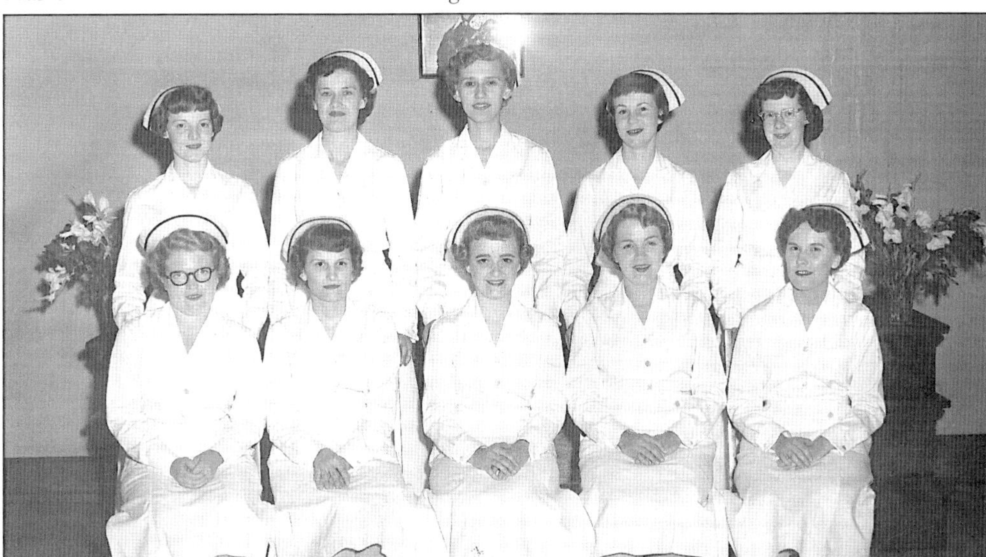

The last graduating class of Miners Hospital finished training in 1954. The class included, from left to right, the following: (first row) Virginia Fisanick Pavin, Janis Roland McMullen, Delores Chuhran Krins, Sally Louchart Macko, Anna Mae Fryer Tibbott; (second row) Mary Jo Kirkpatrick Fenello, Mary Pazlva Drahnak, Jean Whited Galinis, Mary Ann Charney Britsky, and Ellen Adams Whalen. The school was discontinued because of updated trends in nursing education whereby nurses were trained in colleges and universities.

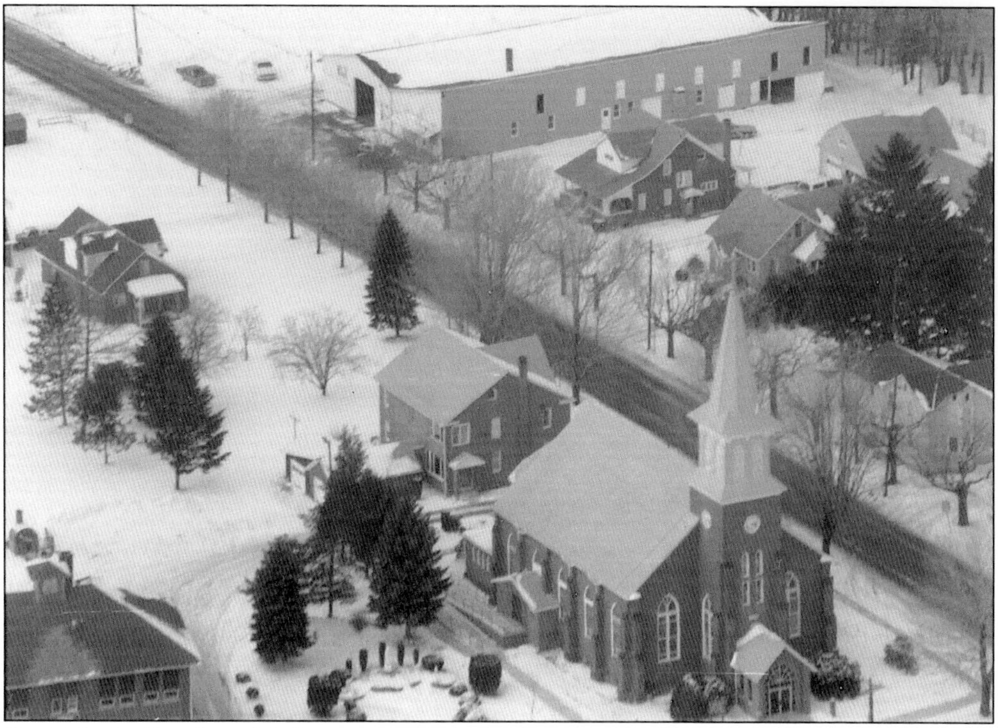

St. Nicholas Parish in Nicktown was formed in 1863, when services were held in private homes. The first church was built in 1867. The church building was destroyed by fire in 1915, and the present church was built on the same site. It was designed much like the first. In this aerial view, the homes of Betty and Herm Kline and John Freck are visible in the background, along with the Krumanaker Builders. The rectory stands behind the church and the school is in the left foreground.

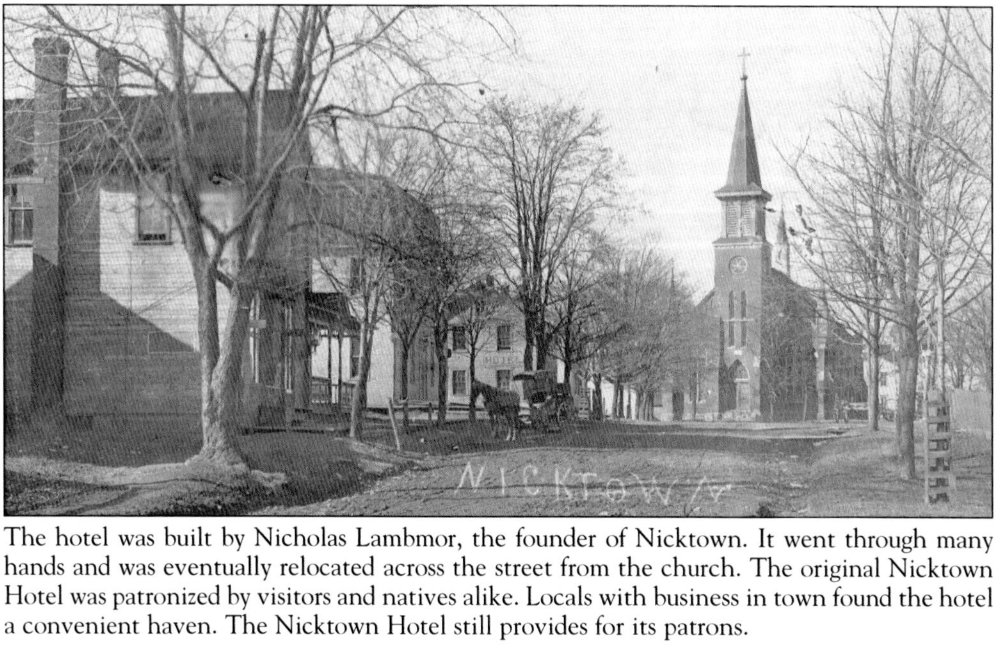

The hotel was built by Nicholas Lambmor, the founder of Nicktown. It went through many hands and was eventually relocated across the street from the church. The original Nicktown Hotel was patronized by visitors and natives alike. Locals with business in town found the hotel a convenient haven. The Nicktown Hotel still provides for its patrons.

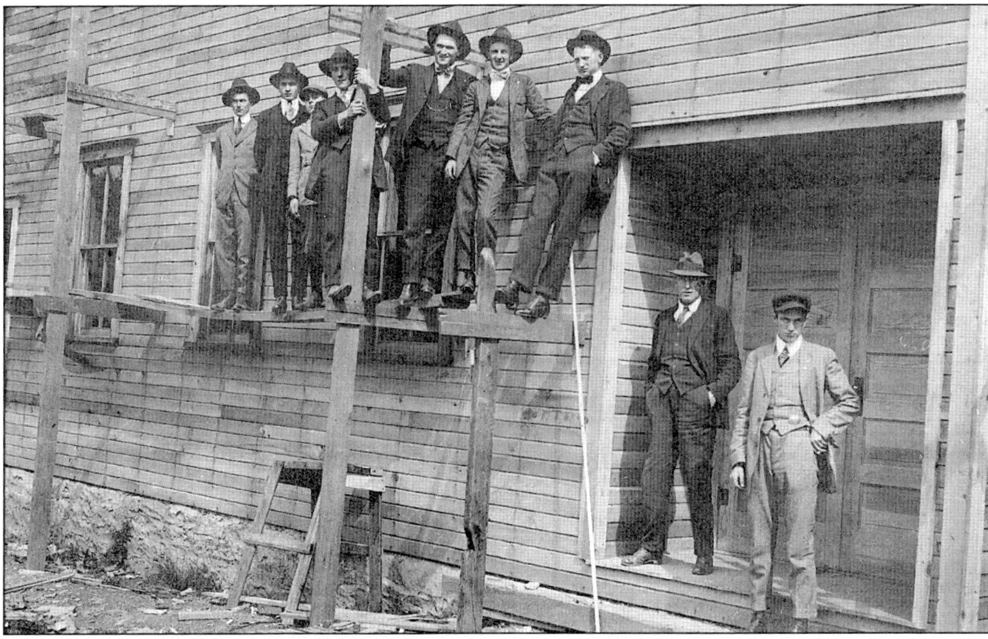

A crew of townsmen completed the St. Nicholas Parish Hall in 1975. Located a few hundred feet from the parish church, it serves as a gathering place for funeral and wedding receptions and many other festive functions. In recent years, the building has been covered with sheetrock. It has long been the scene of the famous annual Nicktown picnic.

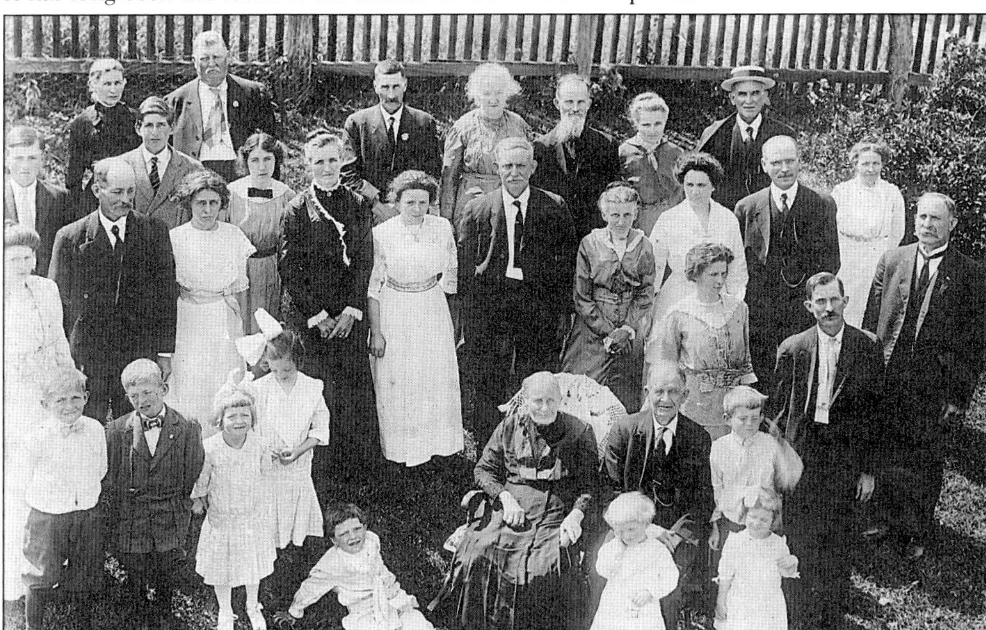

Reunions have always provided intermingling among the mountaineers of Northern Cambria. Peter and Margaret Strittmatter hosted a reunion in 1910. Among the families present were Leonard Holtz; Kate and Simon Schrift; John and Mary Kaylor; Aloysius and Rose Helfrick; Ed, Joe, and Hilda Strittmatter; Isadore and Frances Hoover; Thomas and Edna Drudine; and Anthony and Kate Fahey.

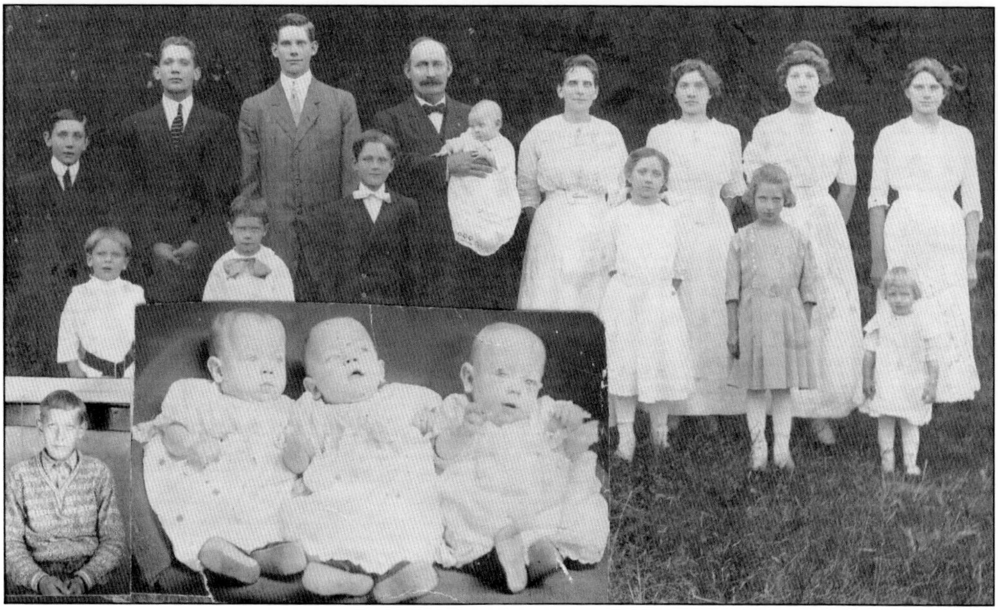

In 1916, the Andrew Kirsch family of Nicktown shows all 17 of their children. Seen here, from left to right, are as follows: (front row) Clair, William, Herman, Geraldine (Sr. Mary Consuella, RSM), Alma, Aline; (back row) Walter, Alucin, Edward, Andrew, the father (holding Merle), Amelia the mother, Demetria, Esther, and Ruth. Marlin is in the left inset. The triplets—Herbert, Harold, and Homer—arrived in 1915.

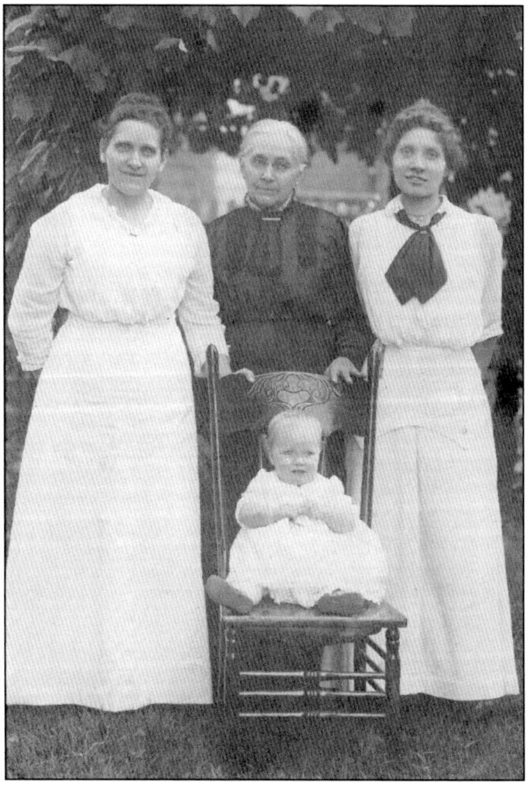

Nicktown has been home to generations of townsfolk who carry on the same agricultural endeavors as their ancestors. This 1916 photograph shows four generations in the same lineage. Great-grandmother Margaret Ager is in the center and grandmother Amelia Ager Kirsch is on the right with mother Demetri Kirsch Dumm on the left. They surround little Helen Marie Dumm, who would later become a Sister of Mercy.

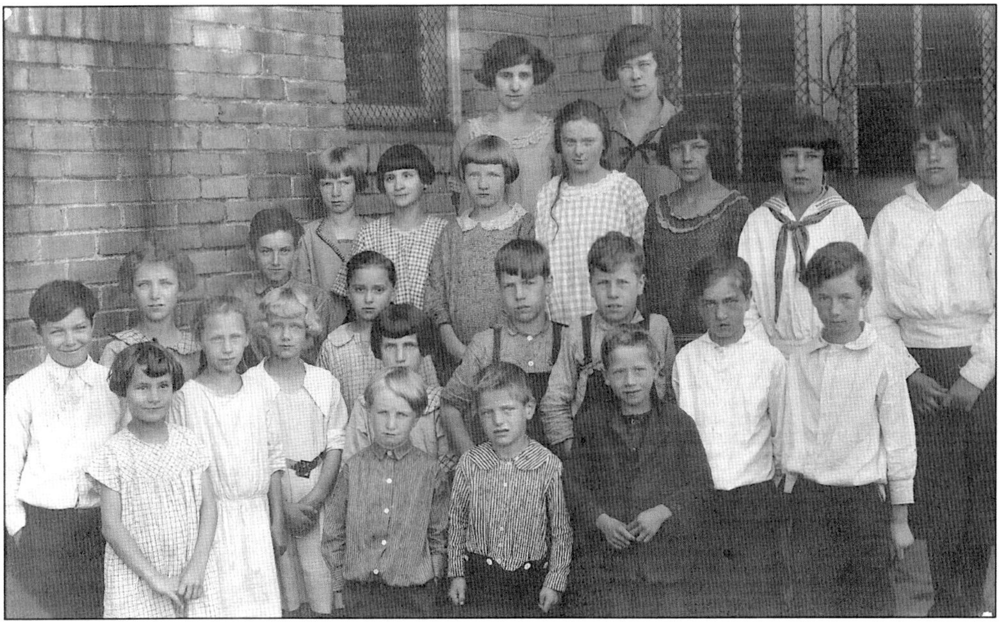

These children attended the Killen School in 1923. They are identified, in an uncertain order, on the back of the photograph as follows: Harry Clevenger, Alex Dumm, Fred Dumm, Helen Dumm, Isabel Dumm, Paul Dumm, Veronica Kirsch, Florence Peters, Grace Peters, William Peters, Blanche Shilling, Francis Shilling, Grace Stuby, Leona Stuby, Walter Shilling, Bernardine Styles, Doyle Styles, Ethel Styles, Jane Styles, Laura Styles, and Veda Styles. Their teachers, Genny Byrnes and Marie Stuby, are in the back.

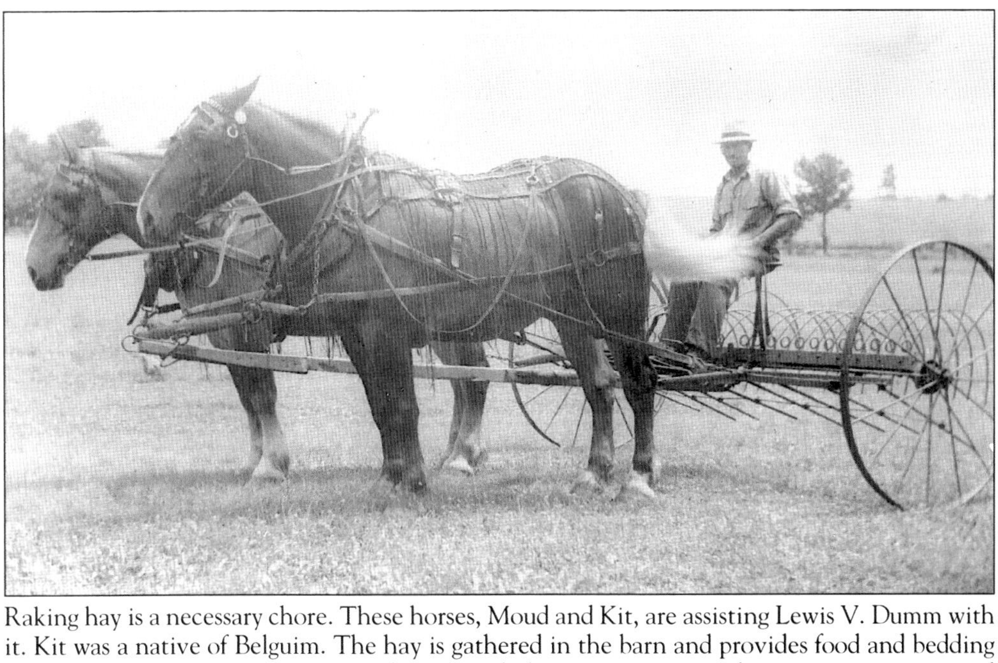

Raking hay is a necessary chore. These horses, Moud and Kit, are assisting Lewis V. Dumm with it. Kit was a native of Belguim. The hay is gathered in the barn and provides food and bedding for the livestock during the winter. Plowing and planting in spring, cultivation in summer, and harvesting in the fall are all part of the farmer's chores.

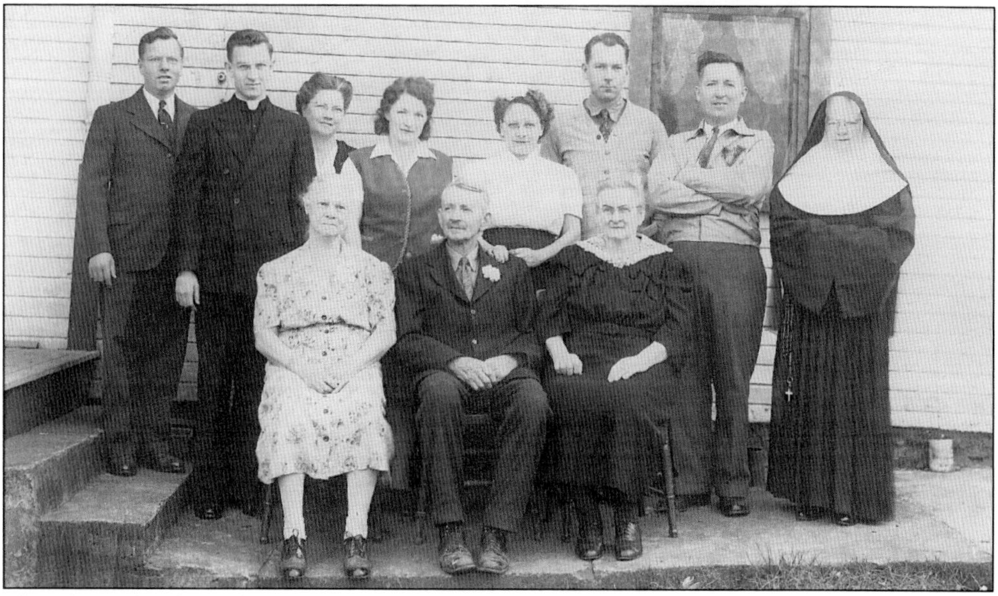

The Pfiester family are direct descendants of the founding father of Nicktown, Nicholas Lambmor. The family gathered for a reunion on November 2, 1946. Those seen here, from left to right, are as follows: (front row) Emma Leimier; Nicholas Valentine Pfiester, who was the first child baptized in St. Nicholas Church in Nicktown; Mary Pfiester Kirsch; (second row) Nicholas Jr.; Reverend Emeric of the Order of St. Benetict (OSB) of St. Vincent's Archabbey in Latrobe, Pennsylvania; Ester Bridge; Kathleen Krug; Irene Abbott; Carl; Joseph; and Sr. Mary Martha of the Religious Sisters of Mercy (RSM) of McAuley Hall, Cresson, Pennsylvania.

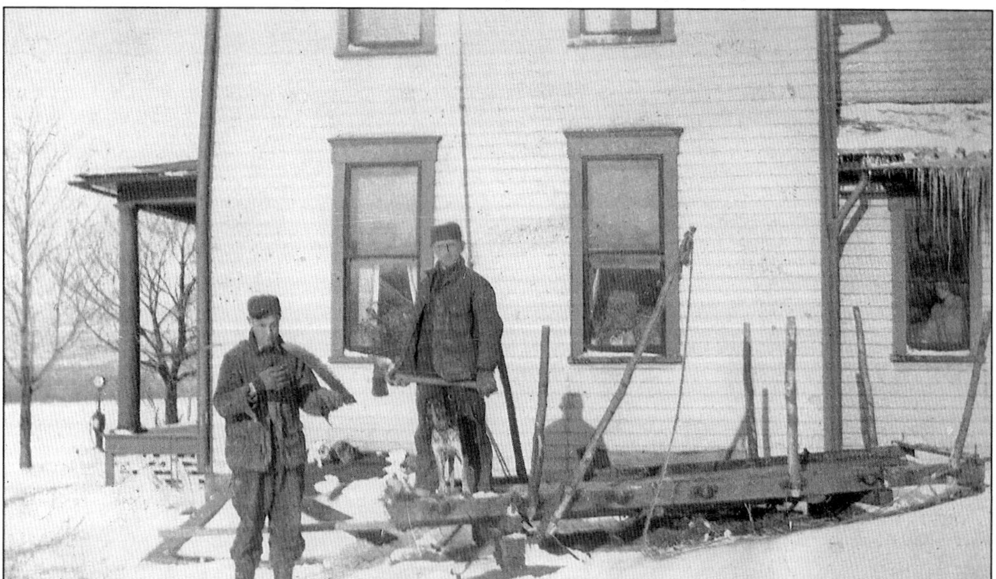

Stanton Ragley with his crosscut saw and Louis with a double-sided ax are using the tools of their trade. Their parents established a lumber mill along Blue Goose Road early in the 20th century. The dense woodlands of Nicktown lent themselves to a profitable lumbering business. The lumber wagon transported logs from the forest that were pulled by horses and, later, by tractor. Note the gas pump in front of the house and the icicle-fringed roof.

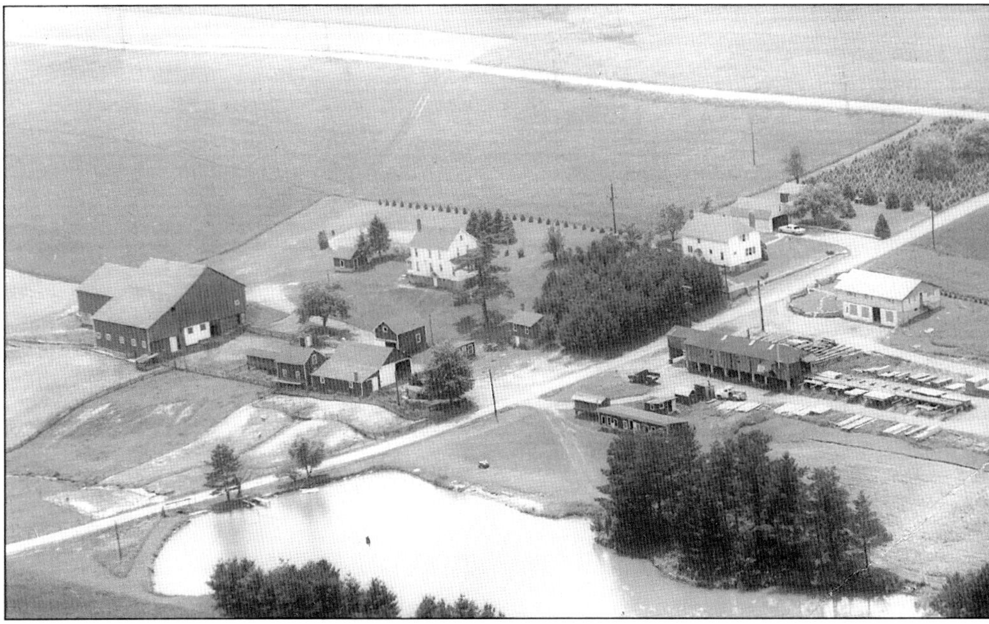

The Albert Dumm Farm was established in Barr Township by Albert Dumm Sr. It is typical of the neat farms that dot the Allegheny countryside. It was passed on to Albert's son, Albert Jr. It is currently operated by Gerald Dumm, the grandson of the founder. The farm chiefly raises beef cattle. This farm is unique in that the machinery is stored in a garage across the road. The farm also features a sawmill currently operated by Gerald Dumm.

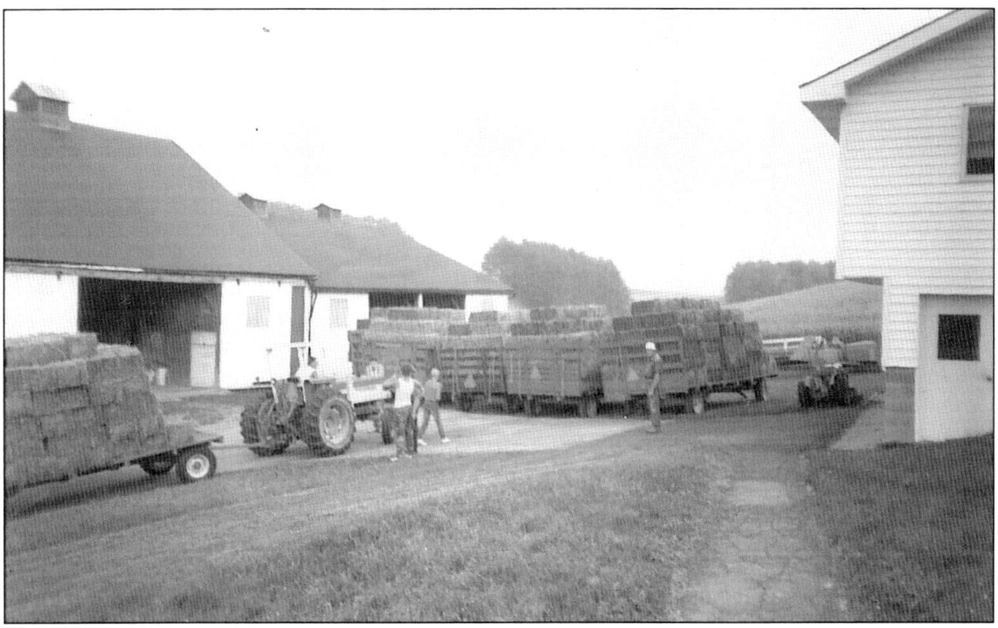

The menfolk have just finished making hay on the Albert Dumm Farm in Nicktown. Today's hay-making differs from that of earlier times. The hay loader of a bygone era is no longer used by the modern farmer, whose machinery does much of the work. The hay is raked, picked up, and put into bailers. The machine gives it a neat, square look. It is then stacked in the barn for the cows.

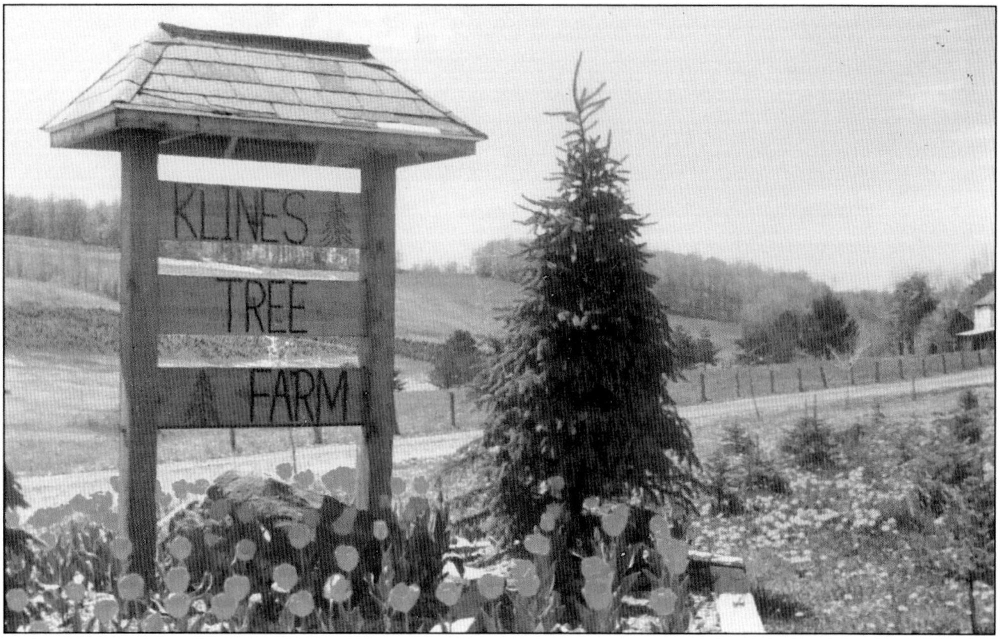

Kline's Tree Farm is located between Nicktown and Spangler. Established by the Kline brothers, the trees are in various stages of maturity. Expansive fields of growing evergreen trees are in the background. The brothers married sisters: the daughters of Albert and Mary Lieb Dumm. Tree production is prosperous throughout the Allegheny Mountain region.

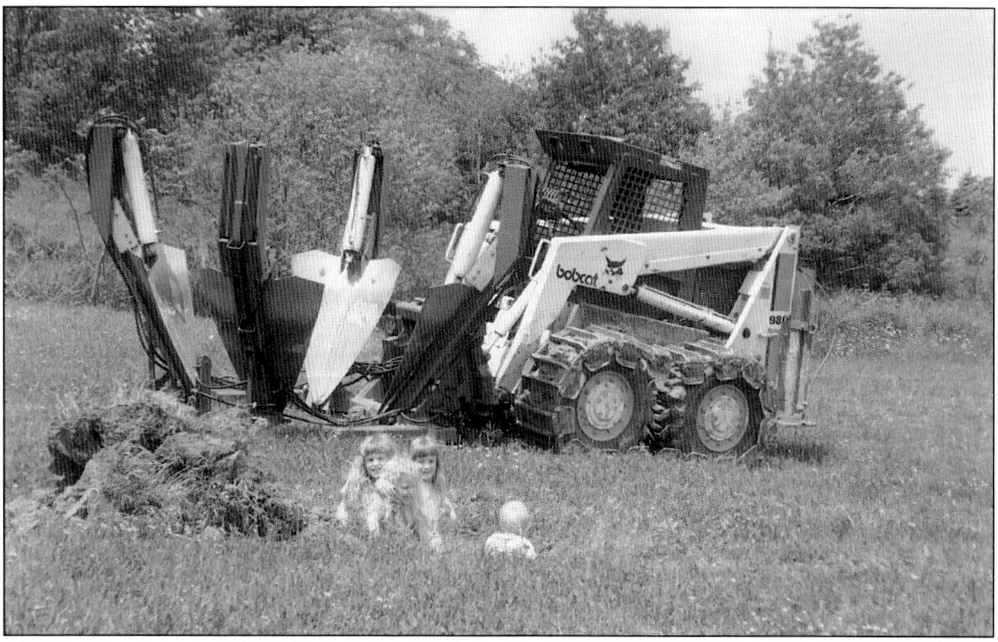

The Bobcat tractor and spade are used for transplanting trees or preparing them for the market. Spraying and trimming are all part of the tree farmer's chores. The trees are shipped in huge balls of soil wrapped in burlap to various markets, often out of state. Cultivated trees are sought for landscaping. Sharon, Libby, Jennifer, and William Kline, the children of the combined Kline families, enjoy watching the Bobcat.

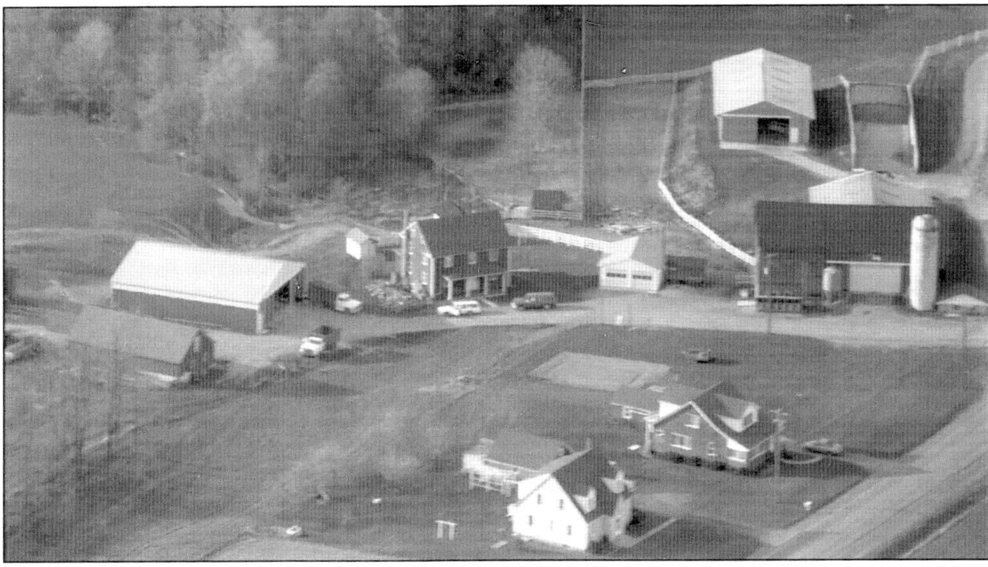

The Barr Ridge Farm in Nicktown has passed through five generations in the same family. In 1861, German immigrant Adam Lieb established the farm. In 1879, his son Joseph bought the farm and built the family homestead. In 1917, Joseph's son Peter took it over. In 1952, Peter's son Herman became the chief farmer, expanding it and making necessary improvements. In 1988, Herman's son Ralph became proprietor. Eighty cows supply milk to dairies in the area of the Barr Ridge Farm.

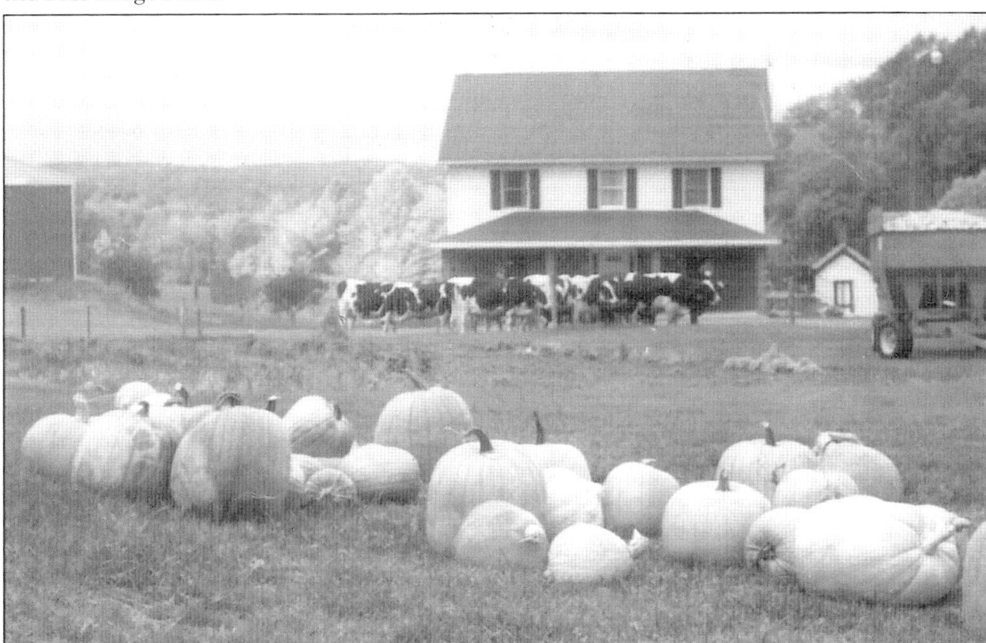

The Lieb farmhouse was built by second owner, Joseph Lieb, before the beginning of the 20th century. It stands on the Barr Ridge Farm in Nicktown. The pumpkins are ready for market. The cows are taking a scenic route to the barn and the wagon is full of corn that will become silage. Milk is sold to dairies that will process, bottle, and sell it. The spring house is in the background.

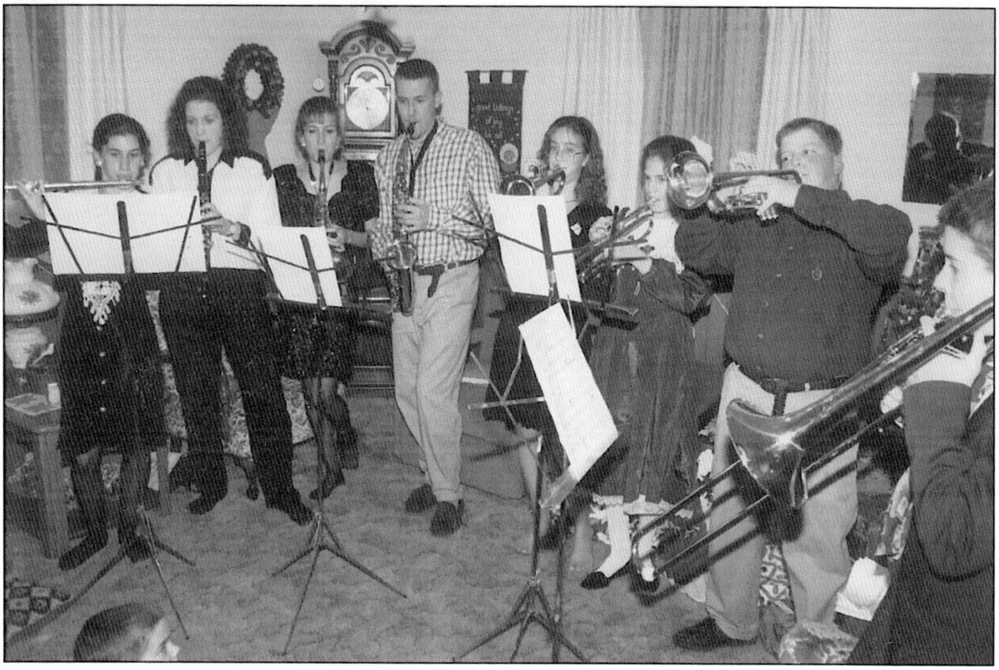

A Christmas concert is given by a group of Lieb grandchildren. It became a tradition that the grandchildren would use their musical instruments to entertain each Christmas Eve when the family gathered together. The musicians, from left to right, are Lisa, Marie, Diane, Scott, Sharon, Tracey, Marty, and David.

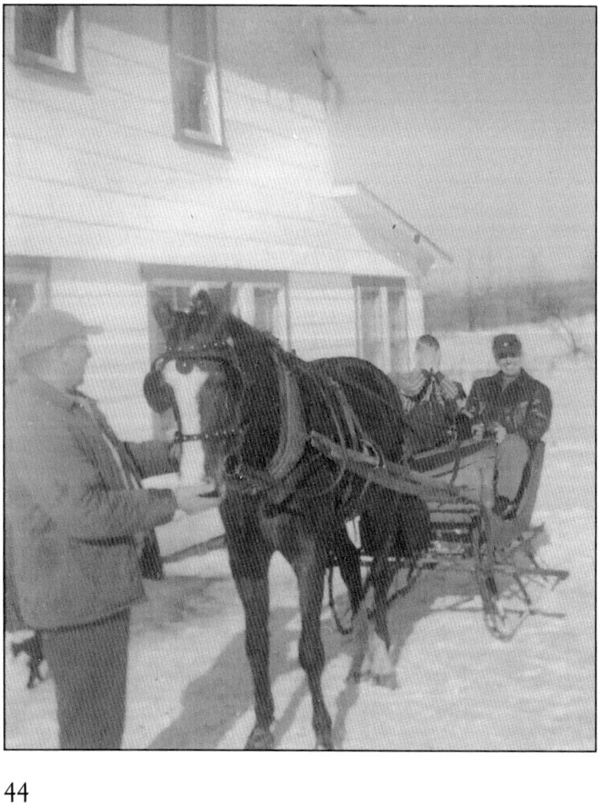

Time is allotted for a genuine old-fashioned sleigh ride. The horse is held by John Nealan. Herman Lieb and son, Ralph (holding the reigns), are ready for the winter fun. The snow of Northern Cambria lends itself to such adventure over a lengthy winter. The "one-horse open sleigh" was a natural reality in the early days of Cambria County.

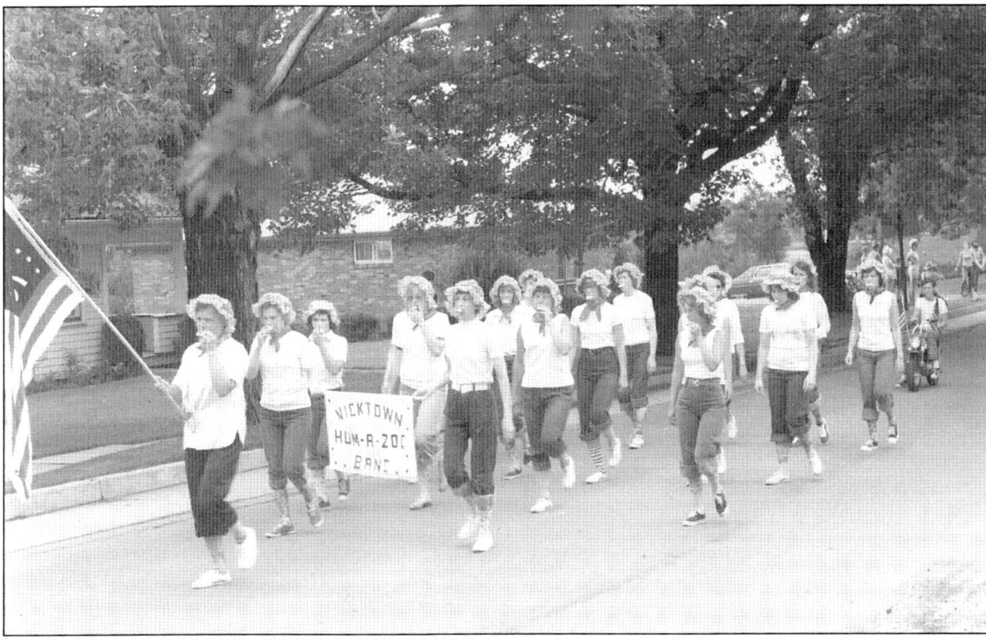

The Hum-a-Zoo Band marches along Nicktown's Main Street in the bicentennial parade. They are led by flag bearer Shirley McNulty. Jane Kirsch and Grace Lieb carry the banner. On July 4, 1976, our country looked back over two centuries of "life, liberty, and the pursuit of happiness." As Americans across the country gathered in towns and villages to celebrate the birth of this great nation, Nicktown joined the festivities with a parade.

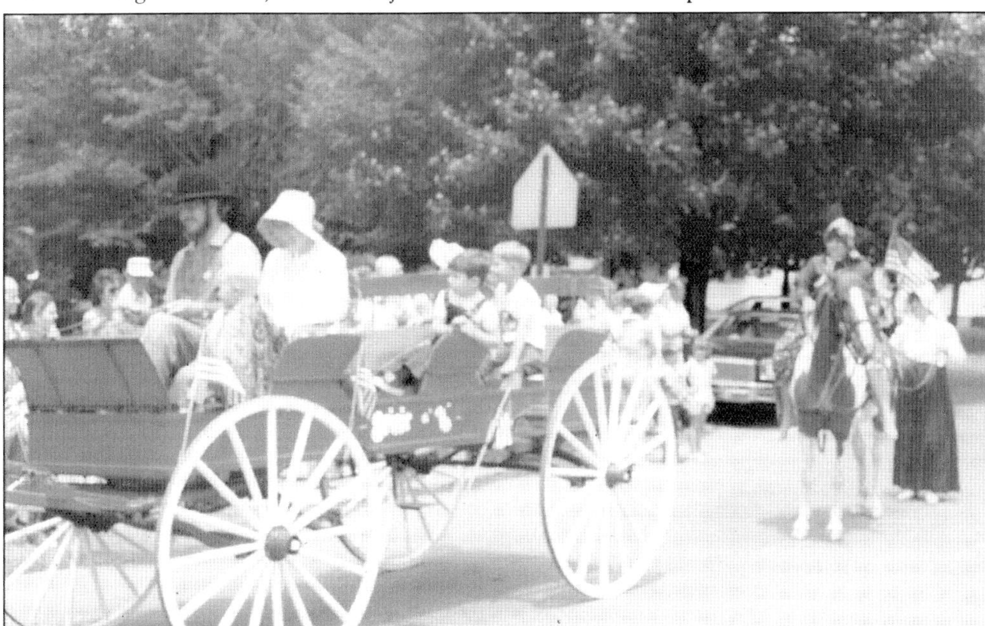

A surrey takes part in the bicentennial parade through Nicktown. The drivers were Edward and Sue Lieb, who were dressed in colonial costume. Their children enjoy the patriotic festivities along the route as they reenacted colonial days. The surrey later became part of the annual Appalachian Wagon Train.

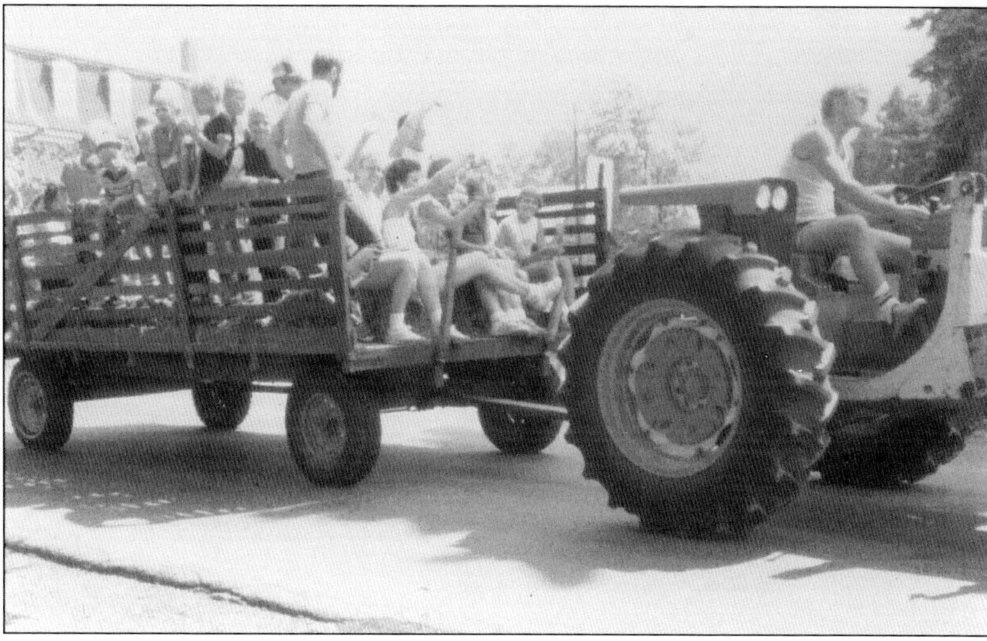

The annual Lieb reunion is accompanied by an old-fashioned hay ride through the area. Mark Dumm, son of Albert and Mary Lieb Dumm, conceived of this idea, and it has become a tradition. He takes a merry group on the rustic excursion. The wagon is filled with bales of hay where the riders sit to enjoy the trek through the woodlands. The horses have been retired and a tractor now pulls the wagon.

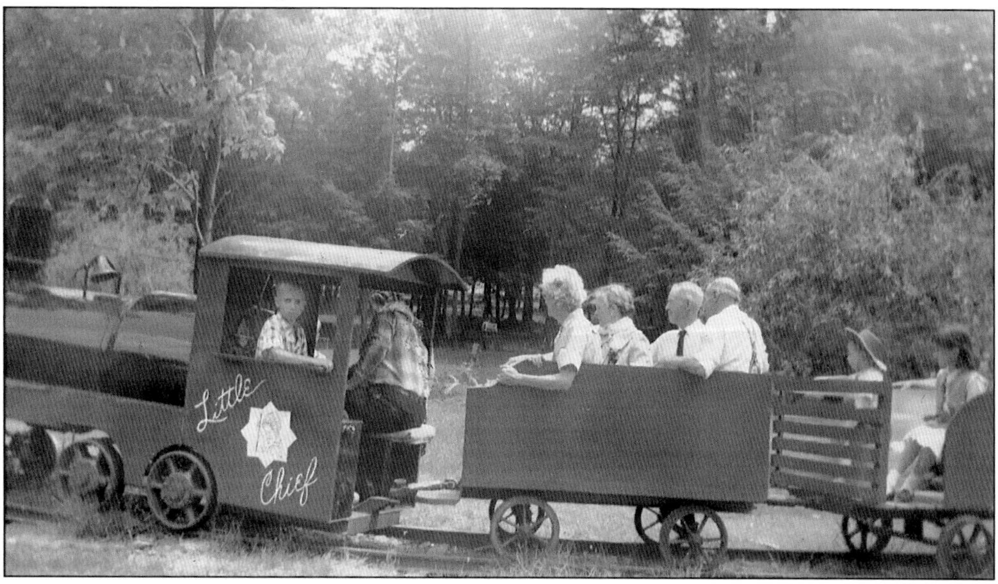

The patrons of Duman Park enjoy an excursion. Duman Lake is a 20-acre body of water located in Nicktown. In 1928, the Sportsman Association built a dam designed for recreation and fishing. In 1953, Fred Soisson convinced the club to establish the 71-acre park with shelters, tables, and recreational facilities. A deep well pump was installed. Long-range planning included a grandstand along the athletic field. The Duman brothers of Nicktown purchased the original 25-acre tract of land.

Three

NAMED BY THE PRINCE

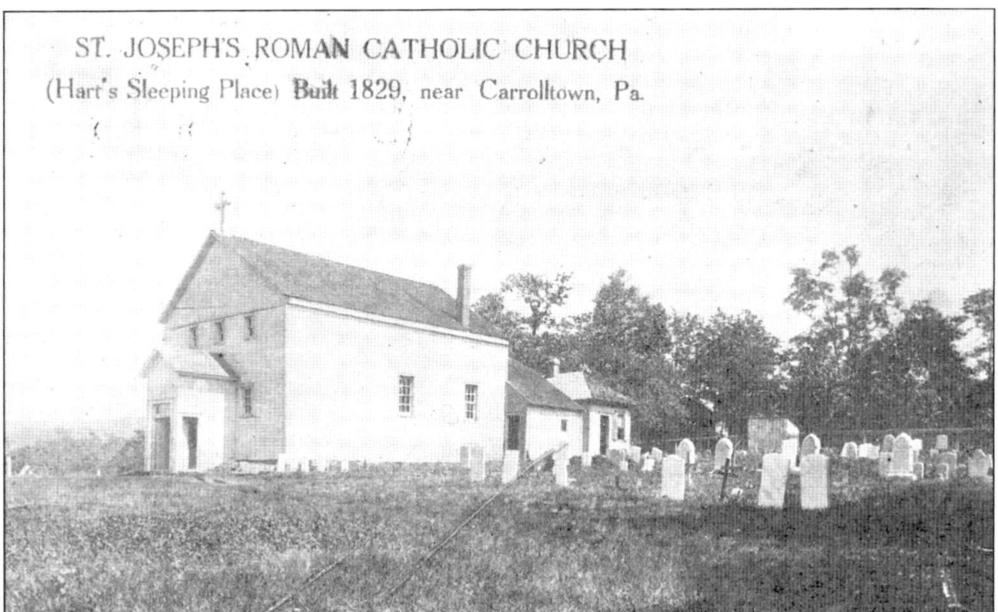

St. Joseph's Church at Hart's Sleeping Place has become a notable historic landmark. The log structure was built by the pioneers of Carrolltown and dedicated by the Prince Priest, Demetrius Gallitzin. Built in 1830, it was the center of Catholicity in the Northern Cambria area for two decades. Nestled in the mountains, the little mission church is surrounded by a cemetery of early parishioners. It has stood for 17 decades on a lone countryside, bearing silent witness to its founders.

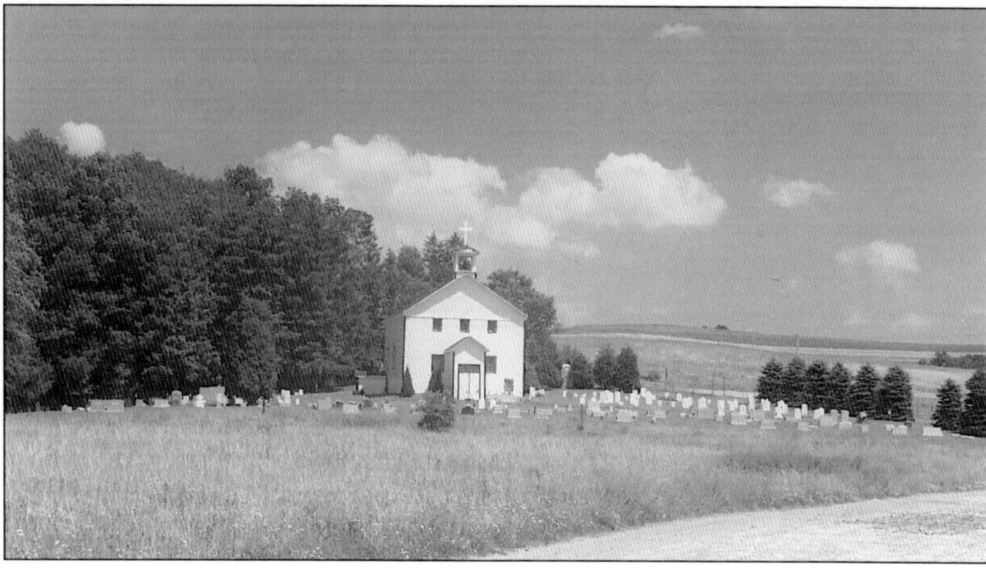

In 1835, the Reverend Peter Lemke was appointed pastor of St. Joseph's Church. He intended to surround the little church with a town, but the population shifted southward toward the main highway. Lemke bought 395 acres south of Hart's Sleeping Place and built a spring house with living quarters and a small log chapel. St. Joseph's Church is the oldest surviving wilderness mission in Cambria County aside from the Chapel House in Loretto. It was blessed on October 10, 1830 and belongs to the Roman Catholic Diocese of Altoona-Johnstown.

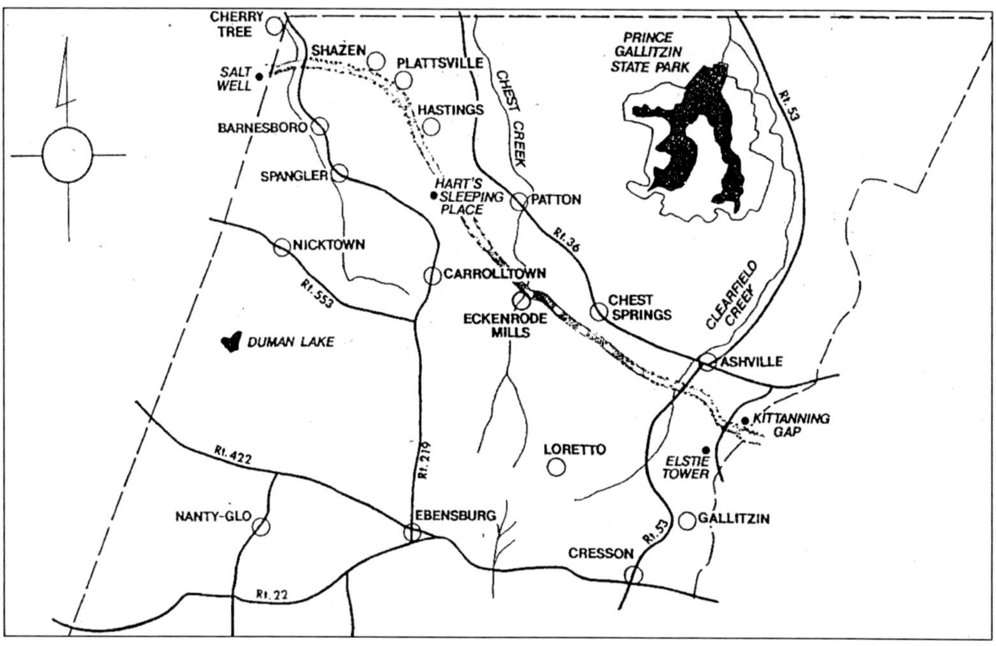

Hart's Sleeping Place is located along an ancient Native American path. Known as Kittaning Trail, it winds through Northern Cambria County. John Hart was a hunter and trader. In 1775, he built a post along the trail at the site we now know as Hart's Sleeping Place. He often rested here while crossing the mountains. The site was long abandoned as a post when Father Lemke, aware of its origin, chose the area for a church.

The Reverend Peter Lemke wanted to name his town Gallitzin after the Prince Priest. He acceded to the wishes of Gallitzin and named it after the first Roman Catholic Bishop to serve in the United States, Bishop John Carroll. He purchased the land from William S. Vaux and established a log chapel at the present site of St. Benedict's Church. This was the beginning of Carrolltown. Lemke was the priest, the lawyer, and the doctor to his mountain flock.

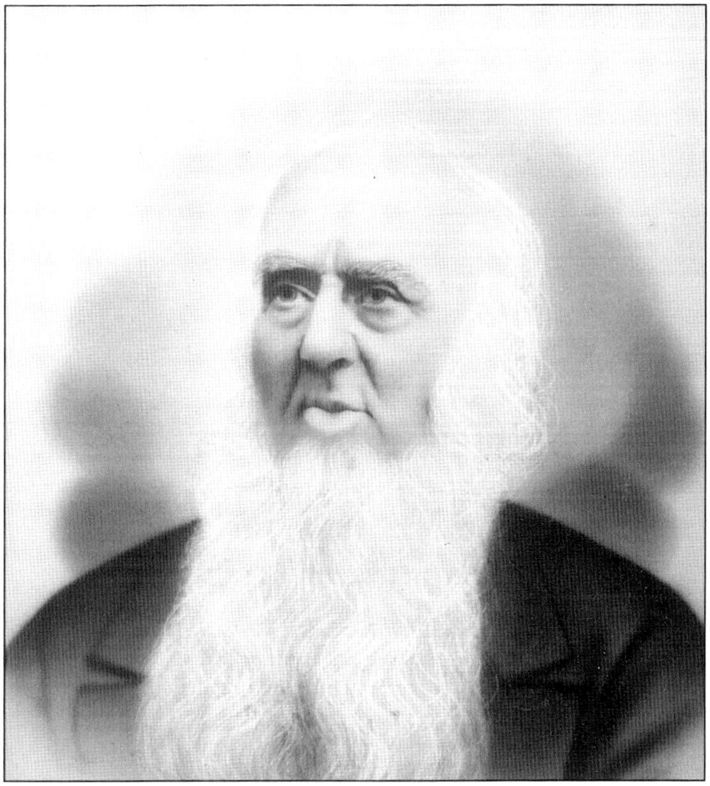

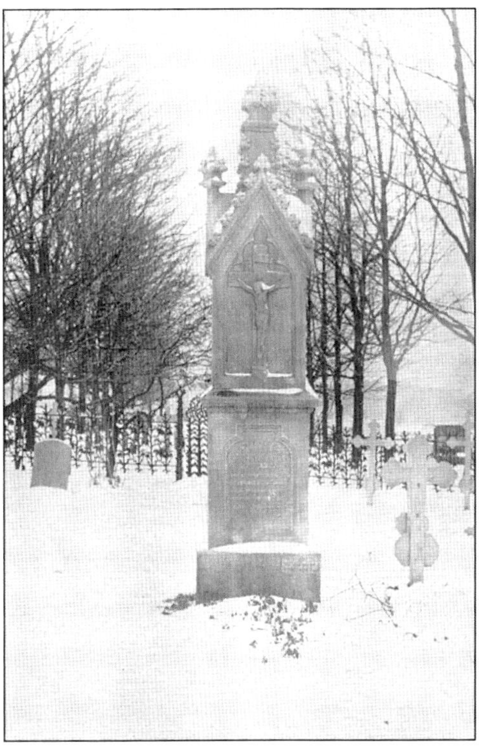

This monument in St. Benedict's Cemetery marks the resting place of Fr. Peter Lemke. He was later known as Father Henry of the Order of St. Benedict and is the founder of Carrolltown. Ordained in Germany in 1826, he came to the Alleghenies as a missionary. In his pastorate at Hart's Sleeping Place, he overcame many obstacles. The first was the death of his good friend, the Prince Priest, Father Gallitzin, in 1840. Lemke later became a Benedictine monk and died in 1882.

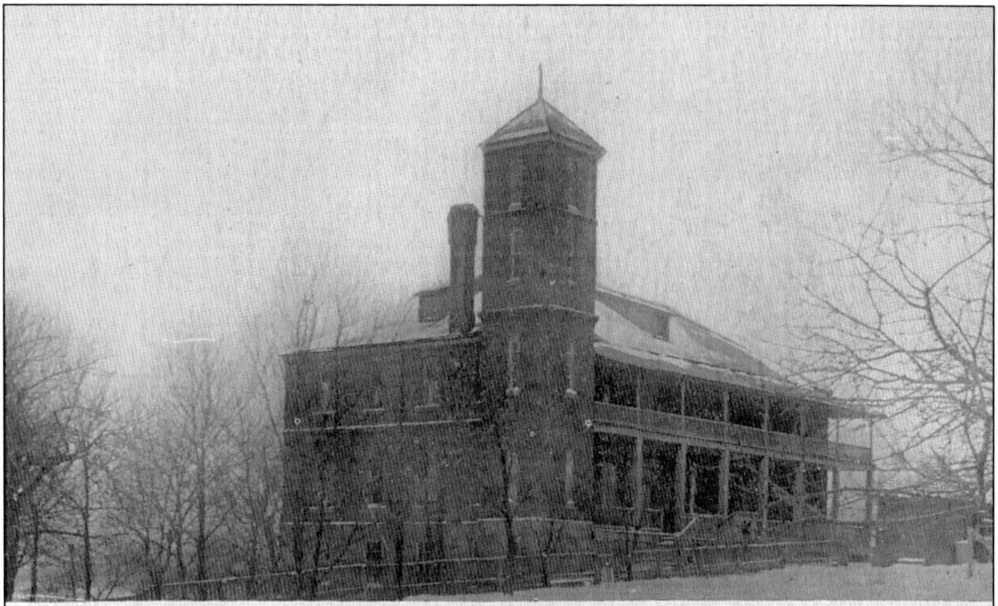

ST. BENEDICT'S MONASTERY, Carrolltown, Pa.

In 1844, Father Lemke visited Germany. He called on the Benedictine Monastery of Metten in Munich and returned with the promise of Benedictine monks. They were offered land for a monastery. In July 1846, four students and 15 lay brothers arrived under the direction of Fr. Boniface Wimmer of the Order of St. Benedict. Their initial stay in Carrolltown was short because Bishop Michael O'Connor of Pittsburgh suggested a site in Latrobe. A monastery was later established in Carrolltown.

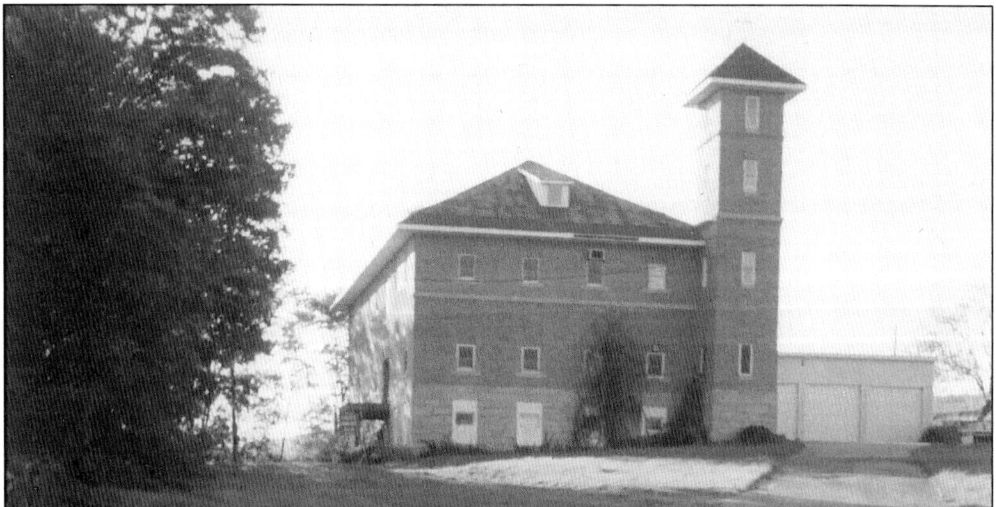

Fr. Boniface Wimmer returned to Carrolltown in 1848 after he had established his community in Latrobe. He bought 298 acres of land from Father Lemke to establish the Benedictine community in Carrolltown. This purchase included Lemke's house and the log church. The first monastery was built in 1846, the second in 1865, and the third in 1902. Now an abandoned abbey, it was a central office for missionary ventures. The Benedictine priests served Bakerton, Barnesboro, Hastings, Patton, Nicktown, Spangler, St. Augustine, and St. Lawrence.

The Reverend Peter Lechner of the Order of St. Benedict was appointed the first Benedictine pastor. His task was building the new church. In March 1849, the contract was signed, and work got underway. The church stands on property deeded by Father Lemke. It is 102 by 28 feet and was dedicated on Christmas day 1850. In 1885, a hand-carved oak altar was imported from Germany. In 1906, a pipe organ was installed.

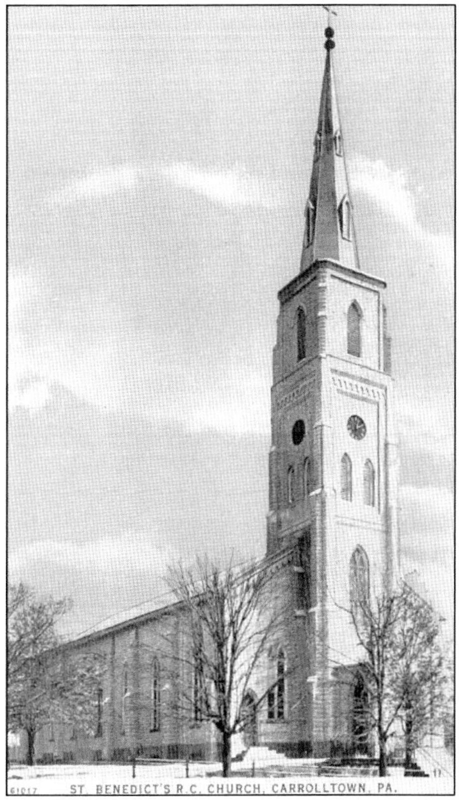

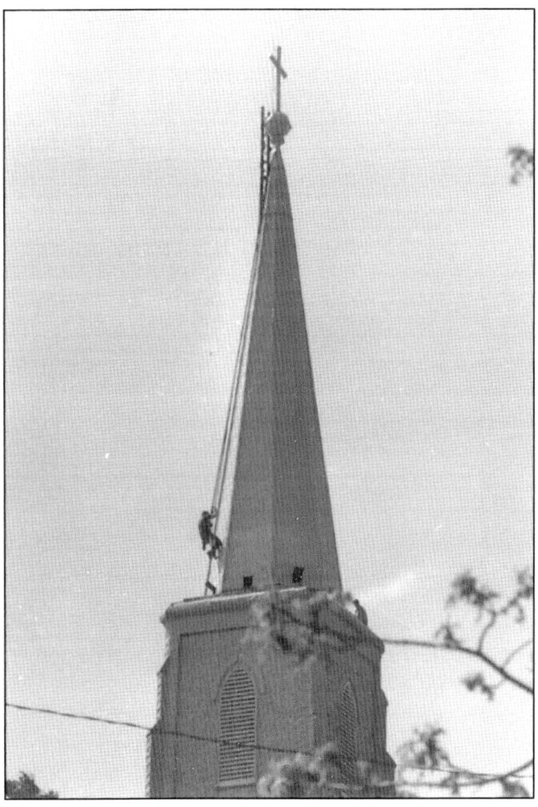

The famous steeple of St. Benedict's Church towers 172 feet into the heavens. It affords a focal point, a landmark almost akin to a lighthouse. This prominent spire was added in 1872. It projects an aura of steadfastness and dependability. Four bells installed at its base still call the faithful to prayer. The grandeur and majesty evoked by the familiar minaret stand out as a beacon. The landmark steeple can be seen for miles in various directions.

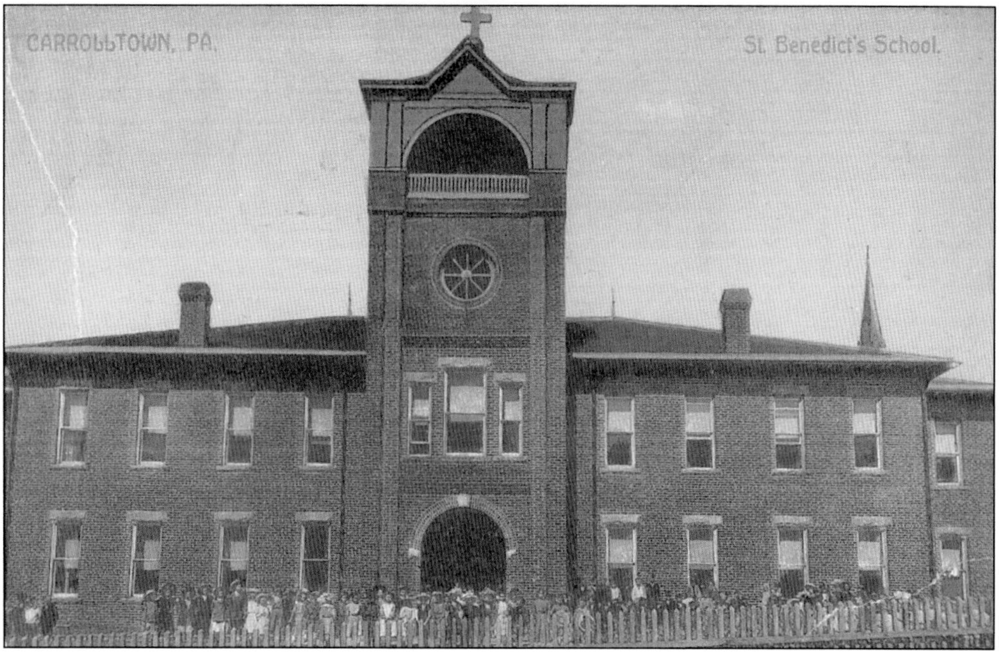

This school dates to 1870, when it was established in response to a rising population. The Benedictine Sisters of St. Mary's, Elk County, opened the school in the church basement. Bricks for a school building were quarried in the monastery brickyard and the lime was donated by John Wirtner from his lime kiln. On October 14, 1878, St. Benedict's School was dedicated and opened with 450 students in eight grades.

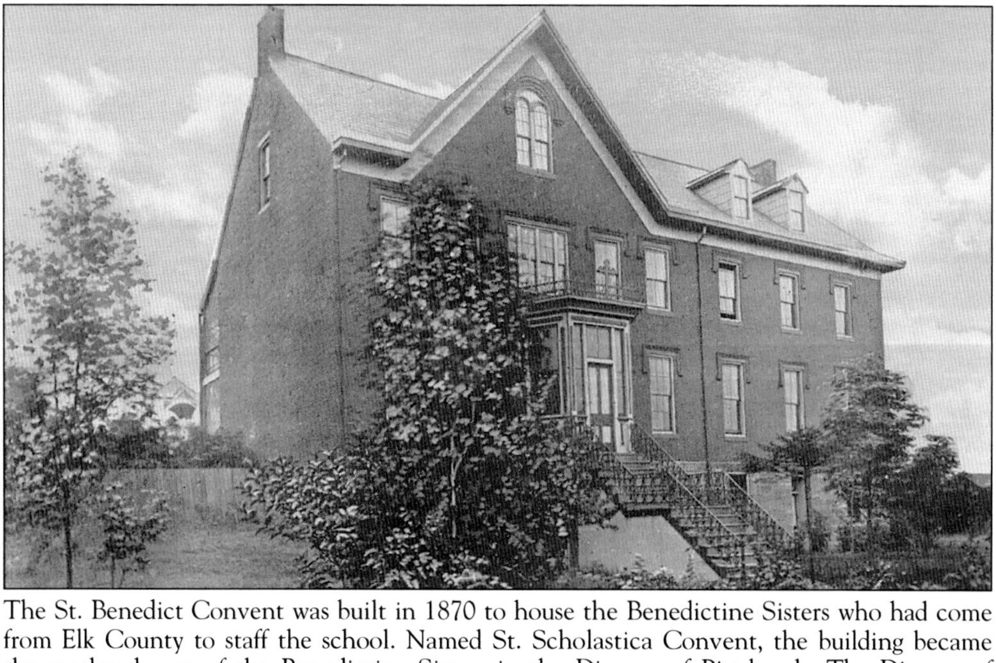

The St. Benedict Convent was built in 1870 to house the Benedictine Sisters who had come from Elk County to staff the school. Named St. Scholastica Convent, the building became the mother house of the Benedictine Sisters in the Diocese of Pittsburgh. The Diocese of Altoona-Johnstown was not formed until 1902. The convent became an old landmark it was dismantled in 1969.

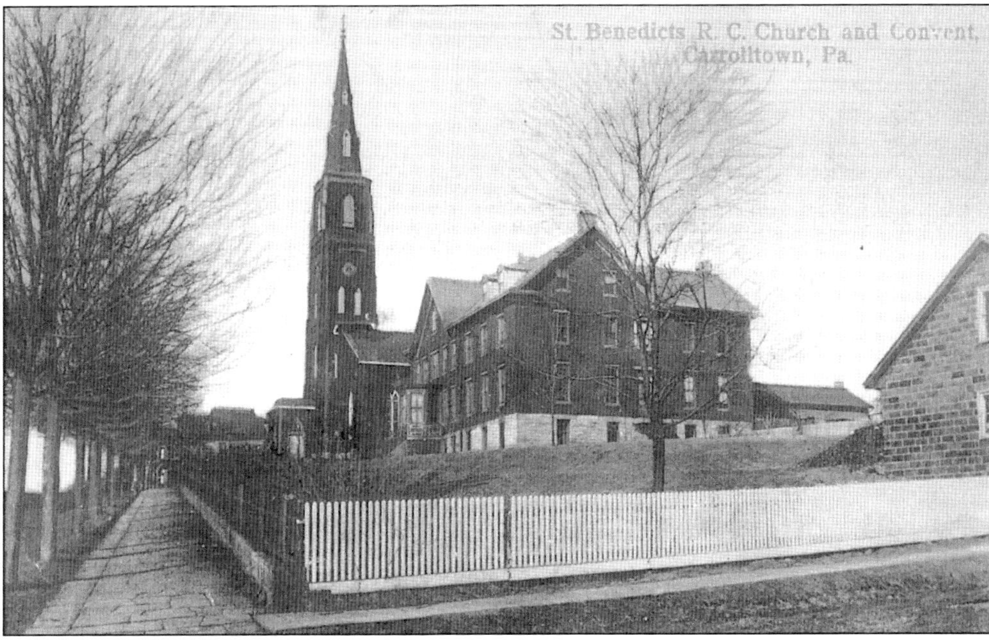

The St. Benedict Church and Convent were surrounded by a crude sidewalk in 1908. Roads were first paved with planks. In 1924, Main Street was widened and cement was placed on the level areas. Brick paving was used on the steep sections to provide traction for horses and wagons. It would be another decade before additional roads in the borough were macadamized. The Main Street was dubbed the "Lake to Sea Highway." We now know it as Route 219.

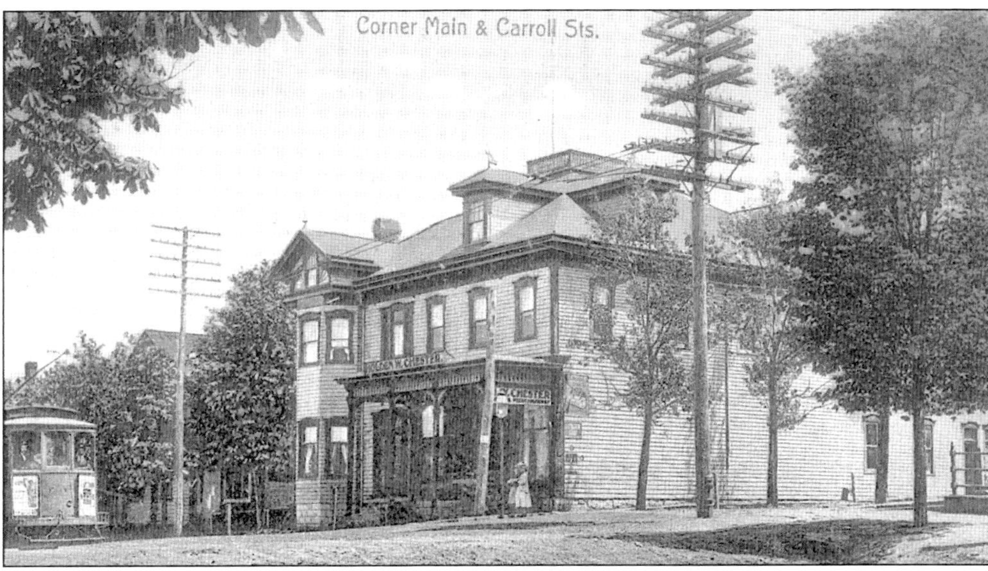

The first store in Carrolltown was located on the northeast corner of Main and Carroll Streets. Dating to 1850, the store went through several owners, such as John Sharbaugh and Andrew Eckenrode. In this postcard postmarked 7 a.m. on June 4, 1912, Holden W. Chester was the proprietor. The trolley travels south, and the conductors can be seen in uniform. This postcard, like many others, was published by Sharbaugh dry goods store, but printed in Germany.

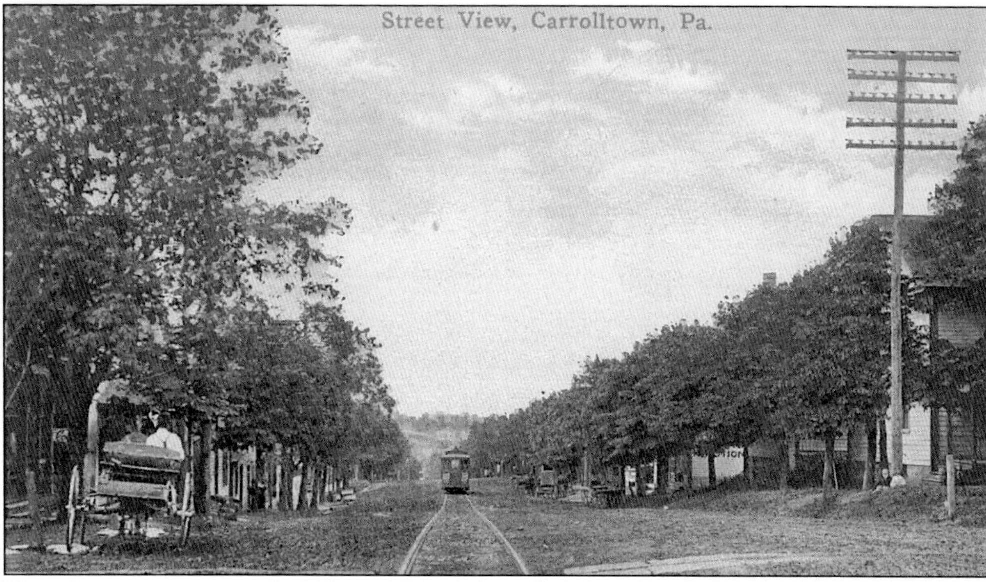

Main Street was unpaved in this 1919 northward view. The P.L. Eck general merchandise store is on the left, followed by Kirsch's meat market and other community establishments. On the right, the H.W. Chester general merchandise store had been established since 1888. This later became the American Legion. Note the width of the road and the wagon on the left. At this time, the Northern Cambria Streetcar Railway Company transported passengers to and from Carrolltown.

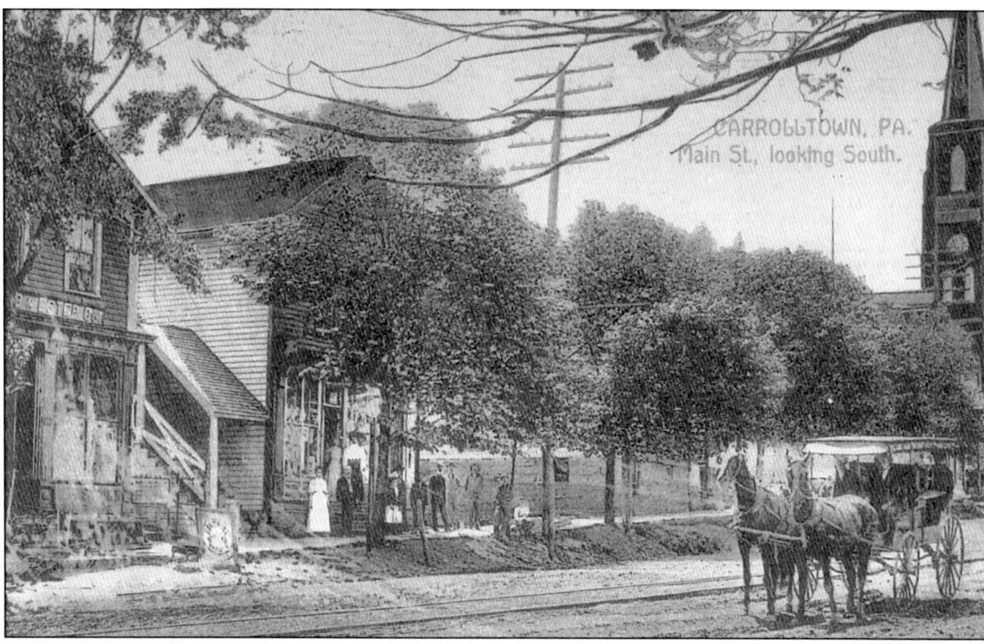

Main Street looking south in 1909 featured a tailor shop on the left, which later became Lieb's family hardware store. On the right and hidden by a tree is the former Lawrence A. Sharbaugh dry goods store. A small music room was located on the second floor of this building, where lessons were given and recitals were held. The tower of St. Benedict's Church rises in the background. Sidewalks were boardwalks, or plank walks, to prevent people from walking in mud.

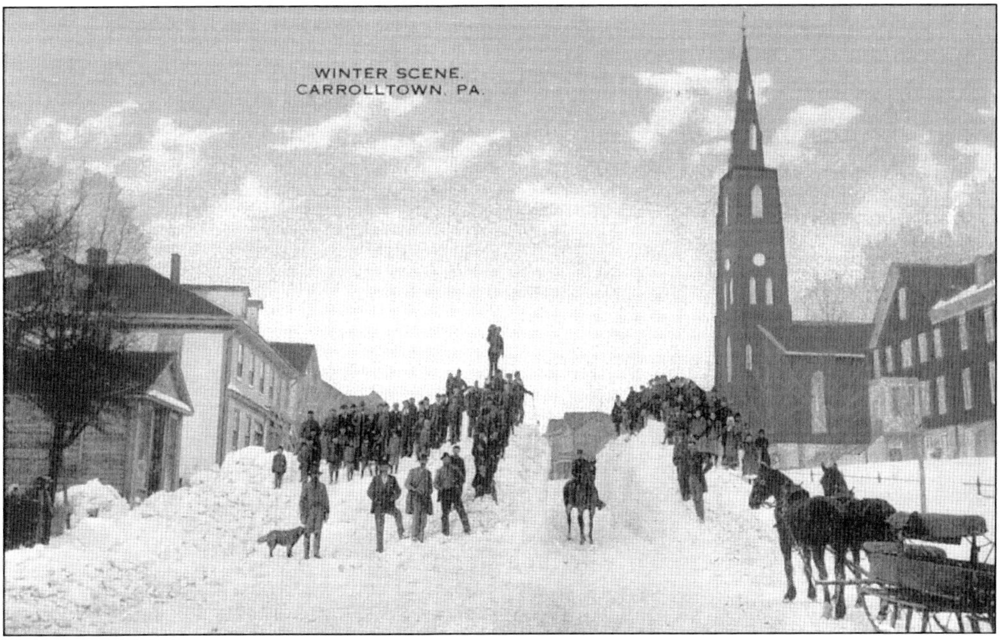

Traveling on Carrolltown's Main Street in the snow of 1936 could be a challenge. This blizzard provided such an occasion for the townsfolk. Adam Fees rides through the drift on horseback, while McAuliffe is atop the highest drift. The liquor store is visible between the drifts. Scanlon's wooden building is on the extreme left, and St. Benedict's Church is on the right. Note the narrow, single lane through the drift

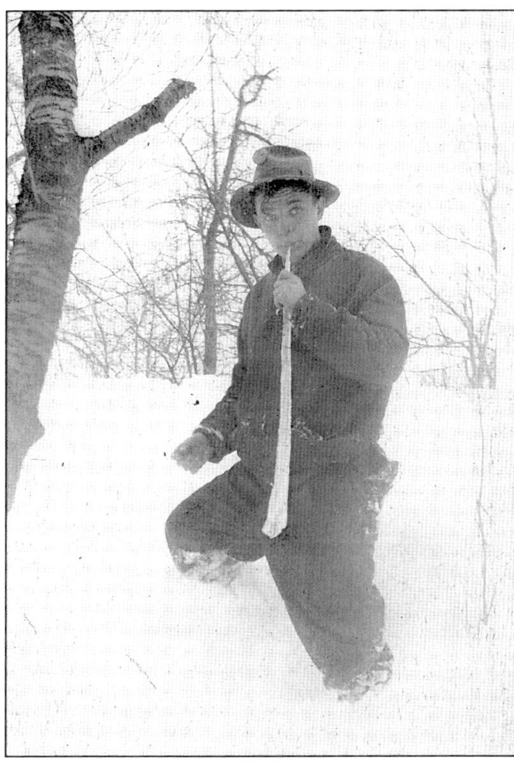

This gentleman is a musician. He seems to be playing "Ode to a Snowdrift." In reality, Dan Connell is enjoying an ice-cold refreshment after cleaning the furnace in his Carrolltown home. The elongated "instrument" grew from the roof in the extreme cold of Northern Cambria County and made an invigorating snack. Icicle-fringed rooftops and picturesque white roadways have always been part of Carrolltown's winter scene. This photograph was taken in March 1944.

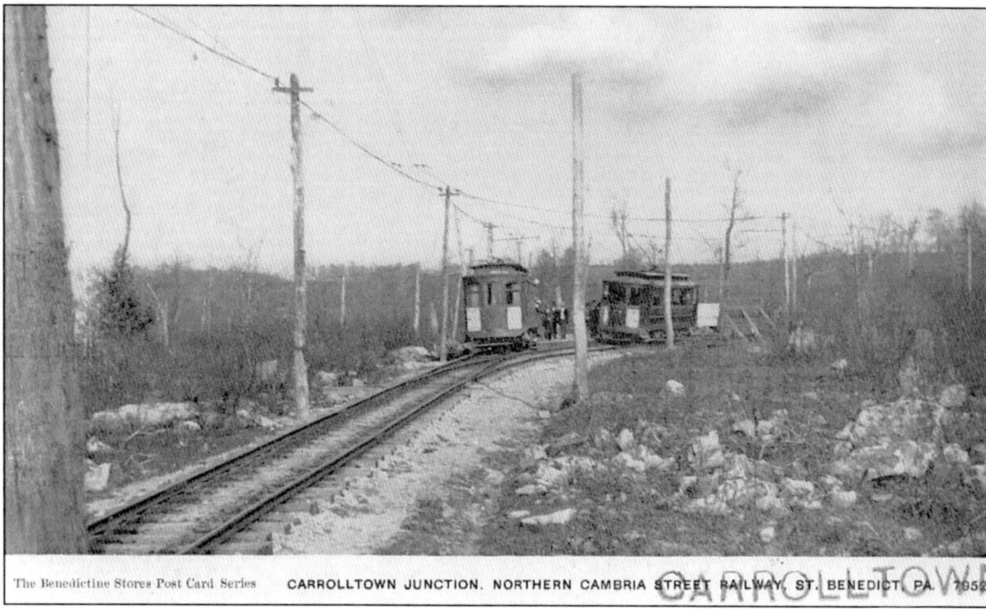

The Northern Cambria Street Railway constructed a trolley line that connected various communities in the north of the county. Baker's Crossing was located at the Carrolltown Junction, midway between Hart's Sleeping Place and Carrolltown. The railway company established a grove and a dance hall. The building gradually evolved into a first-class ballroom surrounded by picnic grounds. The automobile later took over, and both transported young and old to dances, basketball games, and community events at Sunset Park.

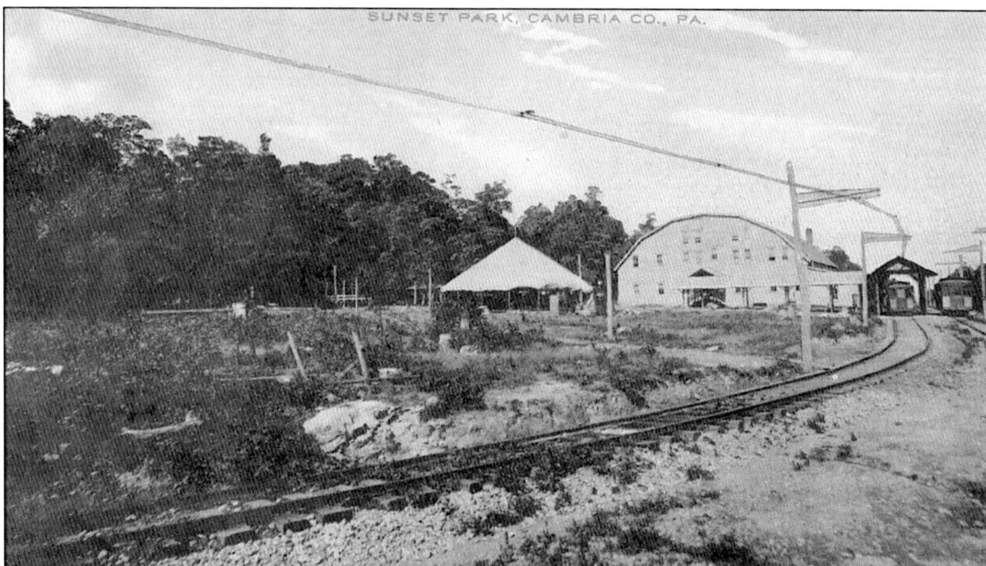

The Sunset Ballroom and auditorium were built by private ownership. The Sunset was known as the world's most unique ballroom and attracted many big bands of the era. Among those who performed were Tommy Dorsey, Sammy Kaye, Glen Miller, Guy Lombardo, Rudy Vallee, Frank Sinatra, Ziggy Orman, Joe Stafford, and the original Inkspots. It was large enough to accommodate sizable crowds and was a source of entertainment very popular in the early 20th century.

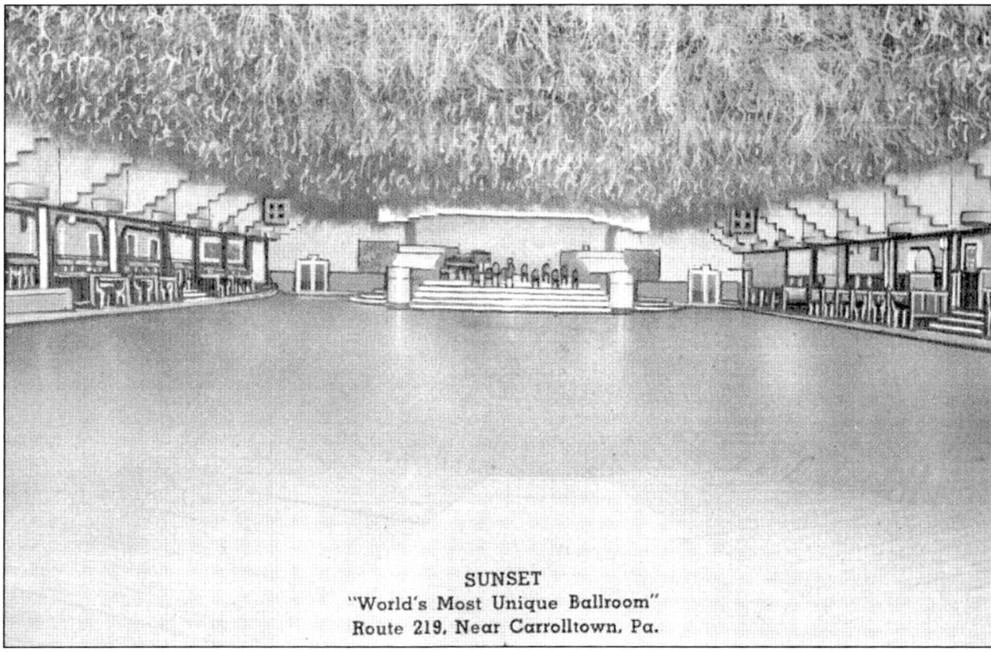

The Sunset Ballroom was often transformed into a skating rink, a basketball court, or a gymnasium. It supplied the needs of large crowds in a recreational mode. Sunset Park was renowned not only in Cambria County, but also throughout the region. The mammoth dance hall was 80 feet wide and 150 feet long. One hundred and fifty thousand board feet of lumber were used in its construction. The formal opening took place on January 1, 1909. Five hundred pairs of skates were bought for the occasion.

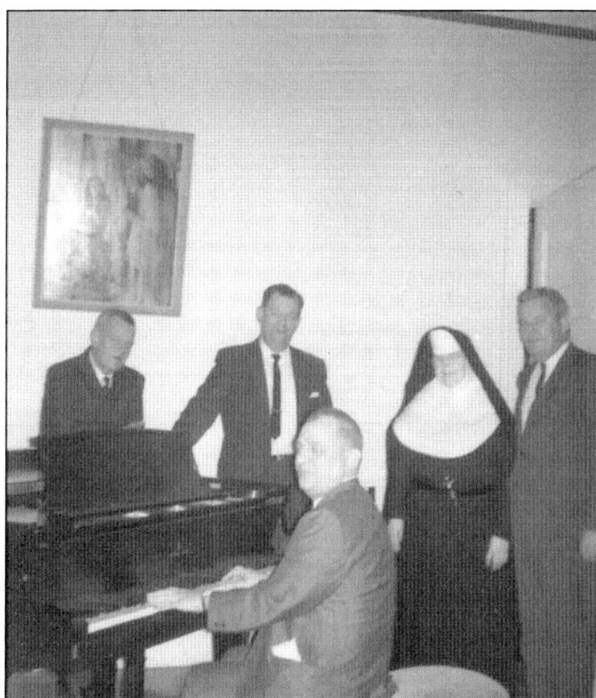

This band was once the Connell Quartet of Carrolltown. Dan accompanied his brothers Joe, Jack, and Dick as they entertained their aunt, Sr. Marie Therese Powers of the Sisters of Mercy on her Golden Jubilee. Daniel was a young accomplished pianist during the era of the Sunset Ballroom. He supplied the music between big band acts and often memorized the latest hit parade songs. He then played for such celebrities as Sammy Kaye and Tommy Dorsey.

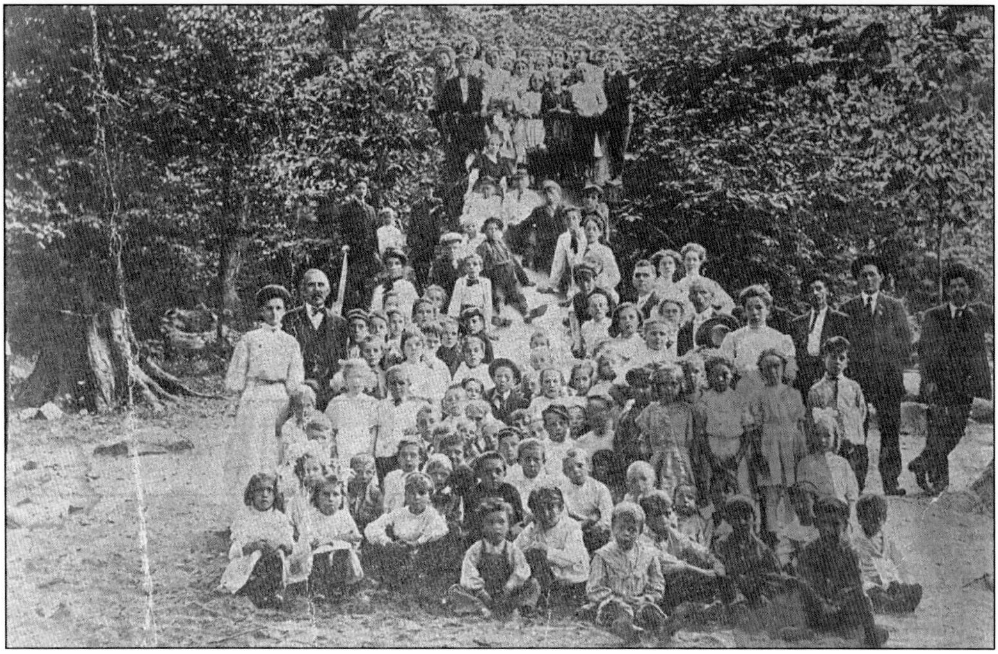

Denlinger's Slide was among the attractions at Sunset Park. William H. Denlinger owned an oil supply business and built a home on Fifth Avenue, which still stands, in Patton. He served as postmaster and was instrumental in the establishment of Sunset Park. The huge slide was named for him. This postcard, dated 1911, advertises "Thank heaven you are not digging in the ditch of Panama Canal—you can visit Sunset Park."

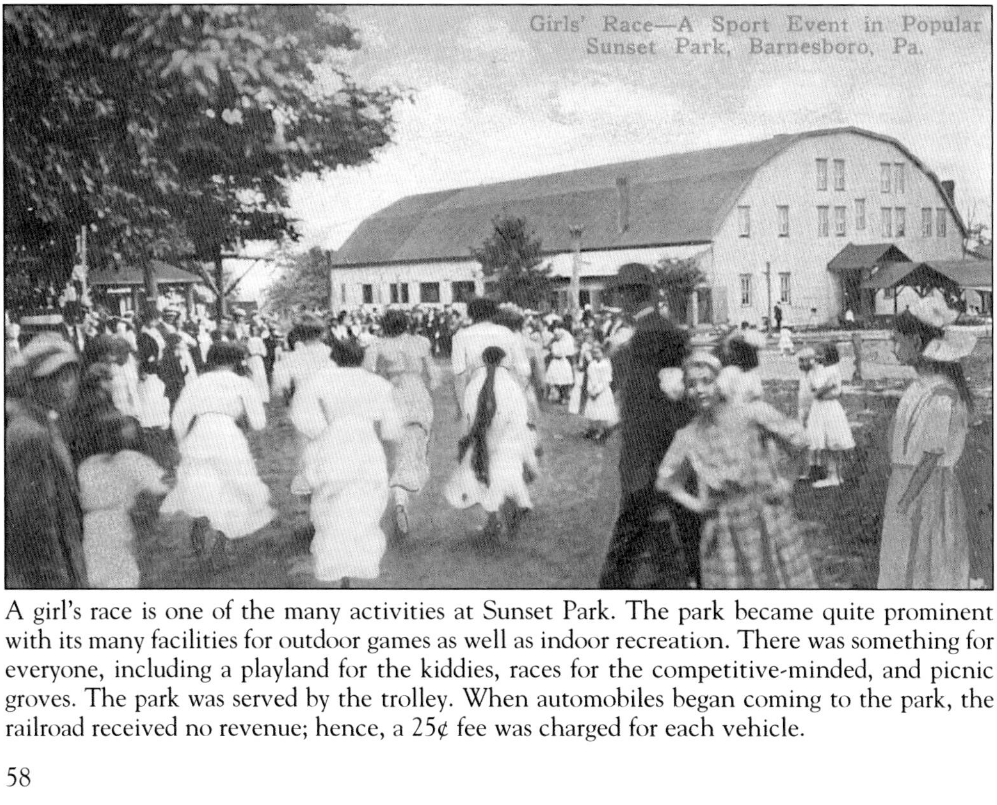

A girl's race is one of the many activities at Sunset Park. The park became quite prominent with its many facilities for outdoor games as well as indoor recreation. There was something for everyone, including a playland for the kiddies, races for the competitive-minded, and picnic groves. The park was served by the trolley. When automobiles began coming to the park, the railroad received no revenue; hence, a 25¢ fee was charged for each vehicle.

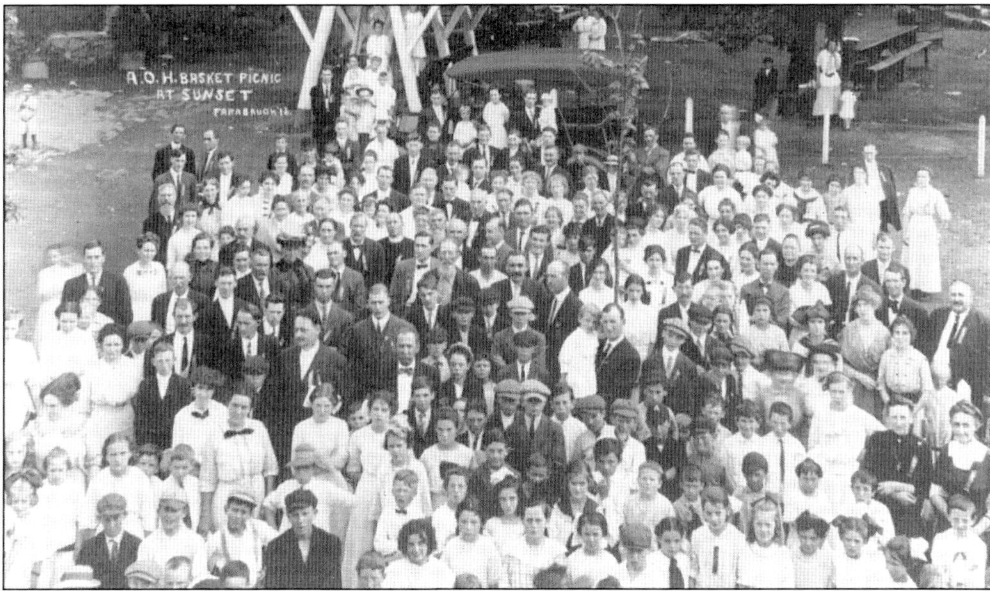

The Ancient Order of Hibernians (AOH) enjoys a picnic at Sunset Park. The AOH originated during penal times in Ireland and consisted of men who guarded the priest while he was offering the Mass for the people in the woodlands. Catholic churches were outlawed during penal times (the interval between 1700 and 1800). The AOH today consists of those immigrants and their descendants who aim to preserve Irish culture. They were among many who came to Northern Cambria early in the 20th century.

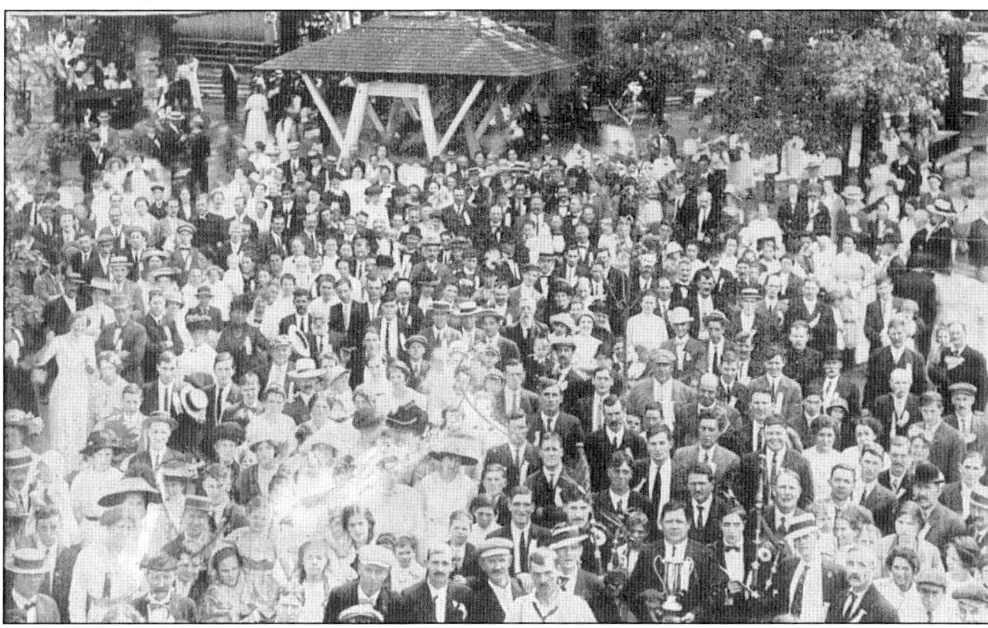

A Scottish picnic is enjoyed at Sunset Park. Immigrants from many lands streamed into Northern Cambria during the first half of the 20th century. Ethnic groups were very strong and ethnic churches were prominent. These institutions kept the culture of the homeland alive. The timber industry and coalmines were attracting forces. Work was always available and the area began blending ethnicities to conform with the American way of life.

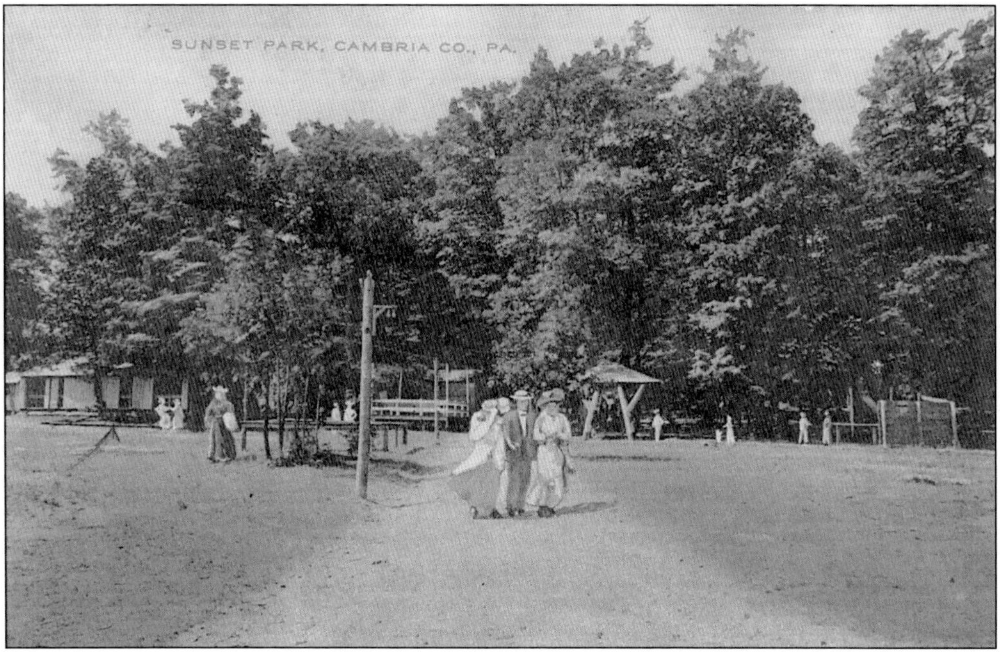

The entertainment at Sunset Park was varied. It included anything from kiddie rides to poker. In 1914, Mrs Lora W. Vandergift, a modern dance instructor from Altoona, was hired to teach modern dance and eliminate the objectionable features in the Bunny Hug, the Turkey Trot, and other such dances. These were prohibited while modern dance was encouraged. Dancing took place from 8:30 to 11:30 p.m. In 1909, an Easter ball was among the festivities. The Spiece Orchestra furnished the music with 300 spectators in attendance.

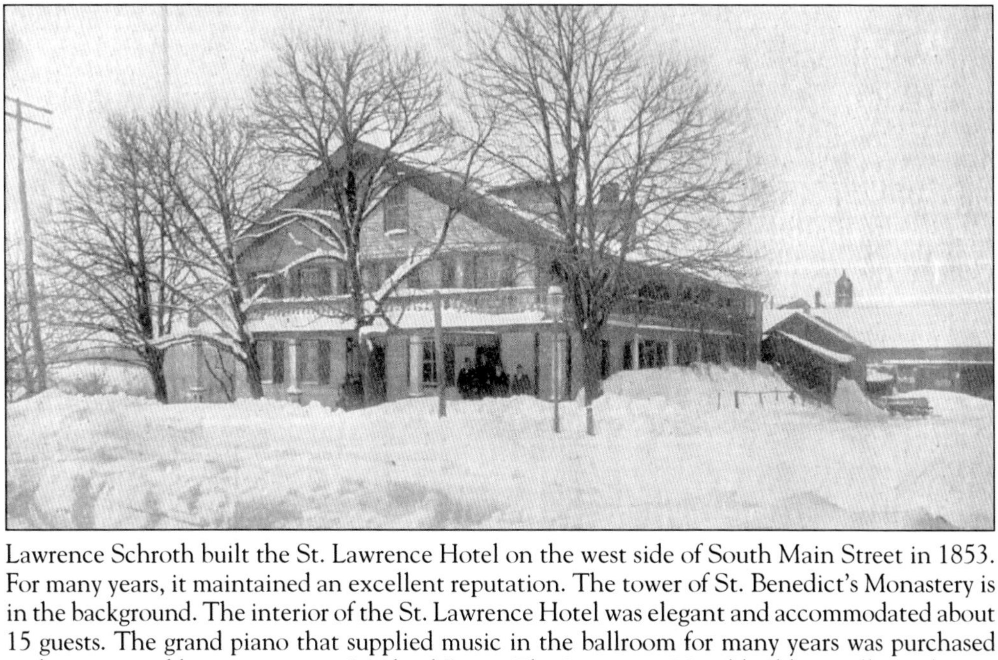

Lawrence Schroth built the St. Lawrence Hotel on the west side of South Main Street in 1853. For many years, it maintained an excellent reputation. The tower of St. Benedict's Monastery is in the background. The interior of the St. Lawrence Hotel was elegant and accommodated about 15 guests. The grand piano that supplied music in the ballroom for many years was purchased and is preserved by a native son, Michael Ryan. The Lawrence Hotel building still stands.

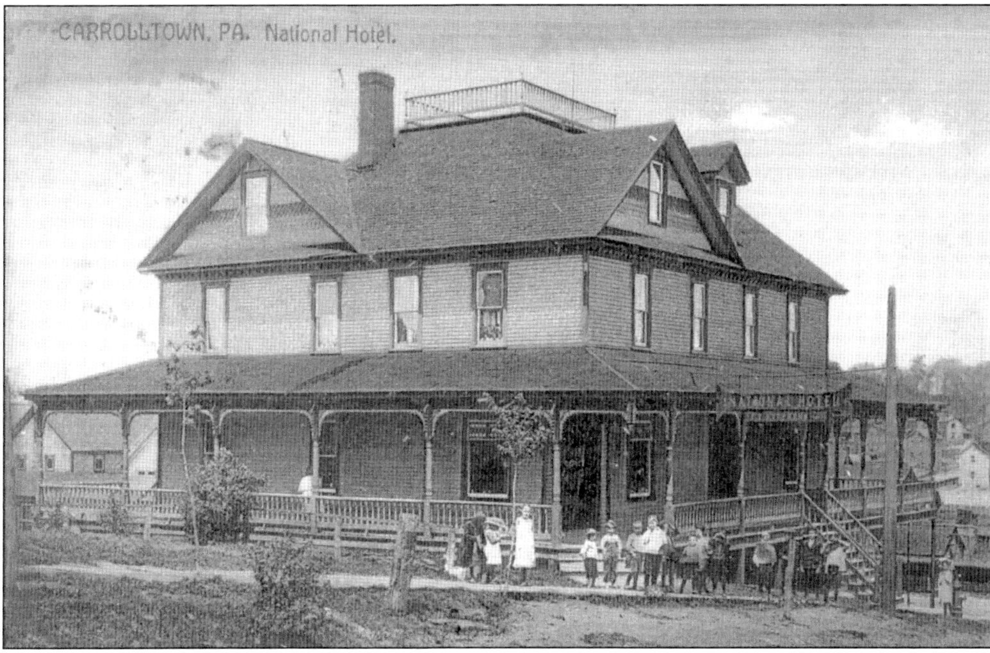

The National Hotel stood on the east side of north Main Street in Carrolltown. The charming building of a bygone era features a square widow's walk on the rooftop. This afforded wives an opportunity to look out to the fields and see when the farmers and miners dispersed for the day. The wrap-around porch afforded the simple pleasure of yesteryear: hotel dwellers could enjoy the evening breezes while chatting with folks passing by.

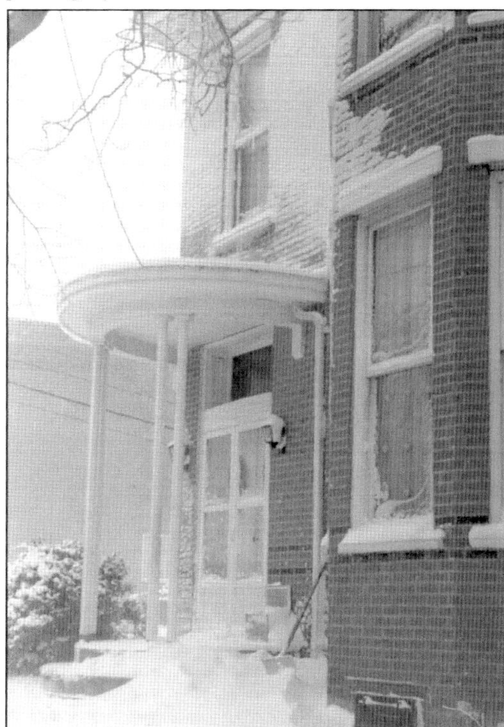

The Eck House was built as a residence by Percival L. Eck in 1873. Eck came to Carrolltown and bought Dr. James O'Tool's building on the southwest corner of Main Street and the Bakerton Road. He established a grocery store and practiced dentistry and photography in the building. That site is now the parking lot for the bank. Eck's home was next door. It was owned by Mary T. Ryan and has since become the Ryan estate.

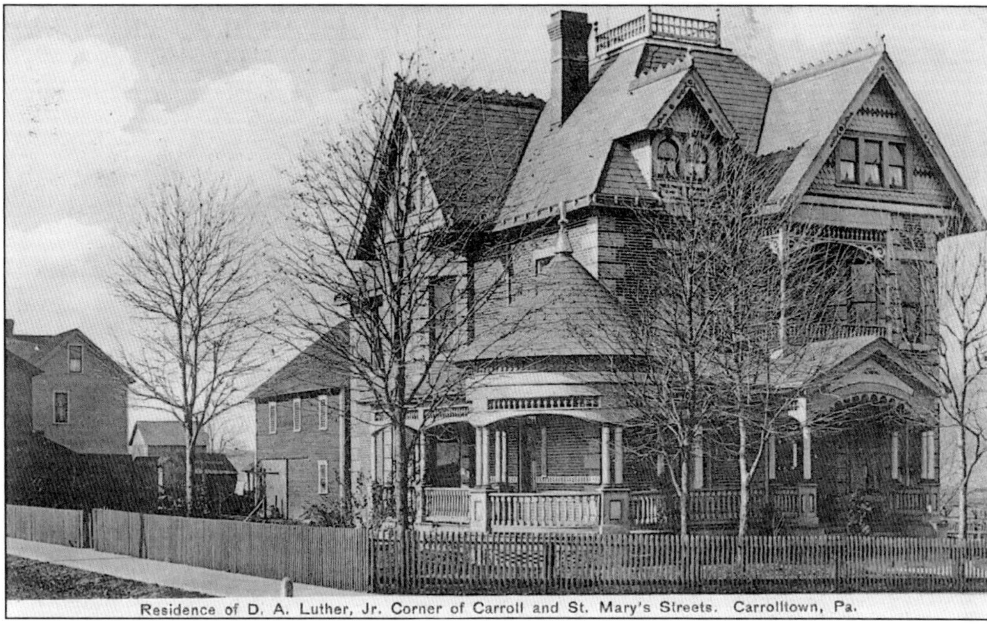

D.A. Luther built his home on the northwest corner of Carroll and St. Mary Streets. A sidewalk in front of the building provided a roller-skating area for the small fry of the hamlet. In 1922, D.A. Luther became the proprietor of the Sunset Ballroom and park. The ballroom was originally built by Alvin Eckenrode; it was later taken over by Eugene Bearer. Luther retained ownership of the Sunset until his death in 1945, at which time his wife continued the tradition.

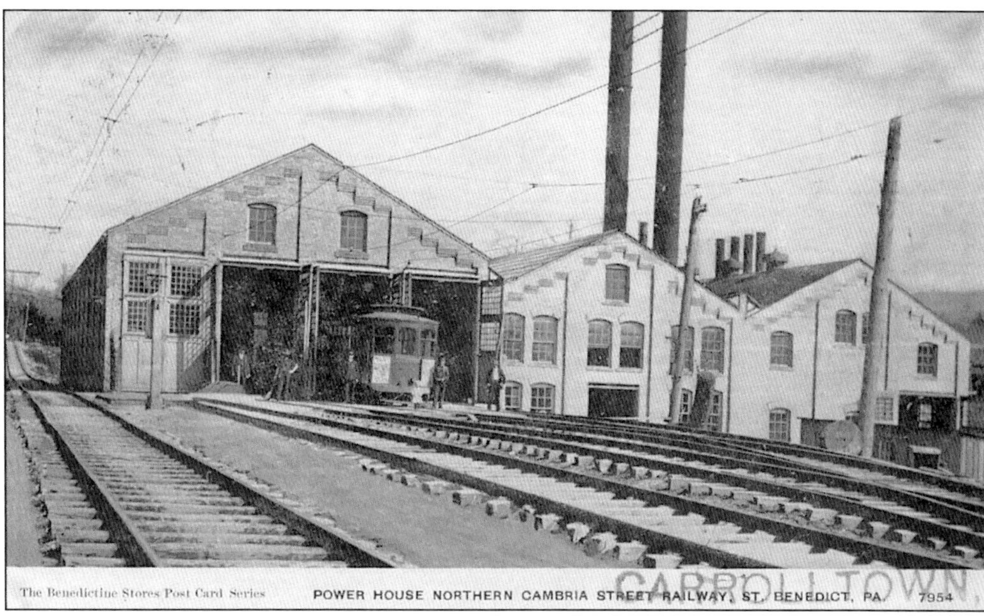

The trolley barn stands along Route 219 between Spangler and Barnesboro. The trolley was controlled by the Southern Cambria Railway of Johnstown. This particular line could always be recognized by the dull green color of its cars. The North Cambria line through the rural locality could not compete financially with the larger trolley lines and was abandoned in 1926.

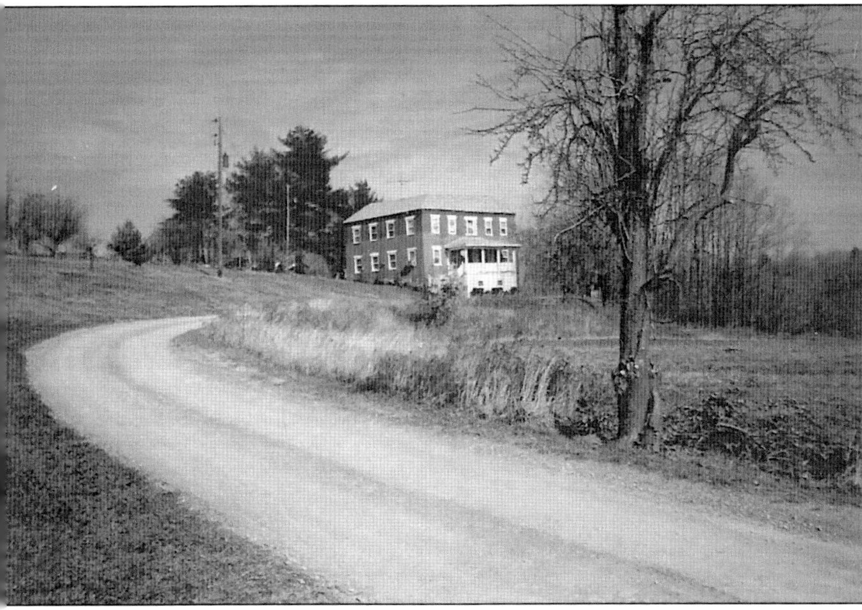

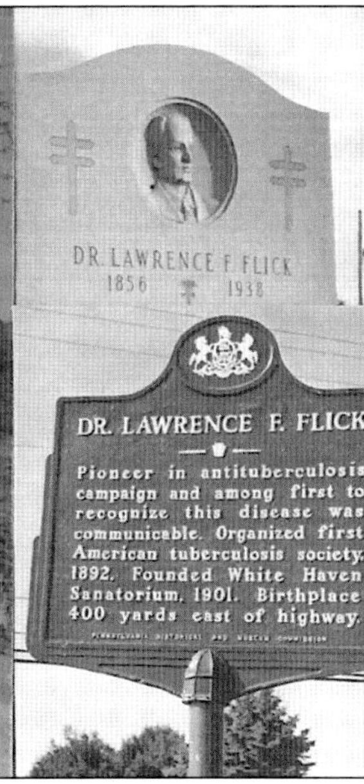

Dr. Lawrence Flick was a man of unusual determination. Born in Carrolltown in 1856, he graduated from St. Vincent's College and Jefferson Medical School. He gained international recognition as a physician with his resolve to conquer tuberculosis. He cured himself of the disease, then led a crusade against the white plague, as it was called. He established sanitariums for those afflicted. One such facility was White Haven Sanatorium. He practiced in Philadelphia, but retained an ardent interest in his hometown.

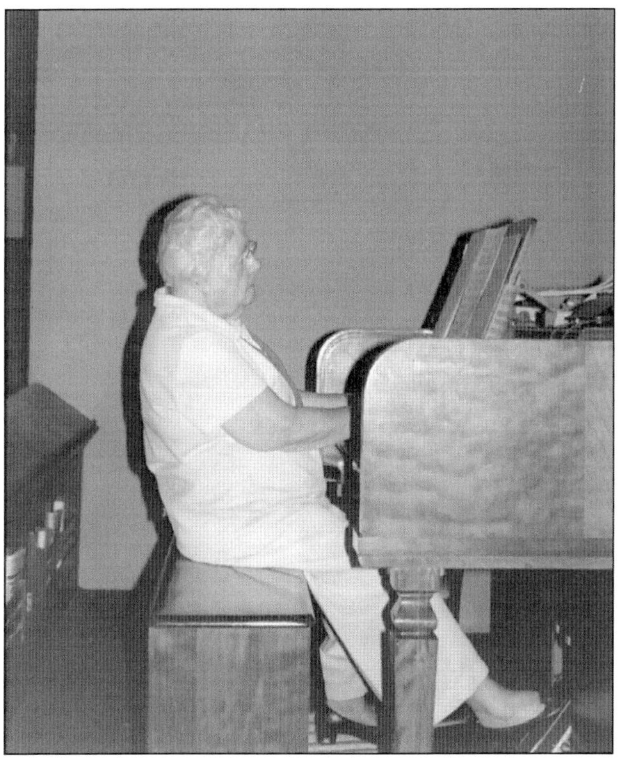

Mrs. Arline Connell began playing the organ at the age of ten. In 1911, she was the organist for the dedication of Saint Francis Church in Cresson. She is a graduate of the Mount Aloysius Academy and the Cincinnati Conservatory of Music. In 1914, Arline married Donald Connell. Their four sons formed the Connell Quartet. The musical ability of the lads was known throughout the area. They entertained at many affairs. Arline was the organist at St. Benedict's for many years.

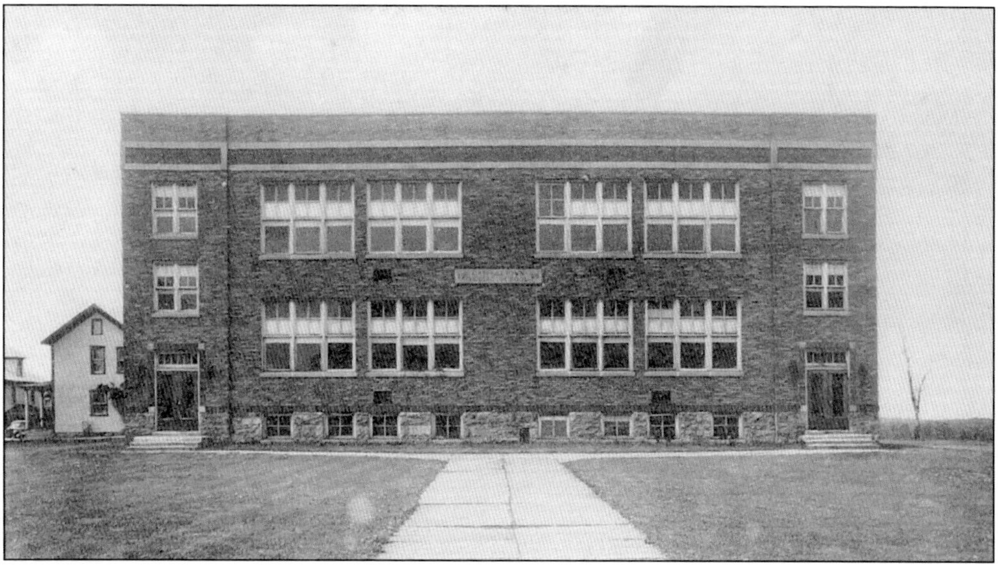

The public school was constructed in 1898 on the north side of Carroll Street. In 1908, eight classrooms were added. Half the building was used for talent shows, card parties, and entertainment. Later, the public school building became part of the Weakland Farm. In 1912, a high school curriculum was introduced. By 1925, the high school population reached 280 students and 8 instructors. A newer building was constructed to meet updated educational trends and a soaring enrollment.

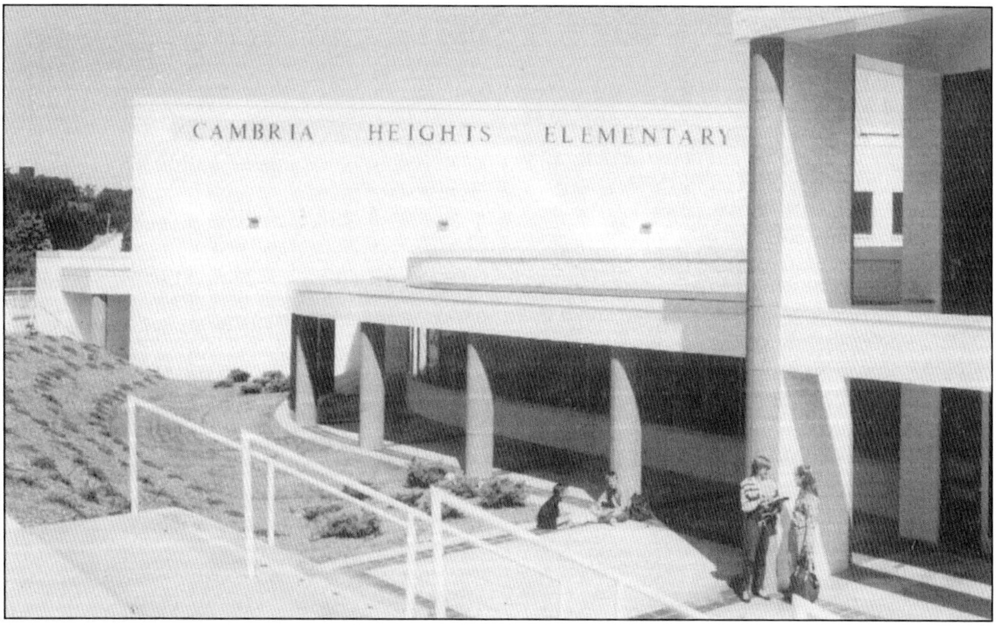

Cambria Heights Elmentary School was opened on Campbell Avenue in Carrolltown on October 5, 1992. Situated on the former football field, the structure was designed to provide state-of-the-art educational programs. Among the special areas are the network computer laboratory and closed-circuit television studio that has capabilities for communications to all the classrooms. The building houses unique science and multipurpose areas and 35 classrooms. The facility trains students facing the challenges of the 21st century.

Four

BENEATH THE ROLLING HILLS

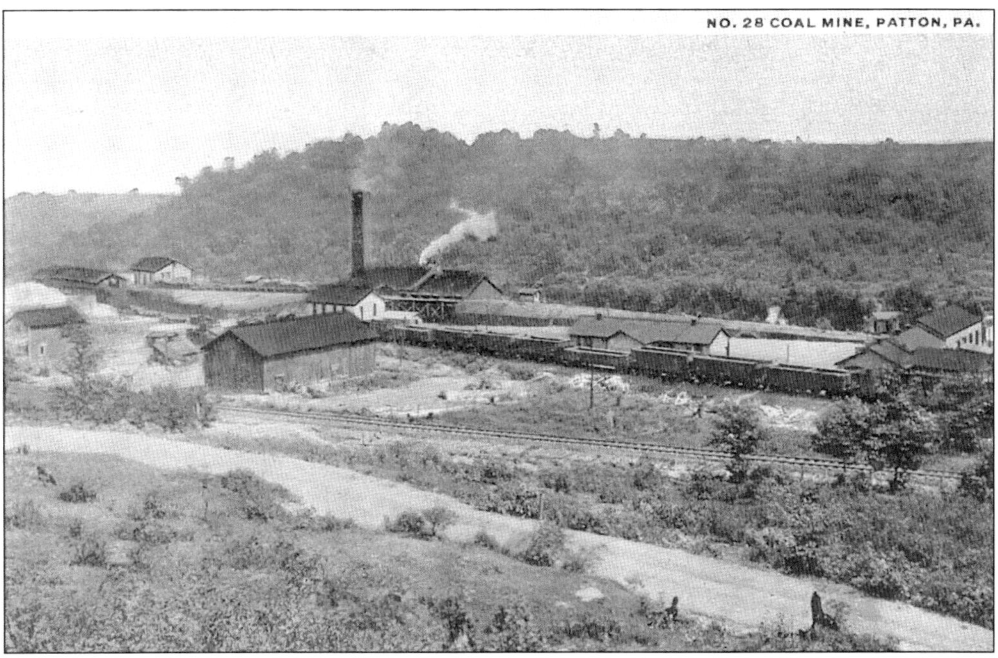

The railroad cars at this No. 28 Mine in Patton are ready to be filled. At this time, steam from a steam motor was used to pull cars in and out of the mine. This process was later converted to cable. Each car rolls beneath the tipple to be filled. Coal is transported on a conveyor belt to the tipple and from there, it is tipped into the cars. There are several types of bituminous coal that have to be sorted.

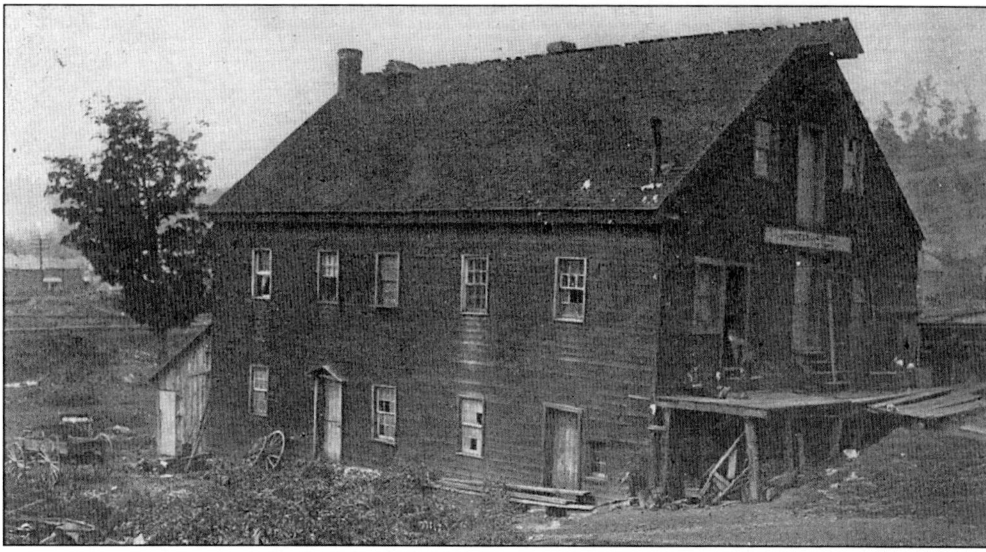

The Marks Mill was built by John McGuire in Patton in 1825. In 1866, it was sold to Ferdinand Marks. The land he acquired became a significant part of Patton. Marks was a miller from Germany and made many improvements in the mill. The area was dubbed "Markstown" and the land around the mill was known as "Marks Mills." It was located near Little Chest Creek on Lang Avenue. In later years, John Otto took the mill over. The building was dismantled in 1914.

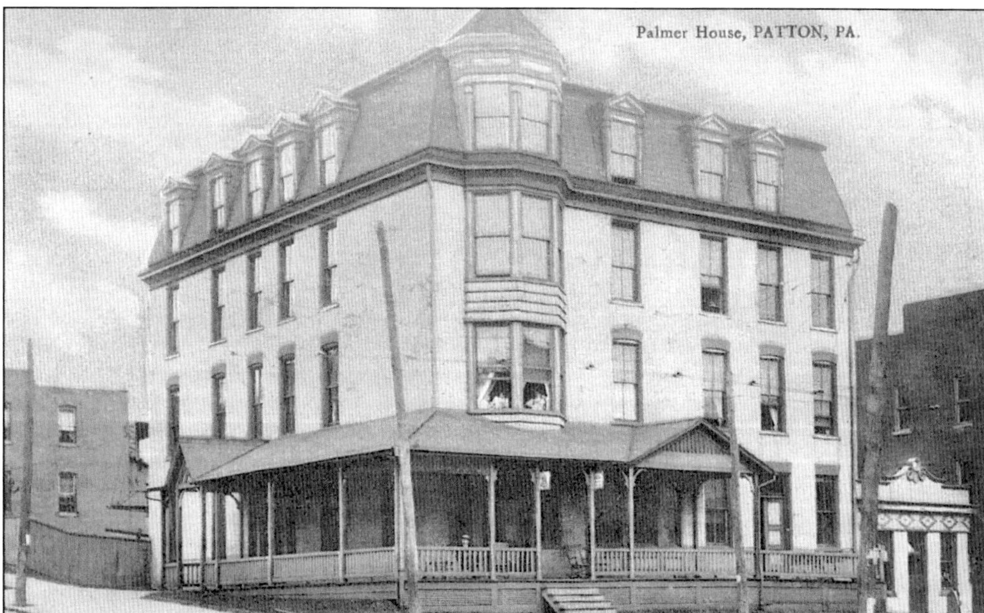

Palmer House was constructed on the corner of Magee and Fifth Avenues in Patton in 1893. The 32-room grand hotel was a 4-story structure spearheaded by the founding fathers of Patton. Expert craftsmanship went into both the interior and the exterior. The building was heated by steam. Brussels carpet covered the floors and the luxurious dining area accommodated many famous guests. The furnishings were elegant throughout the building. In 1904, an annex that kept with the decor of the house was added.

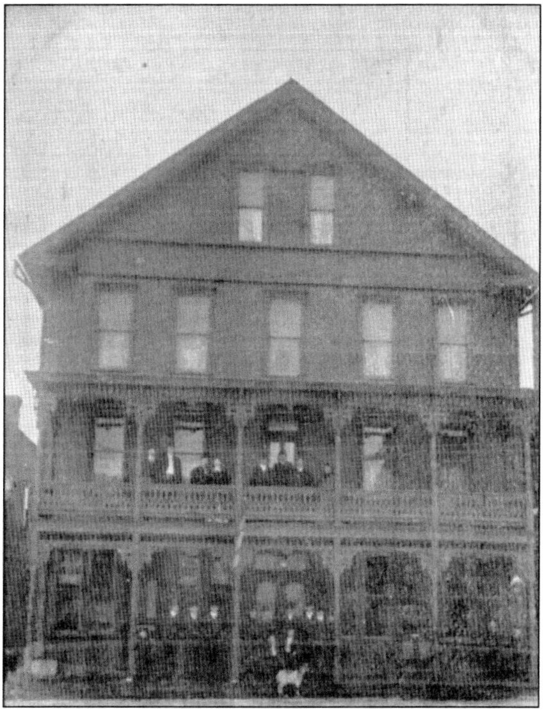

The Commercial Hotel was built by S.M. Wilson in 1893. Located near the depot, it was a three-story structure with a veranda across the front. Its 24 rooms were heated by steam. The furniture was built of antique oak and had yellow pine woodwork. Its elegant dining room served as a banquet hall for community activities, meetings, and special occasions. Later known as the Central Hotel, it has retained its original decor. The Central Hotel has passed the centenary mark.

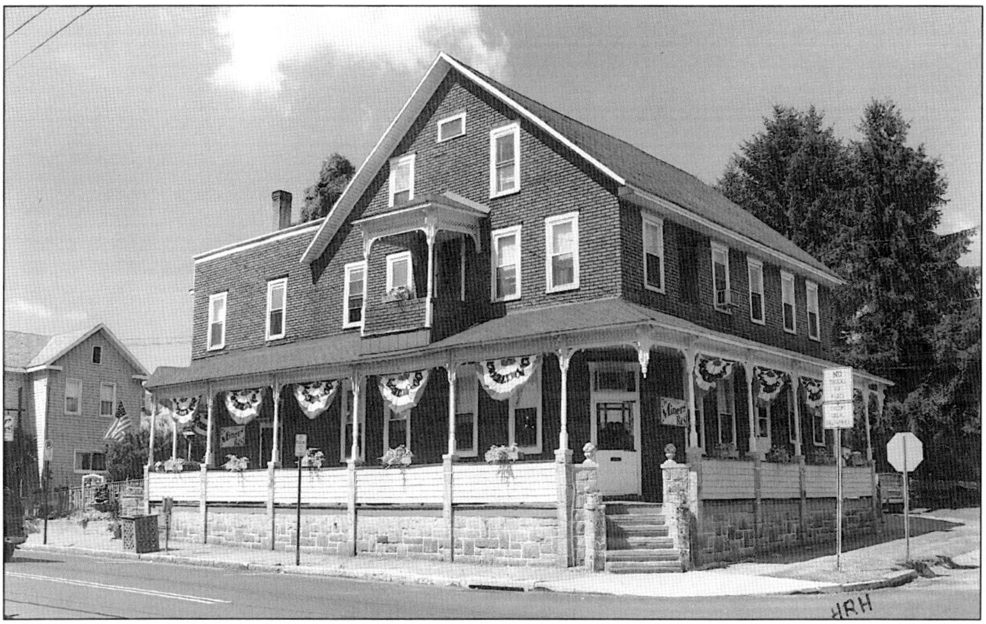

The Miner's Rest Hotel of Patton derived its name from the miners who rested on its porch while waiting in line for their paychecks. Located on the corner of Magee and Fourth Avenues, the three-story hotel contained 20 well-furnished rooms and a dining room that accommodated 30 guests. The business was sold to Anthony Masci, who specialized in Italian cuisine. He removed the antique mahogany and red oak bars to create additional space. These are now in the Brandywine Battlefield, Pennsylvania.

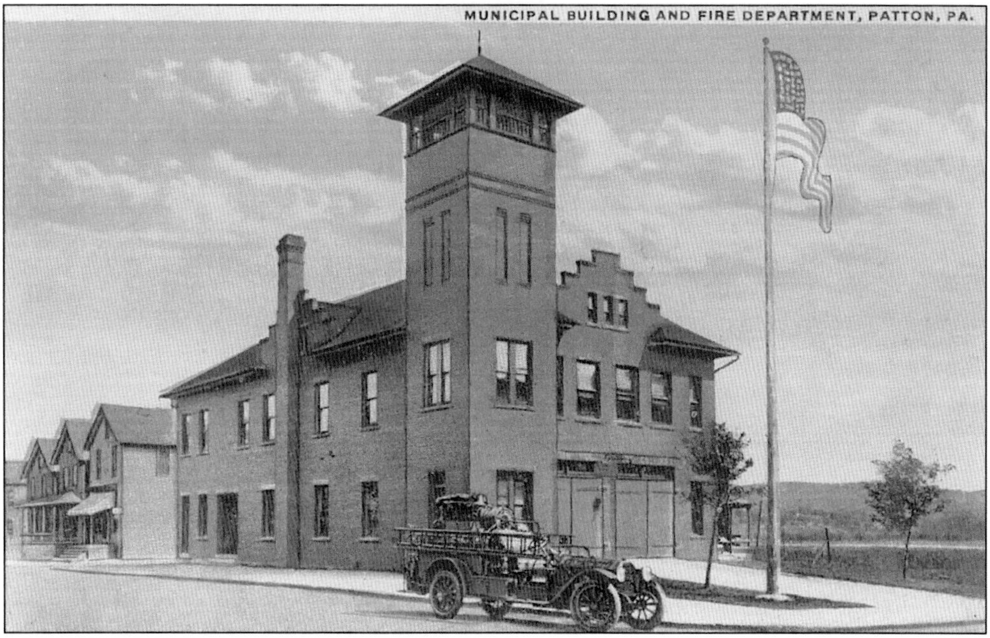

The Patton Volunteer Fire Department was organized in 1893. Firemen met in a store on Fifth Avenue and planned to build a two-story edifice on Lang Avenue to house the equipment. The equipment consisted of a single hand-drawn hose cart with a 40-foot-long drag-line and a 100-foot fire hose. As a municipal building, the fire hall also acted as a gathering place for town meetings, social events, and as an opera house and dance hall. It was erected on the corner of Fourth and Magee Avenues.

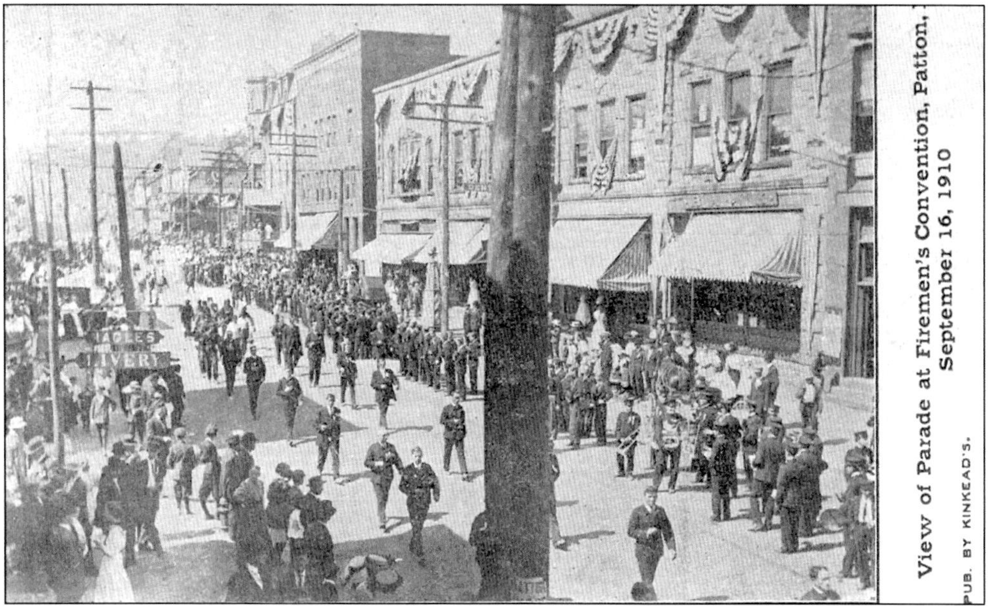

The Patton Fire Department played host to a huge firemen's convention on September 16, 1910. Note the buildings along Magee Avenue decorated in bunting. The town went all out to host the convention and parade. Nagle's Livery is on the left. Fire departments from Hastings, Spangler, Barnesboro, and Carrolltown joined in the festivities.

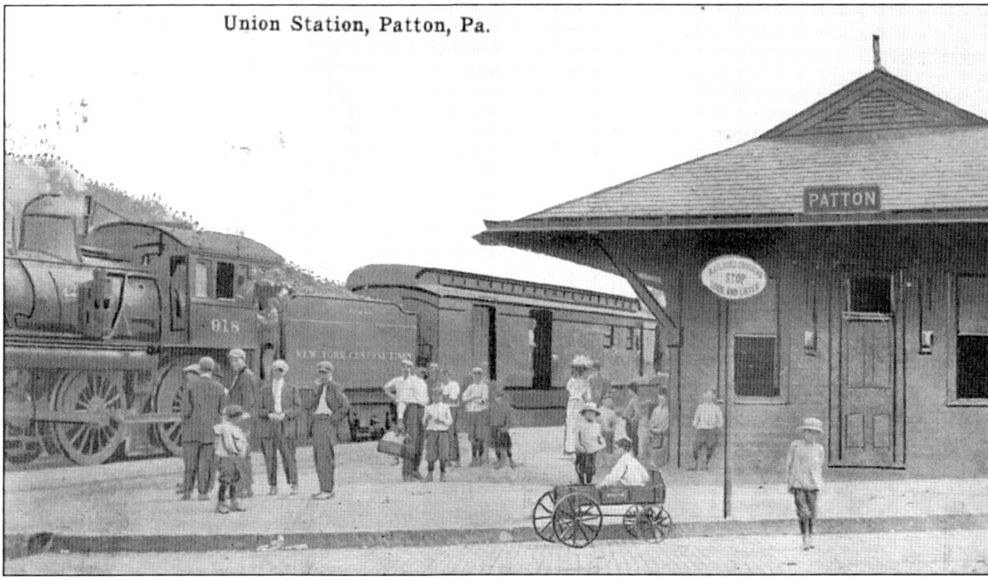

In 1902, the Union railroad station became a reality in Patton. Although the railroad had come through a decade earlier, its primary motive was to transport commodities. The mines, clay works, the brewery, and retail establishments all depended on the railroad for delivery of goods and supplies. Carrying passengers meant additional money. The railroad discredited bike riders, or wheelmen, as they were sometimes called. Patton Paver bricks surround the station.

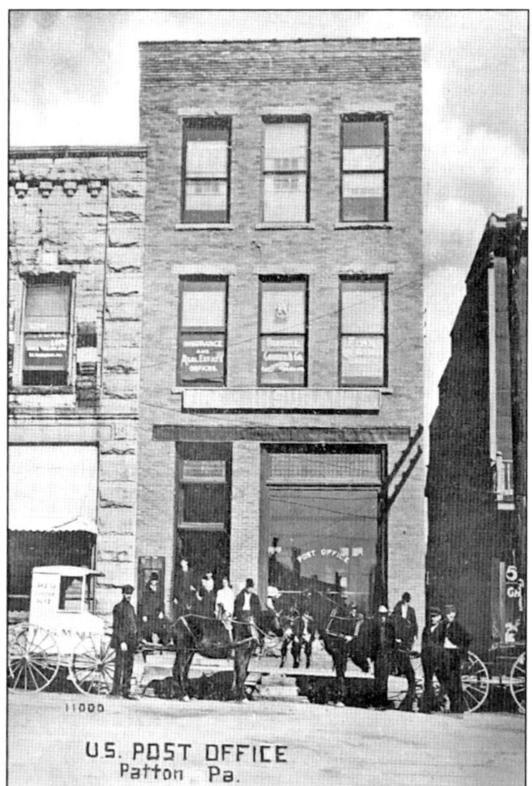

The Patton Post Office had a mobile history. Established in 1888 in the Bender store, it relocated to Leonard's restaurant and was later housed in the Mountain mercantile market. In 1902, it moved to this tall building in the center of town. The window on second floor advertises "Insurance and Real Estate." Mail delivery wagons wait outside. In 1934, another move brought it to the Cimo building. In 1972, the post office finally had a new home of its own on Beaver Avenue.

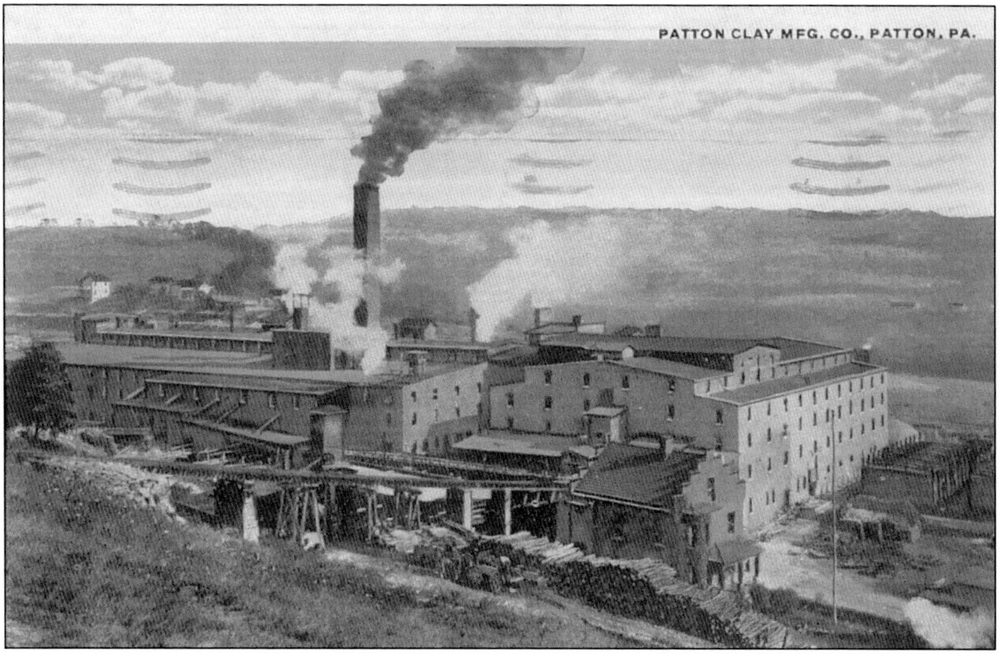

The Patton Clay Manufacturing Company was founded in 1894 by George S. Good Sr. It was located on the northwest corner of Patton in the Flanighan Run Valley. F.E. McElfresh of the clay works in West Virginia first recognized that the clay of Patton was of superior quality. George S. Good, A.E. Patton, and Col. John Magee established the Patton Board of Trade, then visited the West Virginia Plant. They had envisioned a clay works in the area.

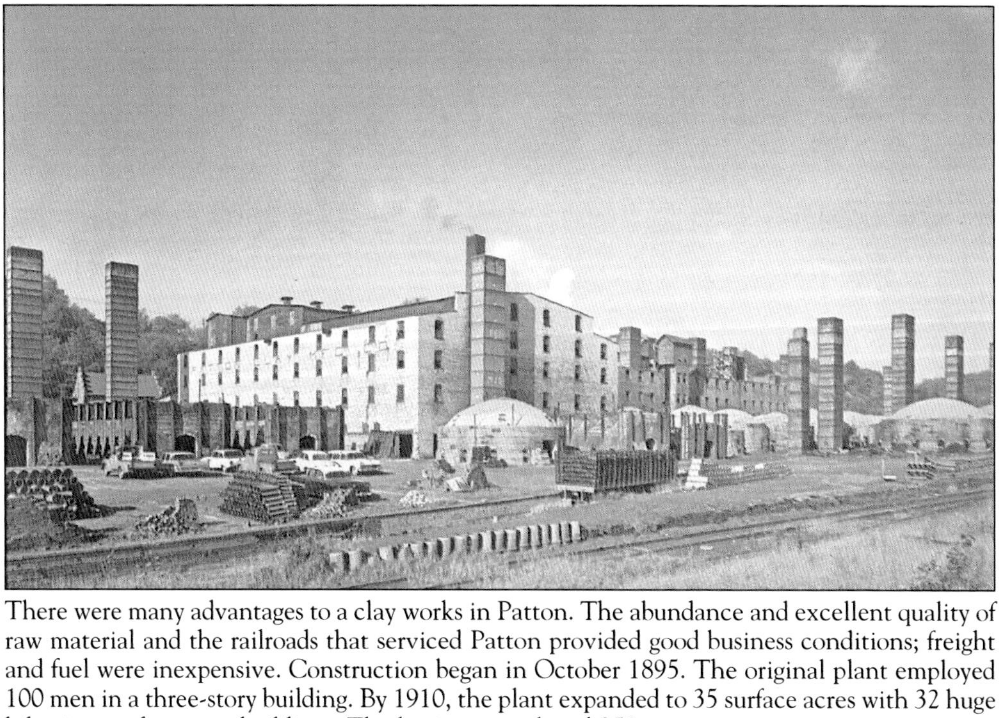

There were many advantages to a clay works in Patton. The abundance and excellent quality of raw material and the railroads that serviced Patton provided good business conditions; freight and fuel were inexpensive. Construction began in October 1895. The original plant employed 100 men in a three-story building. By 1910, the plant expanded to 35 surface acres with 32 huge kilns in two five-story buildings. The business employed 350 men.

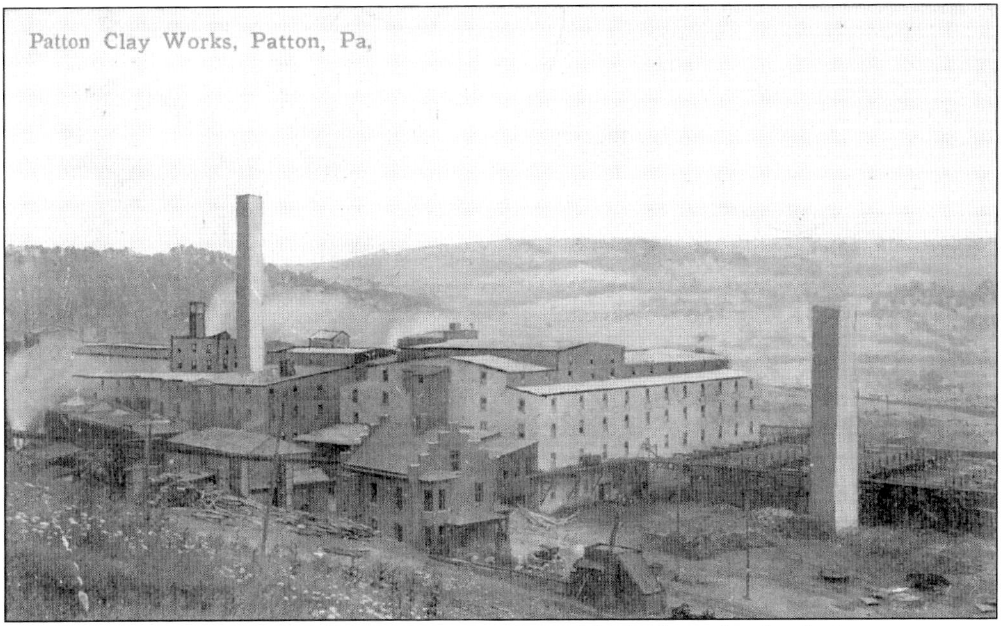

The Clay Works of Patton had its own claim to fame. The high-quality bricks for construction and road paving were considered the best in the world. Veterans and tourists to Rome, Italy, and the base of the Eiffel Tower in France reported walking on Patton Pavers. Raw materials, clay and shale, were brought to the plant and pulverized into fine powder. They were molded, steam-pressurized, and fired in a kiln. The product was then ready for shipment.

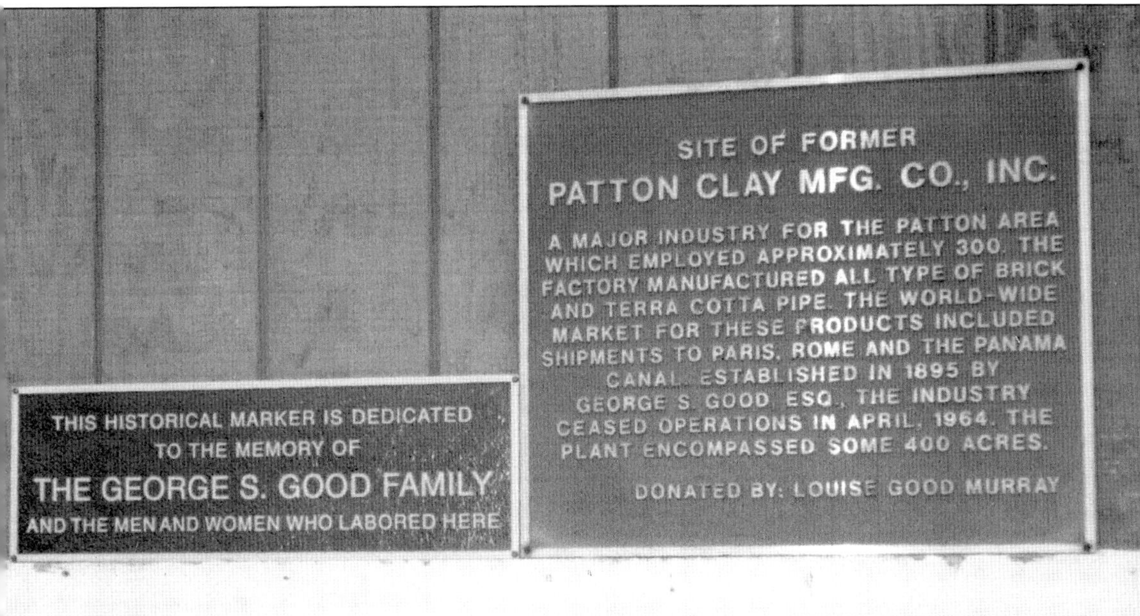

Many employees of the clay works lived in company houses along Terra Cotta Avenue. Following World War II, the economy shifted. More advanced products and production techniques were ushered in, and the need for clay diminished. The plant closed in 1968. All evidence of Patton's famous landmark phased into history. This sign, on a shopping center building, is all that is left of Patton's glorious past.

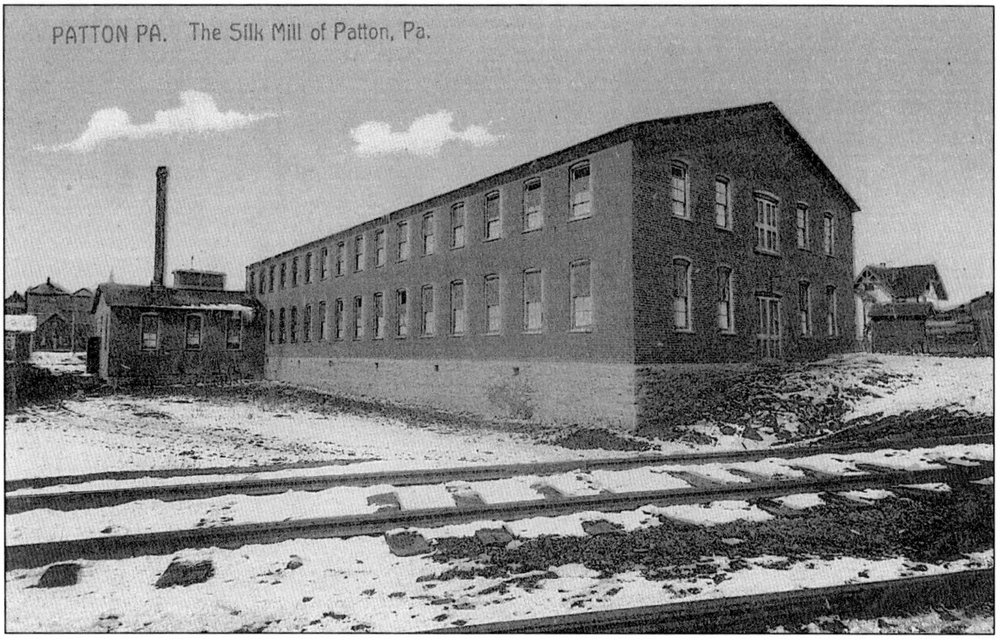

A silk mill was established in 1907 by Ernest and Herman Levy of New York. The two-story structure opened with 19 machines. A year later, there were 66 machines and over 100 employees. The mill was located on Palmer Avenue. The company bought the raw silk from Japan and put it through many processes before it was dyed and converted into ribbon. The plant closed in 1949.

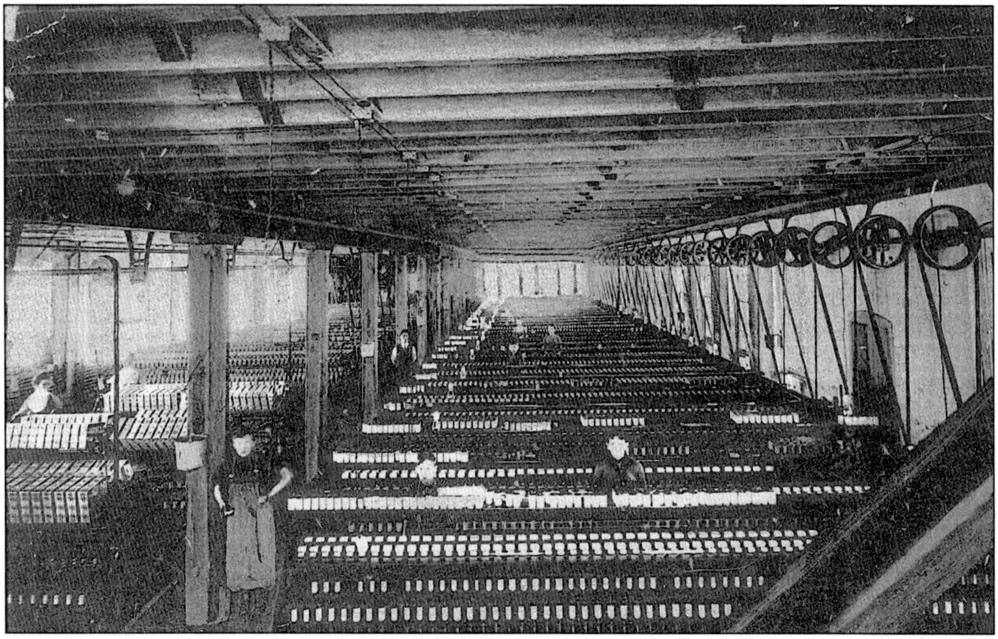

The looms of the silk mill were kept in constant motion for over four decades. During this time, much silk was turned out and sent to the head plant in Patterson, New Jersey, where it was put through further processes. Profits declined and the mill went out of business. In 1950, the Patton Box and Paper Company moved into the abandoned silk mill.

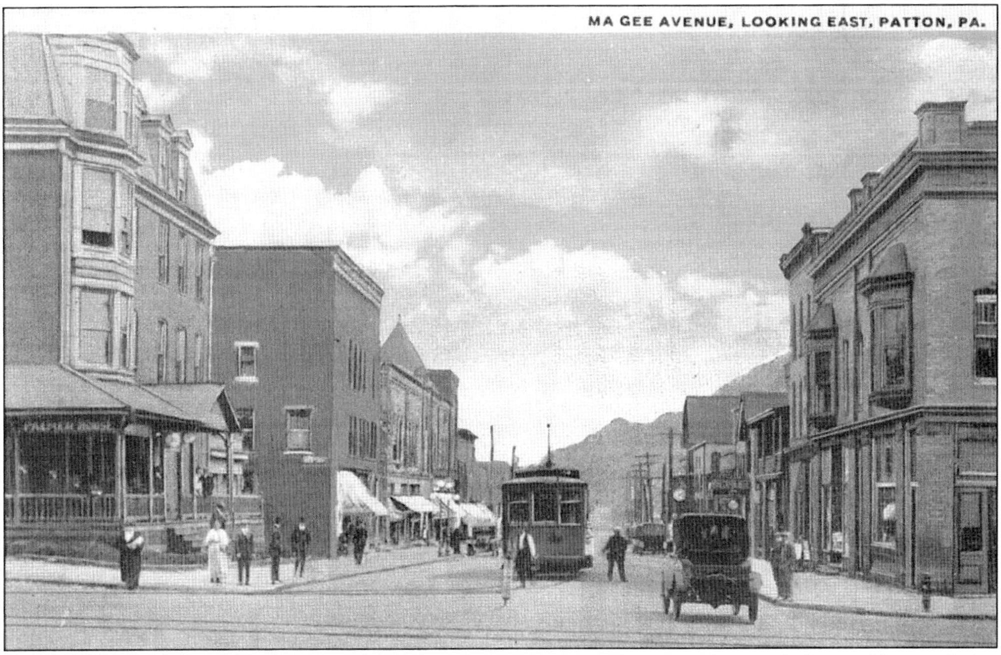

Looking east early in the 20th century, Patton's Magee Avenue featured the trolley and the Palmer house on the left corner. The main street through town was named for George Magee of the New York Central Railroad. He became a partner in the development of coal resources in the Patton area. Magee, Fourth, and Beech Avenues were paved in 1907.

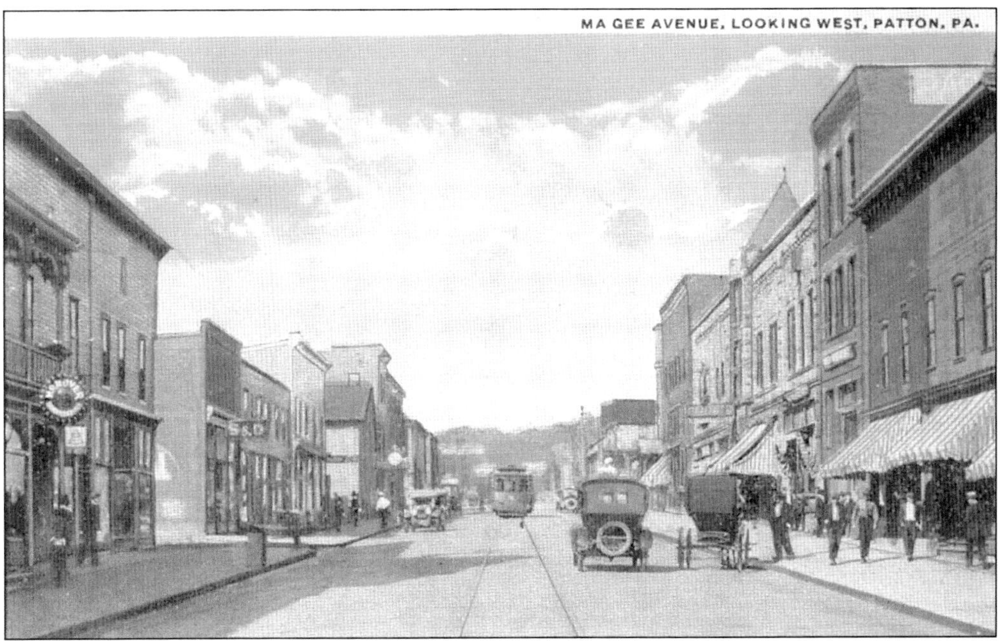

This westward view of Magee Avenue in 1913 affords a rare moment in Patton's history. This photograph captured three modes of transportation: a horse and buggy on the right, a trolley in the center, and an automobile on the left. They all share the right of way. On the extreme left, the porch of the Commercial Hotel is visible.

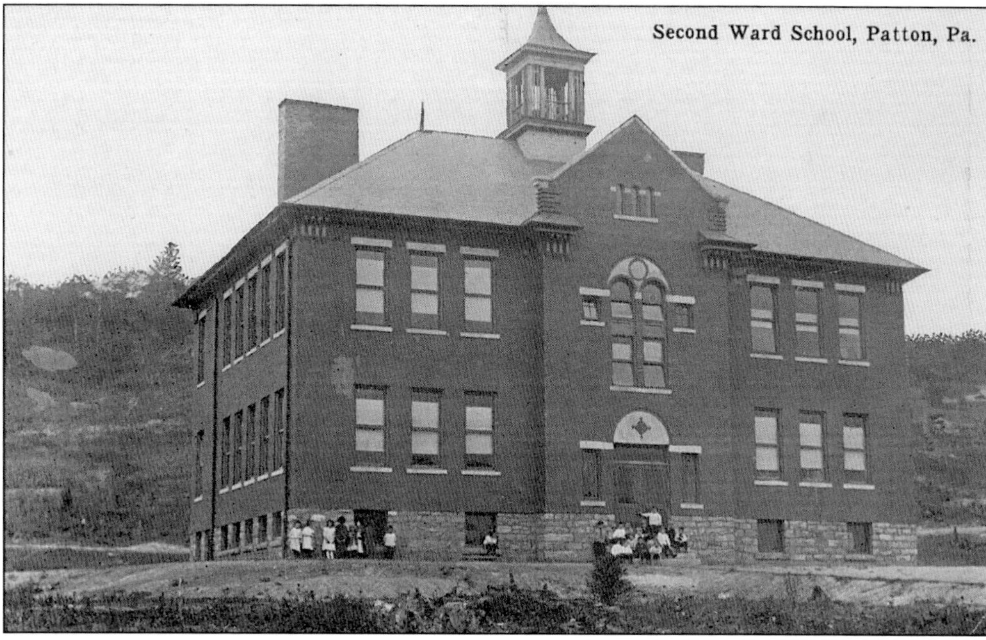

Education in Patton began when a school building was constructed on the corner of Beech Street and Fifth Avenue in 1894. In 1915, a second school building was constructed in the southwest of town. The Beech Street facility became the high school. The Cambria Heights High School formed a joint school for the towns of Patton, Hastings, and Carrolltown. The new school was constructed in Patton and featured 132,119 square feet of space and a capacity of 1,155 students. It was dedicated on November 22, 1970.

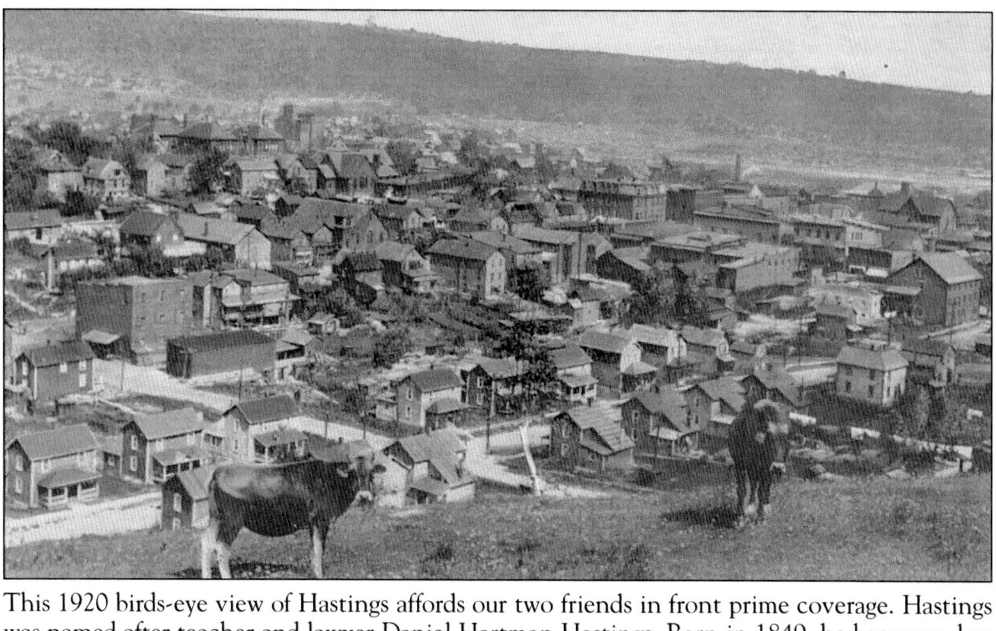

This 1920 birds-eye view of Hastings affords our two friends in front prime coverage. Hastings was named after teacher and lawyer Daniel Hartman Hastings. Born in 1849, he became a law partner with Colonel Spangler. They chartered the Blubaker Coal Company in 1887 and opened the coal lands as well as coke ovens. Hastings was elected governor of Pennsylvania in 1894.

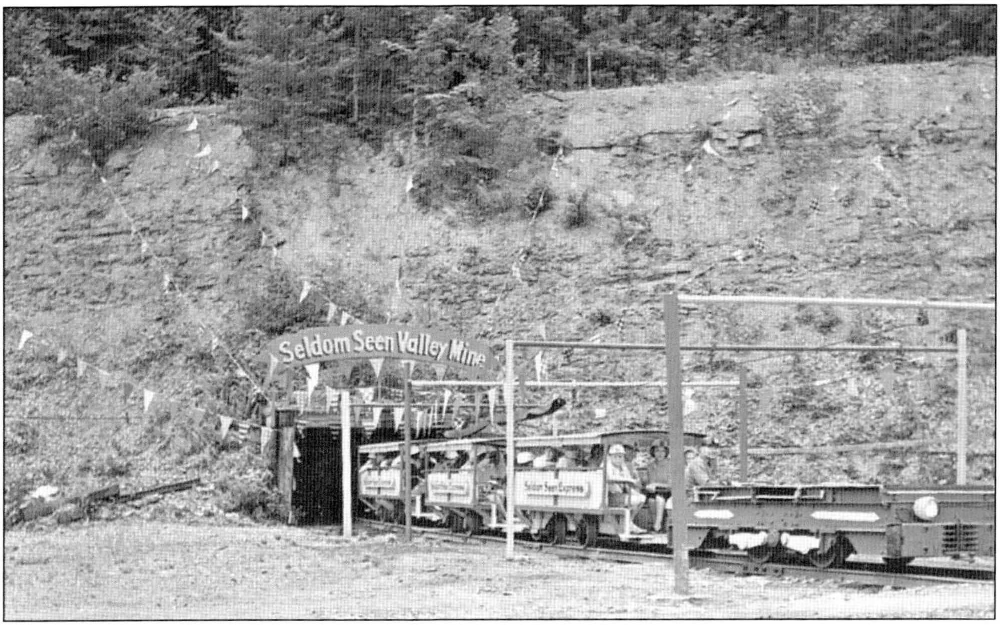

Seldom Seen Mine is Northern Cambria's newest tourist attraction. When draft mines are closed, they are sealed. This mine has become a historical and educational facility. Located in the heart of the bituminous or soft coal region, electric sight-seeing cars carry passengers 2,000 feet deep into the mine. Opened in the 1950s by Dr. Edward Haluska, it tells the story of coalmining and its role in the development of American industries.

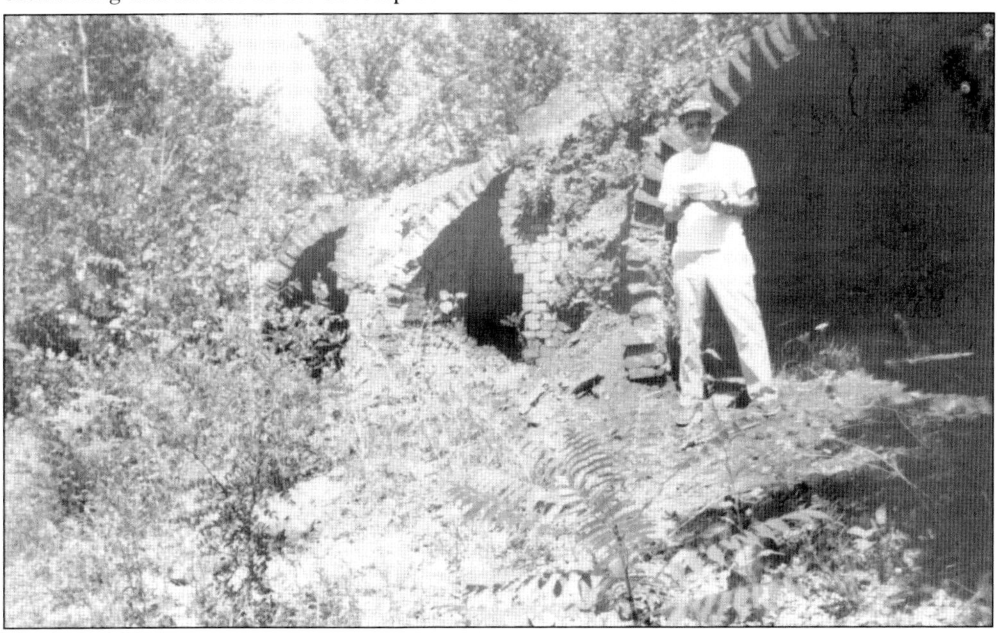

Joe Puffley explains to a group the workings of coke ovens. The small, brick, igloo-like structures were encased in stone. Openings at the top released smoke and gasses. Coking is a method of baking coal and driving off smoke and volatile products, leaving a lump of hard, gray carbon product. Coke was valuable in smelting iron ore. More than one hundred coke ovens were constructed in Hastings. The surrounding area came to be called "Smokey Valley."

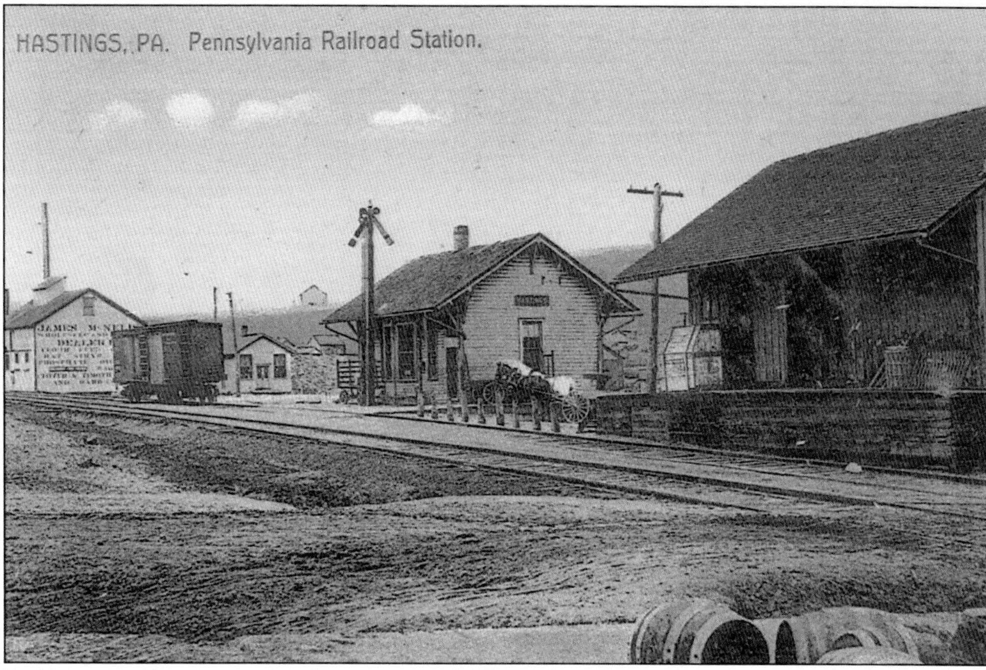

In 1888, the Hastings railroad station was built in the center of town, beside Brubaker's Run, between Third and Fourth Avenues. There were three passenger trains per day. Sylvester Kuhn was the station master from 1913 until 1933. The James McNelis feed mill is in the background.

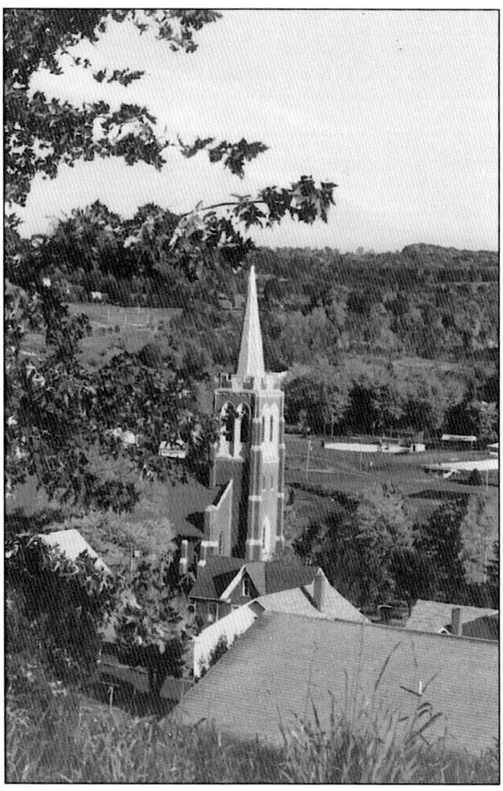

The St. Bernard Parish was established in 1889. Built in the Gothic style, the frame structure is 40 by 110 feet and has a seating capacity of 100. The church was completed in 1890 and dedicated by the Reverend Abbott Andrew of the Order of St. Benedict. Within the first year, all seats were rented out among 175 families. The Benedictine Priests of Latrobe have served the parish since its inception.

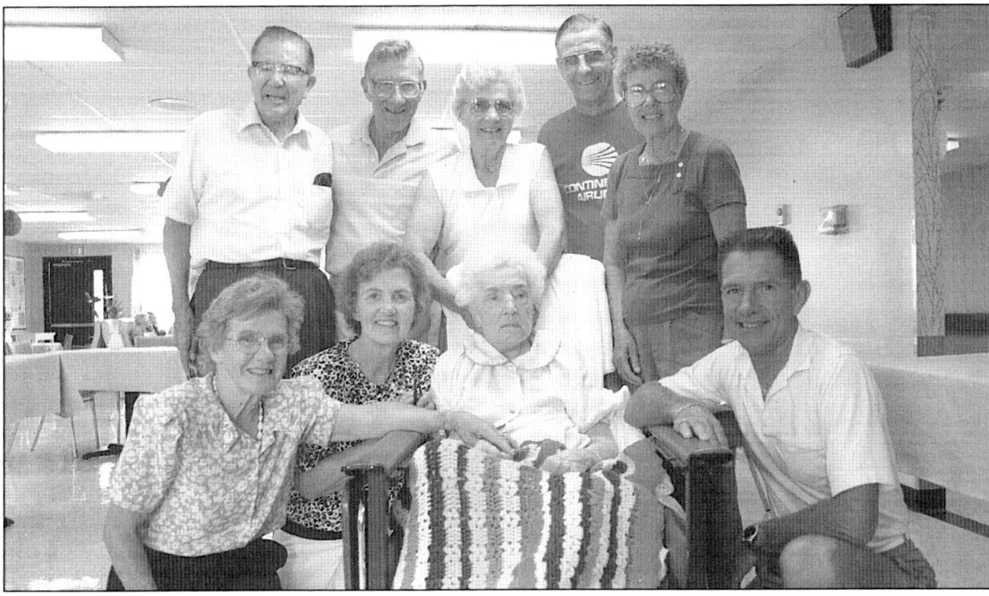

The Victor Kline family gathered at Haida Manor in Hastings to celebrate the 100th birthday of their mother, Rose T. Klein, second from right. Born February 1, 1890, she married Victor Klein and settled on the family farm in Hastings. The children, from left to right, are as follows: (front row) Ann Kanik, Mildred Rosenhamer, William; (back row) Louis, Alfred, Rose Marie Lieb, Richard, and Elizabeth Ariz.

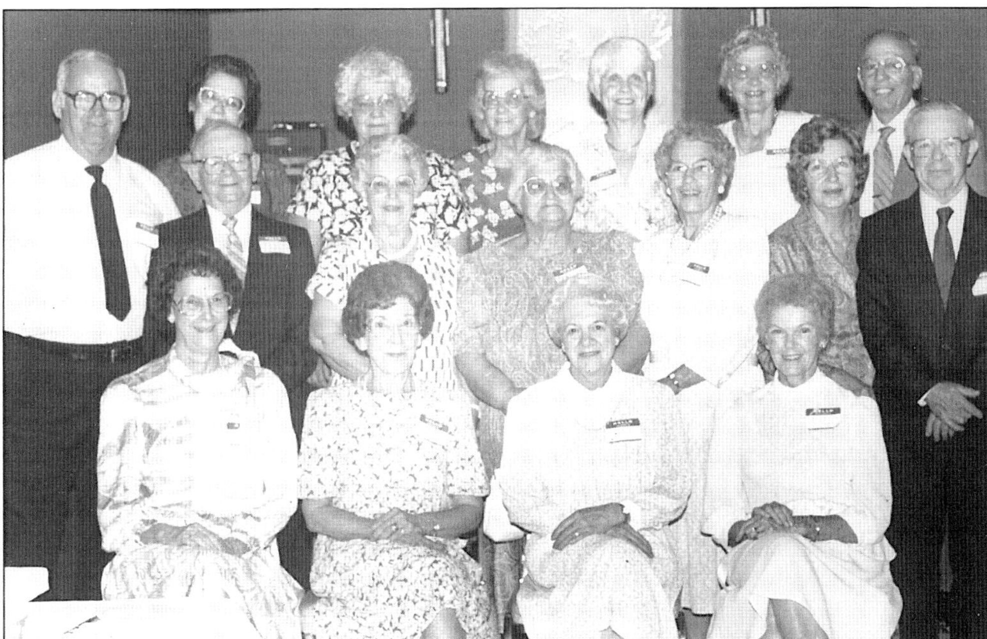

The Hastings High School class of 1940 staged a 50th class reunion. The alumni shown, from left to right, are as follows: (first row) Mary Sullivan Weakland, Hilda Becker Dietrick, Mary Louise Becker Dietrick, Rita Riodan Hicks; (second row) Iwaga Link, Anne Easly Nosik, Anne Skilha Junenko, Ruth Walker Yescavage, Julia Dillon Kline, Leo Kline; (third row) Mary Nelson Busby, Rose Marie Kline Lieb, and Fred Cimo.

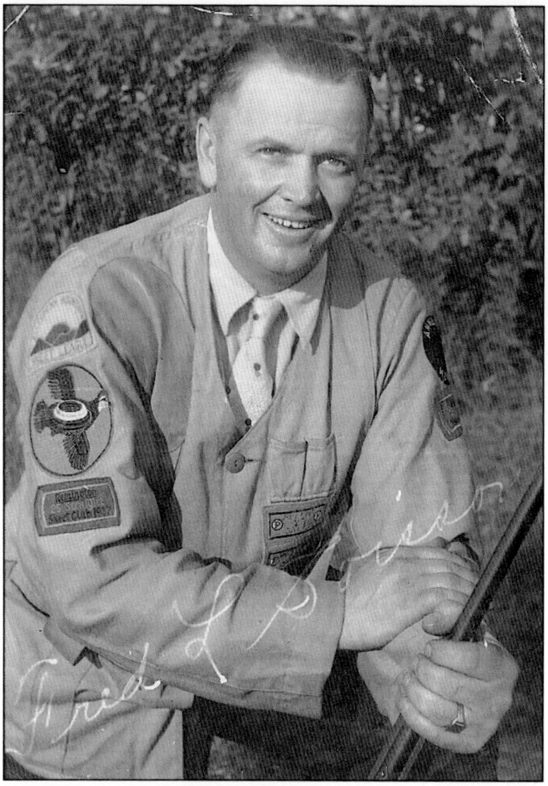

Fred Soisson was a multitalented artist; he was a businessman, a skeet-shooting champion, a trick shot expert, and the father of seven. He was selected for the Cambria County War Memorial Sports Hall of Fame. He gained national distinction when he established the world record as the country's best rifleman at the New York World's Fair, 1939–1940. He was a civic-minded marksman who also served as a sheriff and the mayor of Hastings. A staunch advocate of hunting safety, he taught gun safety, the use of firearms, and civil defense.

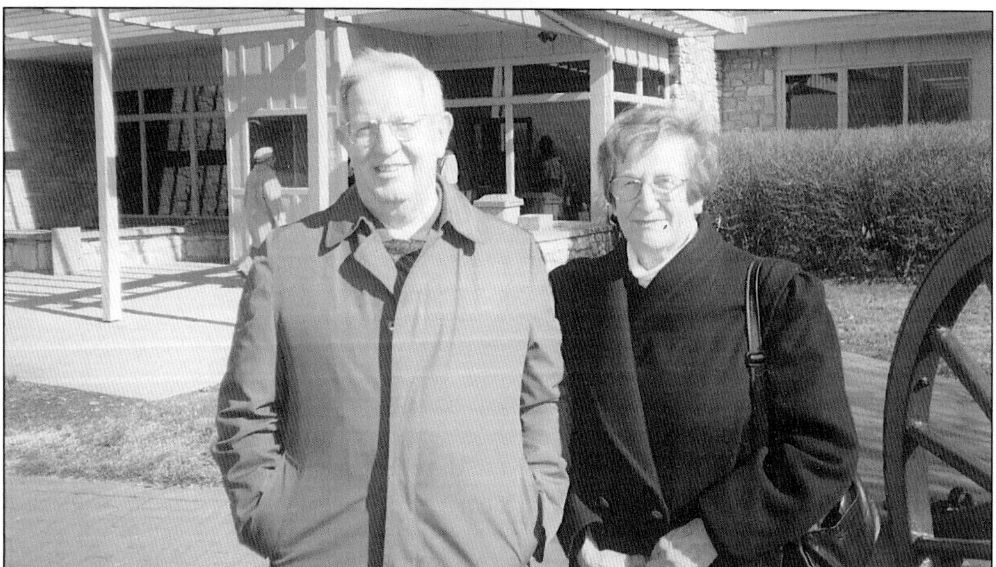

Dr. Fred Soisson is presently the Cambria County commissioner. A graduate of Spangler High School, St Vincent's College, and Georgetown University, he obtained a medical degree in 1955. He interned at Fitzsimmons Army Hospital in Denver, Colorado, as an Air Force lieutenant. Dr. Soisson set up practice in Johnstown in 1963. He was chief of obstetrics and on the board of directors at Mercy Hospital. He and his wife, Dorothy, are the parents of nine children. Dr. Soisson received an honorary doctoral degree from St. Vincents College in 1982.

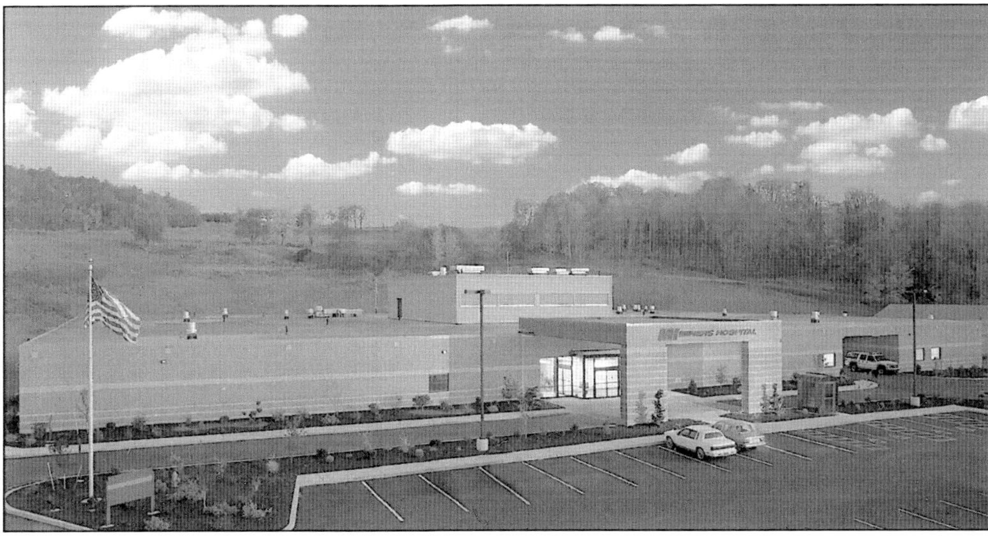

The new Miners Hospital opened in September 1999 in Hastings. It officially transferred from Spangler to a new modern facility. Located in Hastings Industrial Park, the 30-bed hospital was constructed at a cost of $12.7 million and covers 70,000 square feet. Current medicine requires expanded outpatient services. This conveniently located and state-of-the-art facility efficiently serves all on one floor. Two thousand people attended open house. All vital services have been improved, updated, and reorganized.

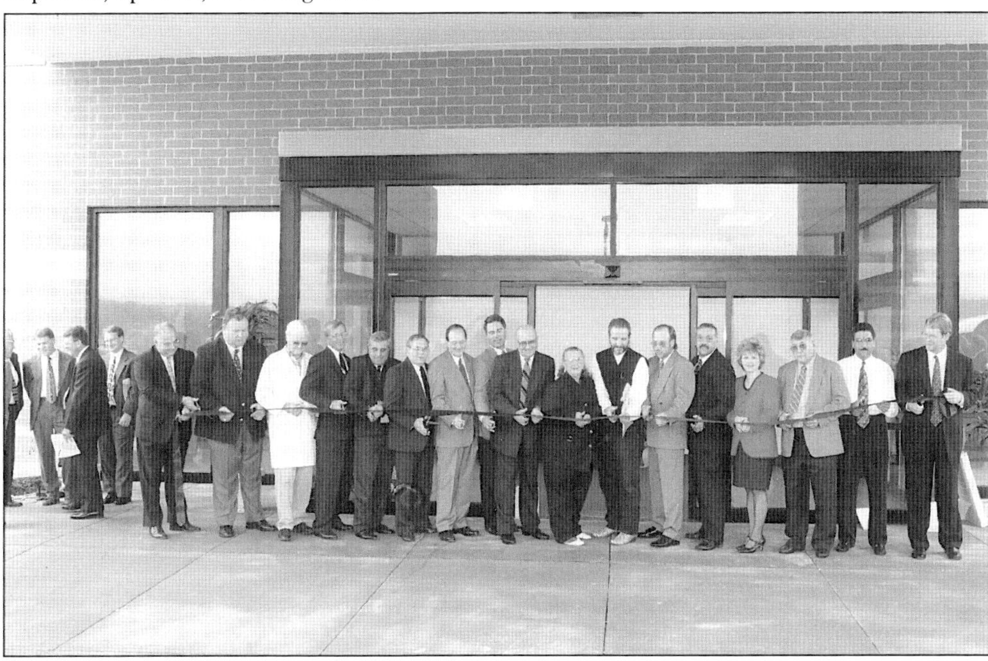

The Miners Hospital Board of Trustees was part of the ribbon-cutting ceremony in Hastings on September 19, 1999. Attendees included, from left to right, Larry Sherwin, John Bem, Dr. Timothy Patrick, Frank Cammarata, Timothy Whited, Thomas Marino, Raymond Ponchione, Warren Rhyner, Salvatore Valenty, M.Virginia Eckenrode, Dr. William Paronish, C. Gregory Hoover, Michael Glova, Peggy Watkins, Carl Galiczynski, John Rezk, and administrator of the new facility, Roger Winn.

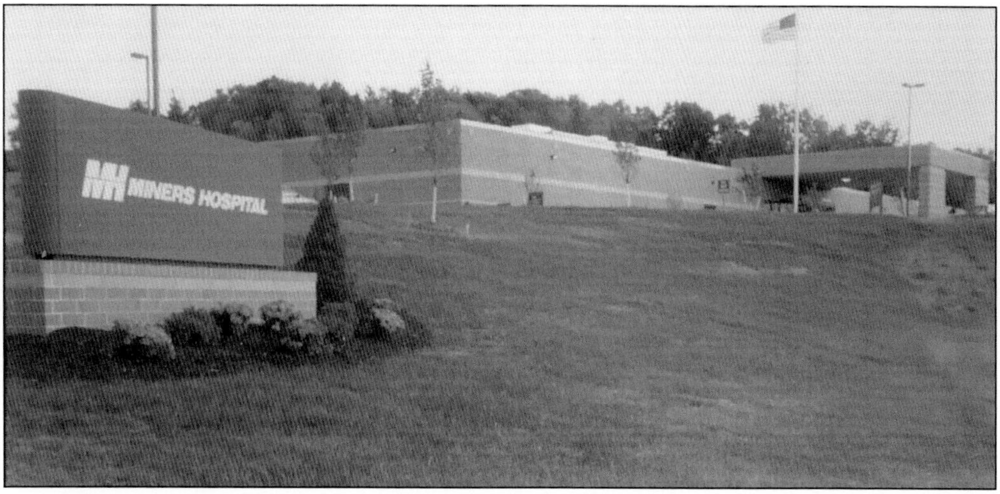

The property on which the new hospital stands is part of Hastings Area Industrial Development Association (HAIDA). The decline of employment in the coalfields prompted the town fathers to establish an industrial park in 1995. Its purpose was to attract employment and housing. Ace Footwear Incorporated was the first company to initiate the new shell building. Other industries gave employment to townsfolk. These helped keep Hastings a vibrant community.

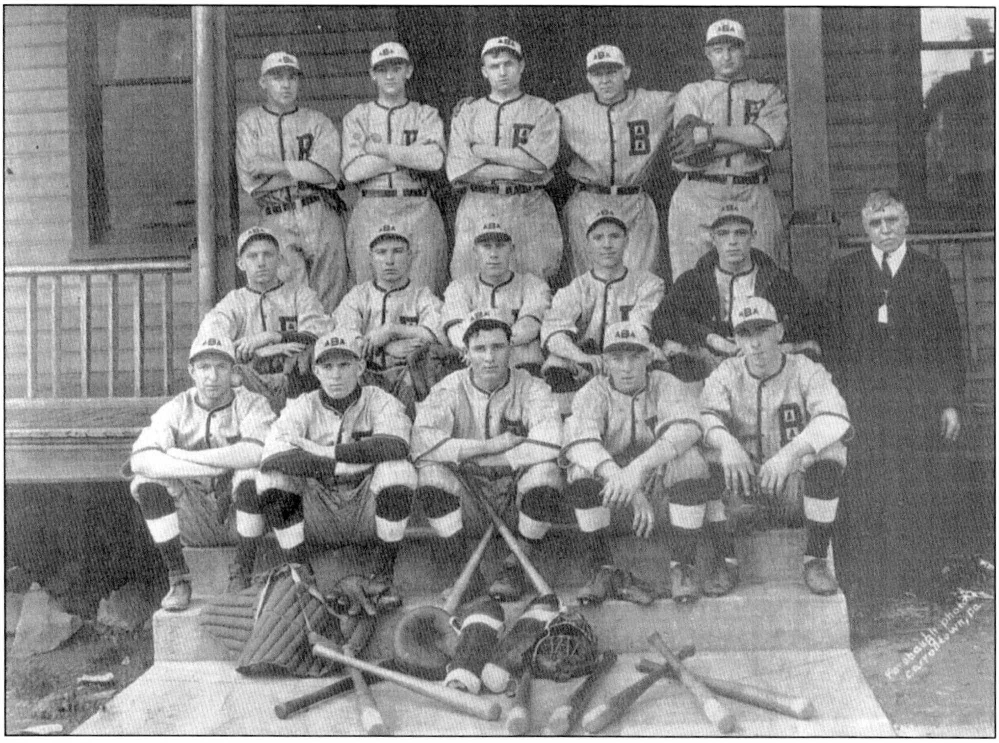

The Bakerton baseball team of the athletic association were champions in 1921. Assembled for this May 8, 1921 photograph are, from left to right, as follows: (first row) Tom Harris, Eugene Murphy, Ed Crouse, Jay Harris, Joe Venesky; (second row) James Callahan, Ray Foster, William Wiseman, Vince Nedimyer, Joe Stephenson, manager Jake Harris; (third row) Pat Teklinsky, Albert Michel, Matt Farrell, Jack Handley and Pete Strong.

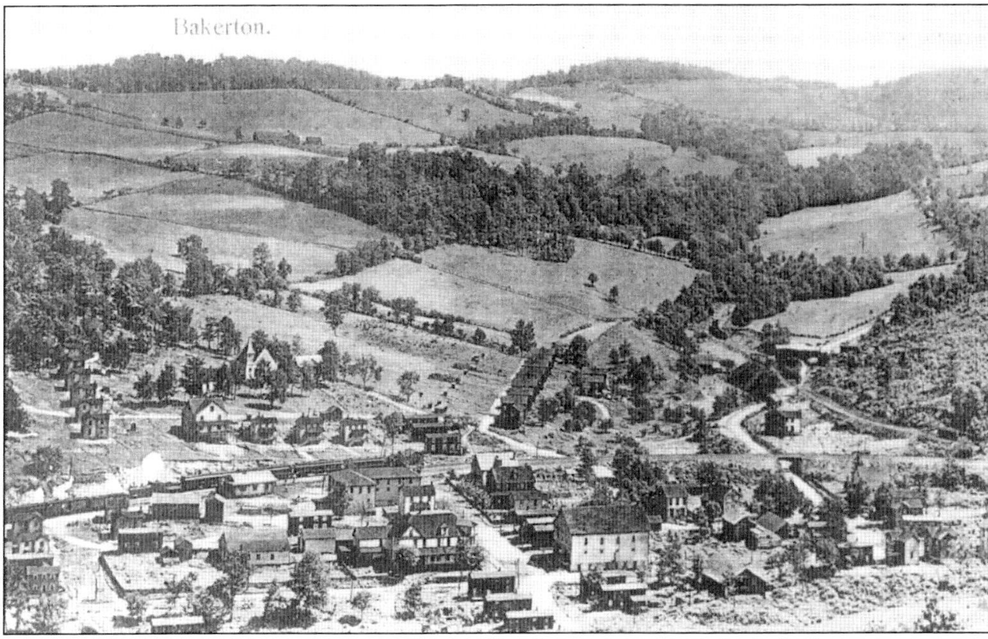

Bakerton affords a glimpse of the rolling hills characteristic of the Allegheny Mountains. Bakerton was a valley of lumbering and farm lands until the Sterling Coal Company opened its first mine. Company houses dot the landscape in both the left and middle of the photograph. The Sacred Heart Roman Catholic Church rises in the left and the railroad makes its way through the town. There is a unique ethnic and religious merging of many cultures. Intermarriage is prevalent.

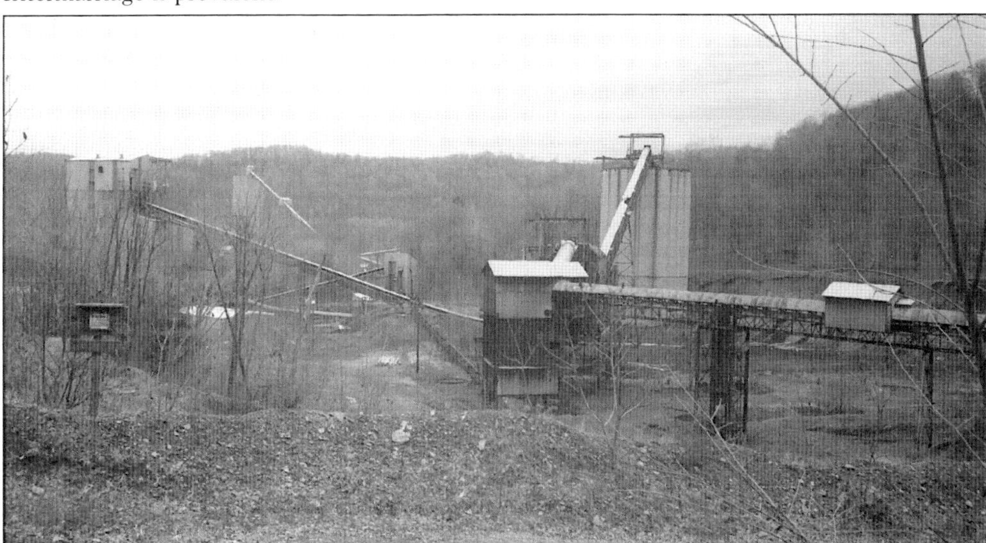

Barnes and Tucker Mine No. 15 demonstrates the several tipples of a coalmine. Three conveyor belts and tipples serve the same mine. Coal is sent up a shaft to a tipple. It can be stored or tipped into coal cars or trucks. The tipple is similar to a silo in that it stores coal. Bakerton is located in a North Cambria Valley at the source of the Susquehanna River. Farming and lumbering preceded coalmines in the hamlet. Coal gave Carroll Township two major communities—St. Benedict and Bakerton.

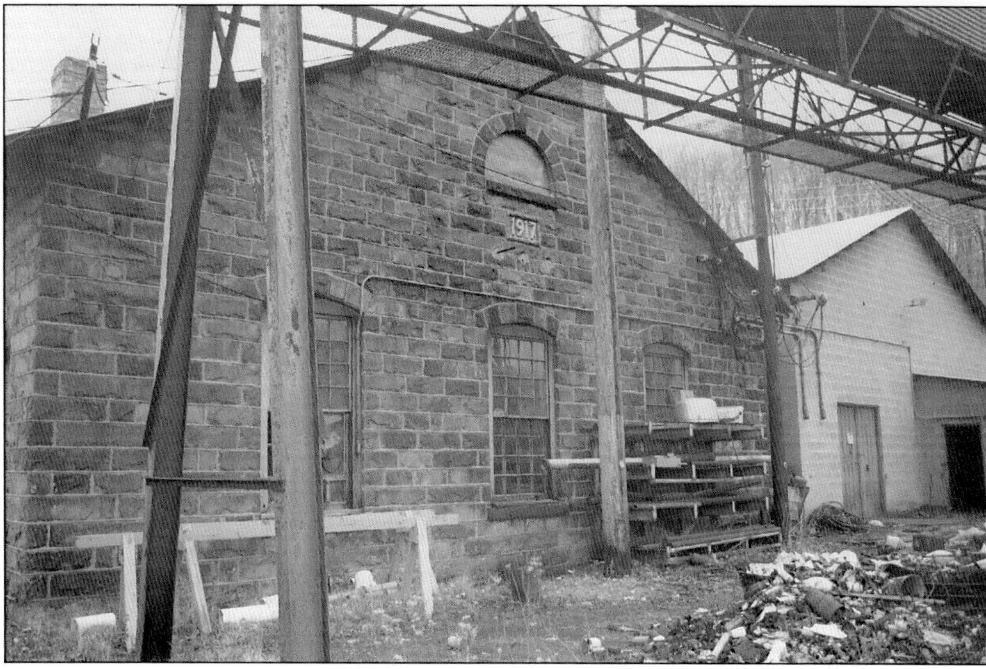

The engine house is where miners prepare for the day and keep their equipment. Colonel C. Baker, a native of London, joined with Robert H. Powell of Philadelphia in operating a mine in 1887. He became the secretary of the Sterling Coal Company in 1887 and vice president in 1902. Baker was president of the Sterling Coal Company and owner of the Powelton Barge Fleet, a coal shipping firm in New York Harbor. Bakerton was named for him and another prominent citizen, John S. Holton.

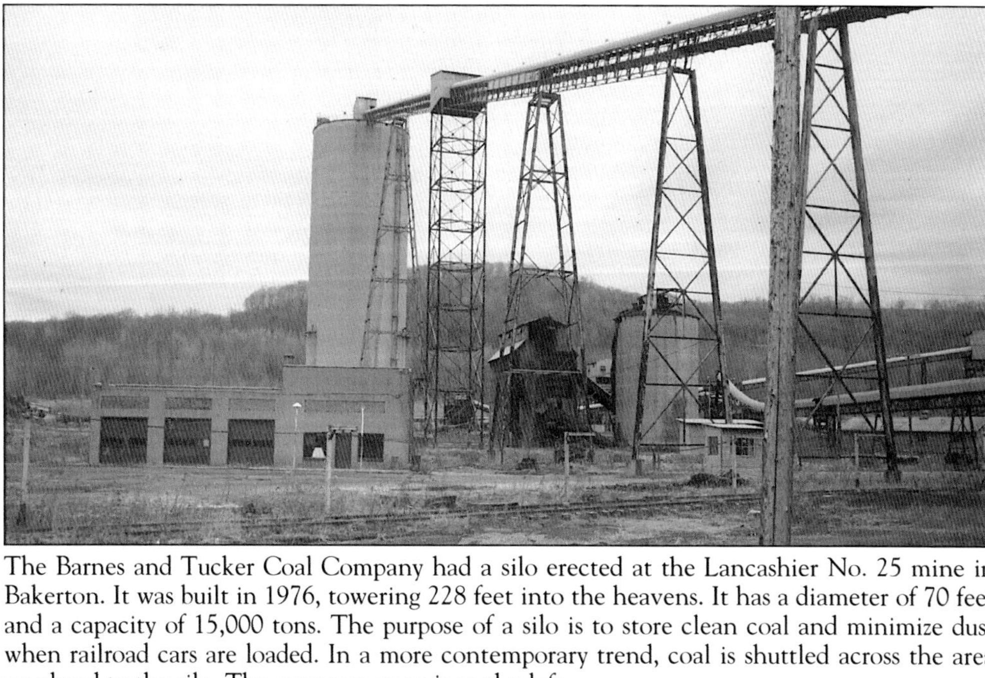

The Barnes and Tucker Coal Company had a silo erected at the Lancashier No. 25 mine in Bakerton. It was built in 1976, towering 228 feet into the heavens. It has a diameter of 70 feet and a capacity of 15,000 tons. The purpose of a silo is to store clean coal and minimize dust when railroad cars are loaded. In a more contemporary trend, coal is shuttled across the area overhead to the silo. The company store is to the left.

Five

By the Waters of Glendale

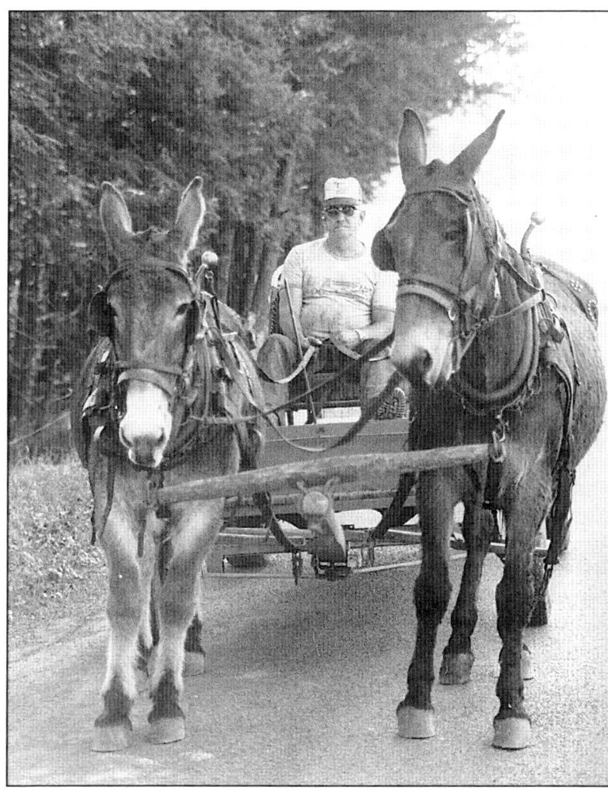

Charles Krug can be seen with his team of mules, Jack and Pete. Contrary to popular belief, mules are usually gentle and obedient. If treated with kindness, they react accordingly. Their strength, adaptable personality, and sure-footedness make them ideal riding and working animals. They take part in the annual Appalachian Wagon Train trek. This family-oriented event highlights historical sites or events that took place in the Appalachian region of Pennsylvania.

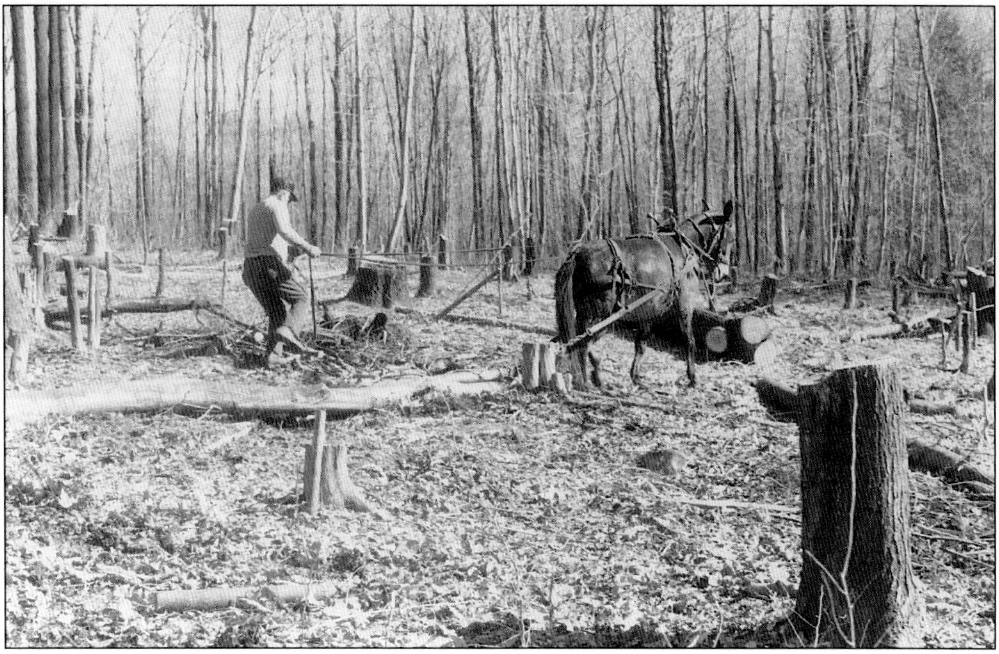

Logging and clearing land were always a necessity of our ancestors. Charles Krug and Jack the mule work together to clear a parcel of woodland to build a new house. The dense forests of western Pennsylvania are still rich in oak, white pine, hemlock, cherry, poplar, chestnut, beech, and birch trees. The Allegheny Mountains provided ideal conditions for the dense, virgin forests, which our ancestors found and which we continue to enjoy.

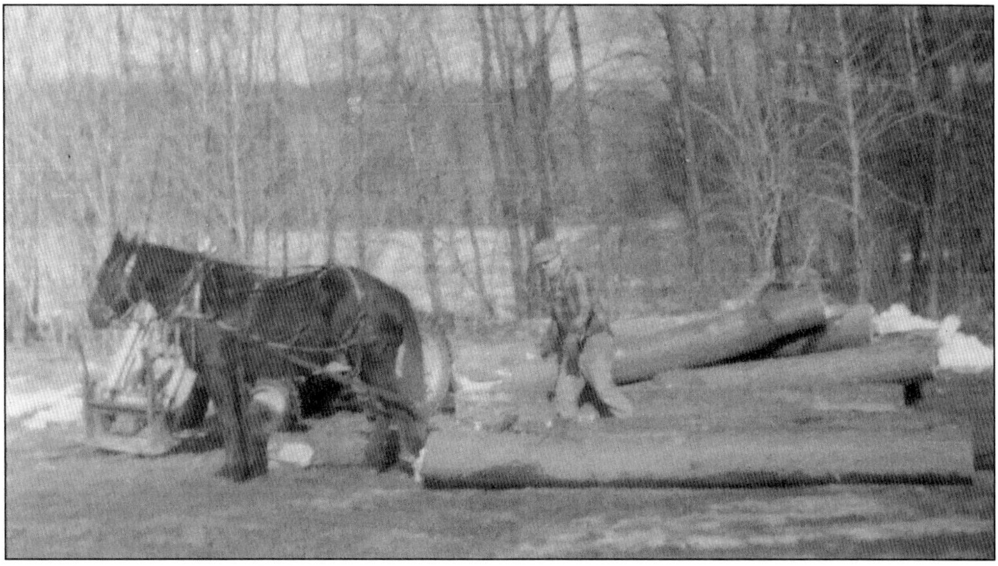

Jack, the mule, assists Charles Krug as they log. The numerous virgin forests of the Allegheny Mountains have always been a source of employment for those who choose to work above ground. Timber was a necessary commodity for expansion. The choice woodlands of the Allegheny Mountains provided a perfect setting for sawmills. Logs were floated down a waterway to the lumbering capital of the world, Williamsport. There, they were sorted and identified.

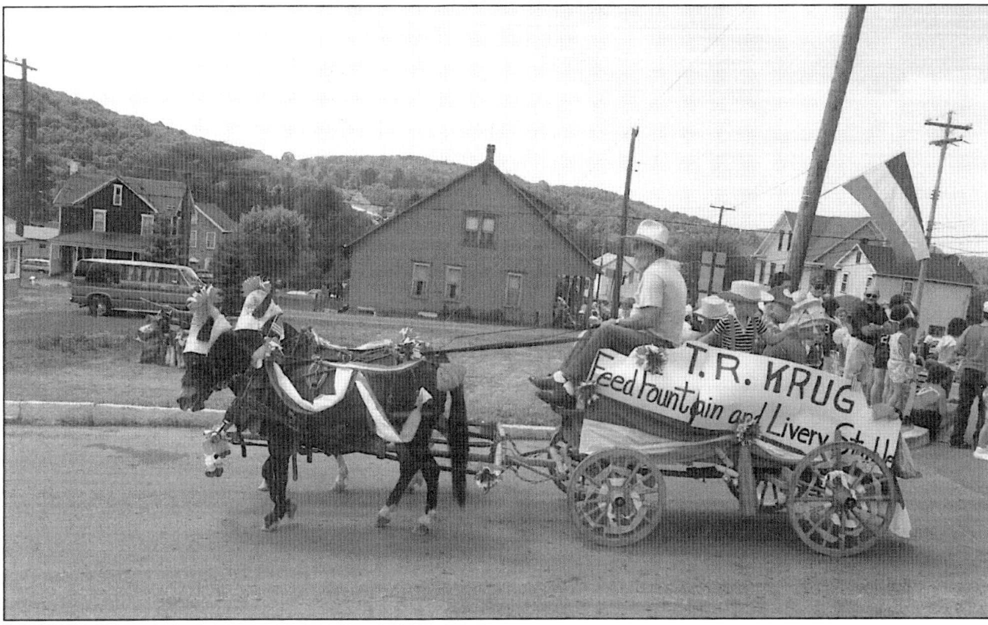

Ashville celebrated its centenary as a borough in 1987. Thomas R. Krug, father of the driver, had a livery stable in the area of Gibbons Funeral Home. In memory of his father, Charles dressed his mules, Gus and Festus, and hitched them up to advertise, "T.R. Krug Feed, Fountain and Livery Stable." The mules are trotting east along Route 36 as they join in the centennial parade through town.

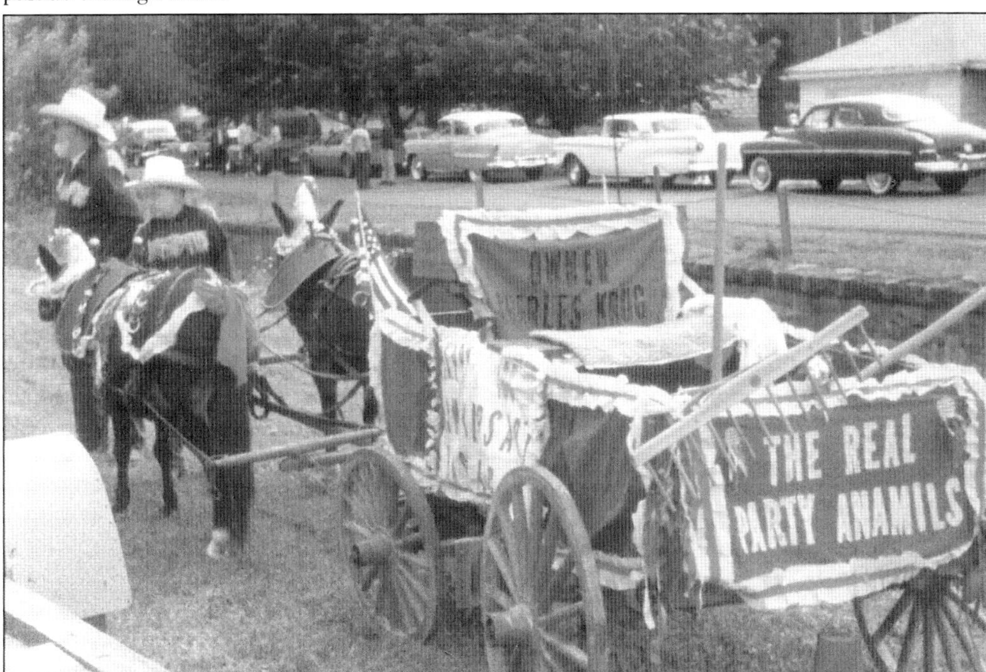

Charles Krug and his son, Jake, took part in the Hastings centennial celebration in 1989. The mules, Gus and Festus, pulled the wagon from Ashville to join in the festivities and parade. Antique cars are parked across the street.

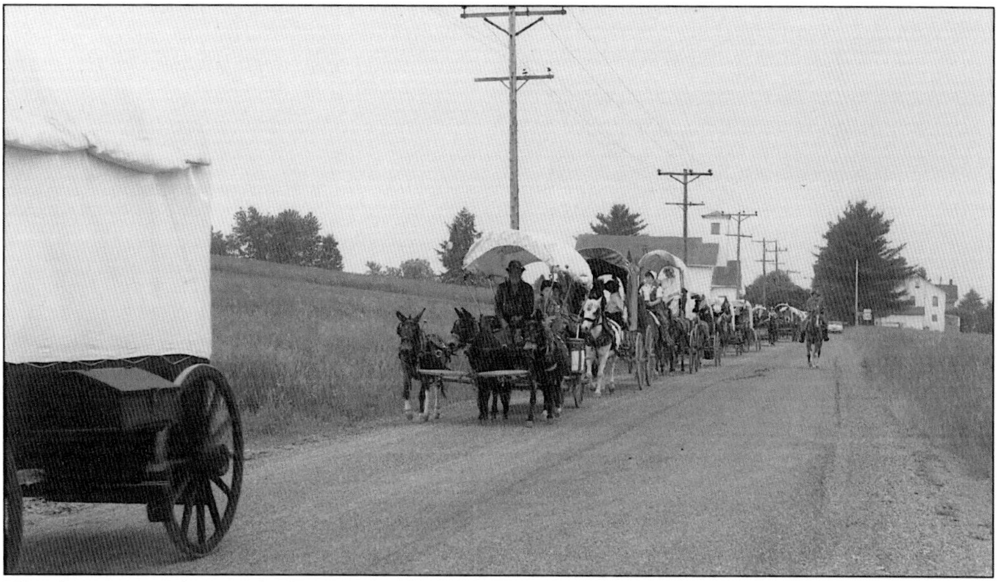

The bicentennial Appalachian Wagon Train became a reality in Cambria County when the tourist council arranged a meeting of interested citizens and encouraged them to plan a celebration of our country's 200th birthday. Visits to historic monuments, festivals, and parades followed. Pony clubs became post riders and everyone became a pioneer. The project was so well received and enjoyed that it continues into the millennium.

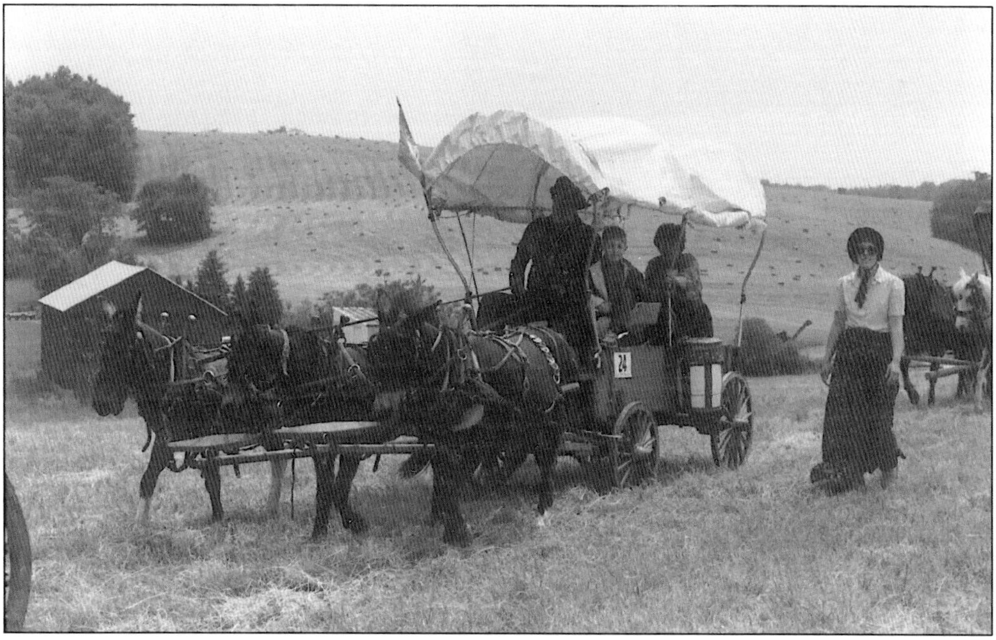

The Appalachian Wagon Train, in canvas covered wagons, rolls along the ancient Native American trails. Charles Krug and family are traveling with his three-mule team. Many rules were established to make the trek enjoyable for everyone. Each wagon travels with its own support, including chuck wagons, souvenir wagons, and water. The Appalachian Wagon Train moves on the third Sunday of June and travels from Monday until Friday. On Saturday, a parade finishes the week.

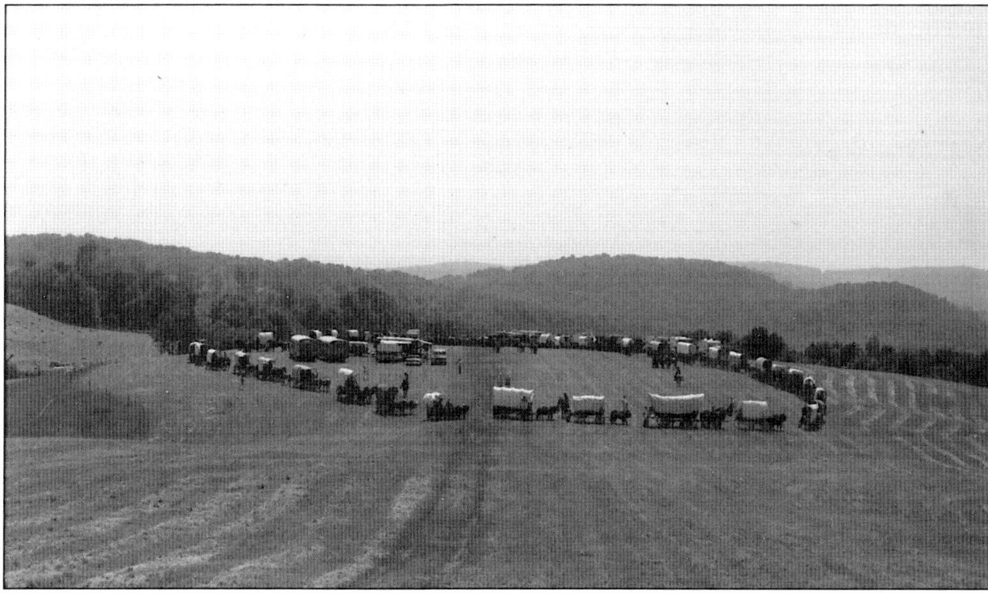

Wagon trains form a circle to prepare for the night. A field at least 10-acres in size is needed for a campsite. The number of wagons vary from year to year. Colonial ladies appear and ministers become circuit riders. All participants are required to dress in colonial attire. The dress code also applies to night attire.

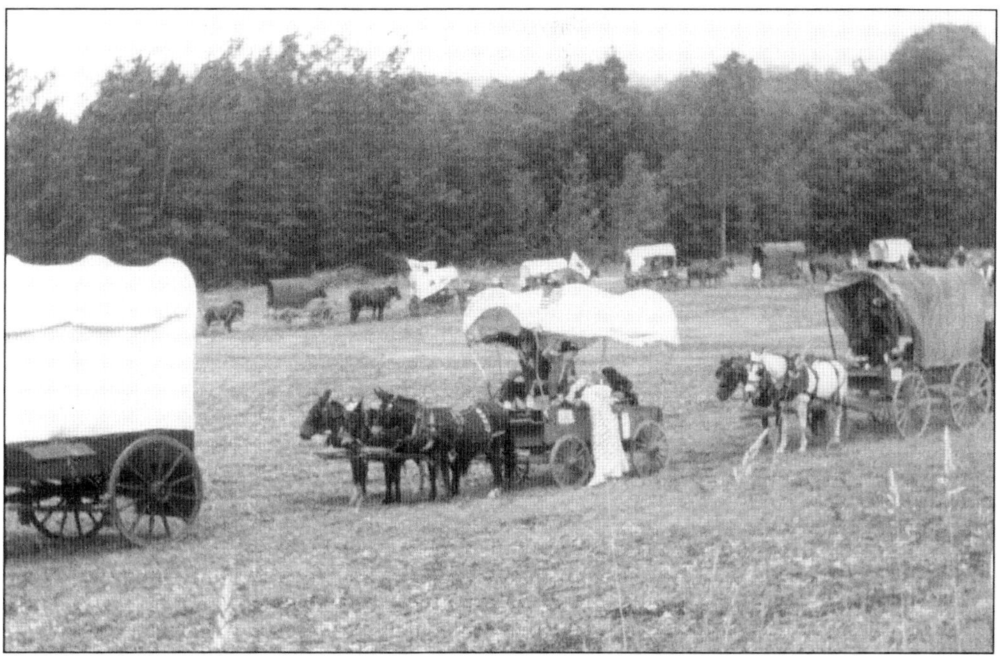

The wagon train prepares to continue the trek. In Cambria County, the Appalachian trail was initiated when Jean Kimmel learned about wagon trains and traveled to North Carolina to take part in the Daniel Boone Wagon Train. It was so enjoyable that she came back to Sommerset with the idea. The Appalachian Wagon Train Association resulted and the first trek occurred from New Baltimore to Ligonier in 1970.

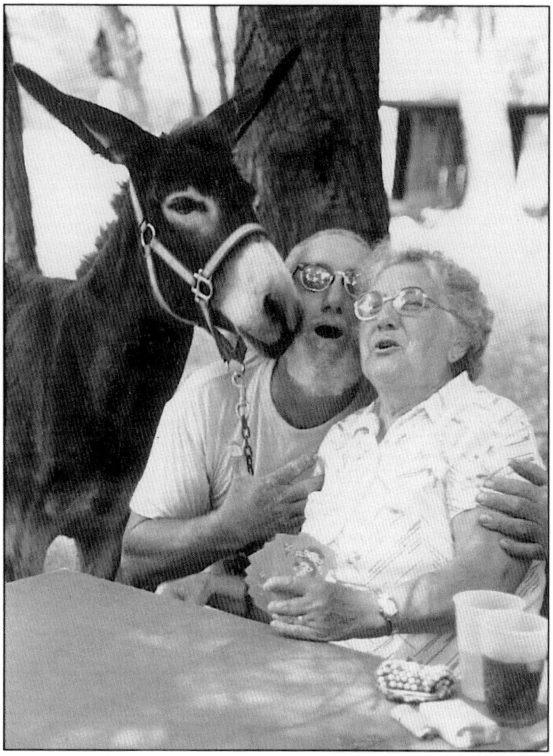

This unusual trio is entertaining with a sing-along. Charles Krug and his sister, Margaret, are joined by Margaret the burro in the songfest. The burro is a working donkey with a calm and amiable disposition. The Church of the Assembly of God in Altoona requested that Margaret the burro take part in a Christmas pageant inside the church. She played her role well and seemed to enjoy assisting Mary and Joseph to Bethlehem.

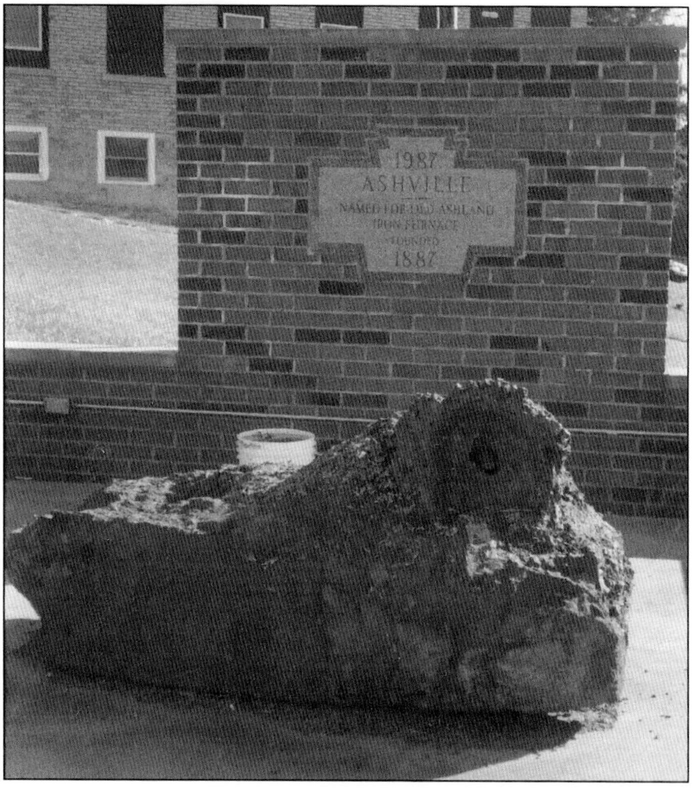

The Ashland furnace gave Ashville its name. In 1842, Joseph A. Conrad purchased 180 acres in what is now Ashville. He established an ore bank in 1845 and hauled 12 tons of ore to the Elizabeth furnace to be tested. He sold out to Hugh McNeil, who continued the business. McNeil produced 6,300 tons of metal and hauled it to Duncansville in 1851. This predated the Pennsylvania Railroad. At that time, distant hauling was not a profitable goal. In 1851, Ashland went out of business.

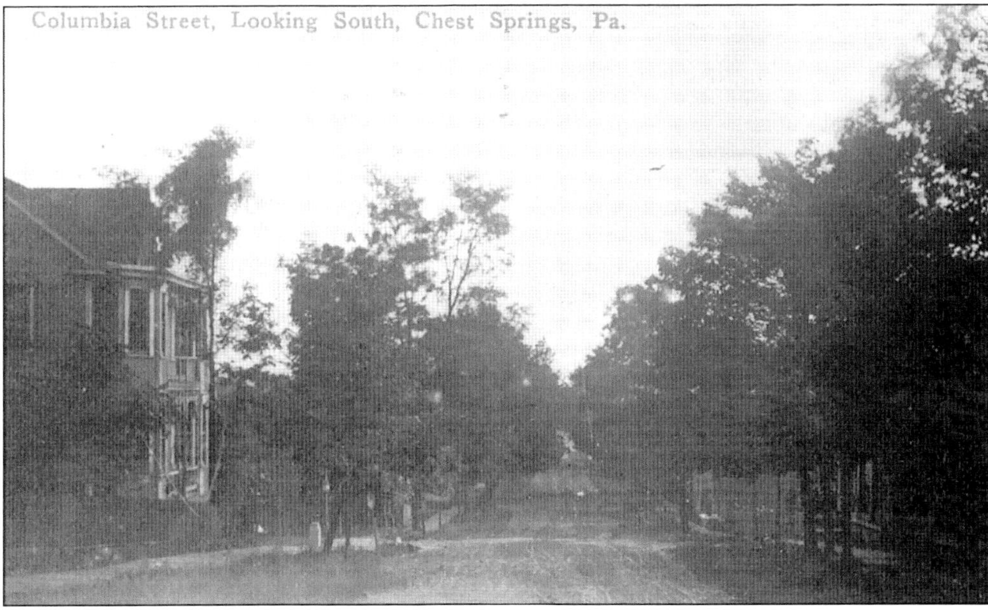

Chest Springs holds the distinction as one of the oldest boroughs in Cambria County, but the smallest in population. In 1754, the Iroquois sold Cambria County to William Penn. In 1769, the land was surveyed and Chest Springs was derived from an abundance of chestnut trees in the area. "Springs" came from the springs along Kittanning Path. The borough was incorporated on May 10, 1858. Many early inhabitants came from Maine. The Nutters and the Perrys settled here and established a lumbering business.

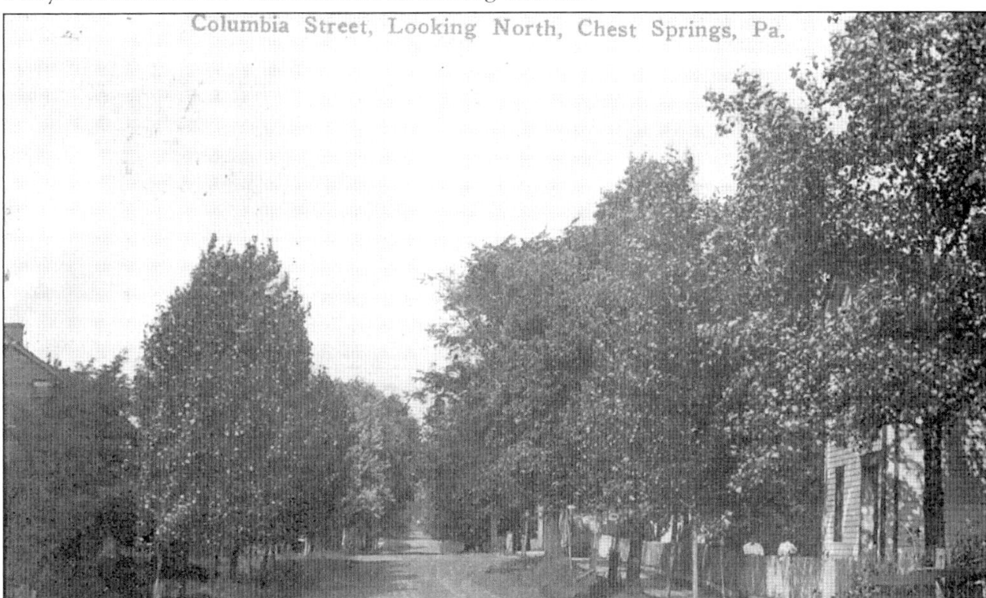

Chest Springs was once a thriving hamlet. Eben Nutter built a boardinghouse for men who worked at the sawmills. An one-room log schoolhouse served the children. The post office was opened on May 4, 1839 in Perry's general store with Andrew McGuire as the postmaster. Flour from the famous rolling mills of Chest Springs was the first to reach Johnstown after the 1889 flood. The village also had a blacksmith shop and a shook shop that turned out barrels.

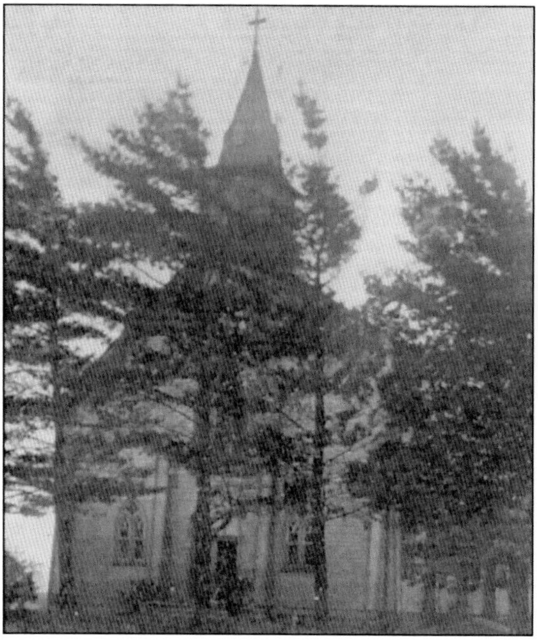

St. Monica's Roman Catholic Church was established in Chest Springs in 1858. The original wooden frame church was built in 1889. The parish was served from St. Augustine until 1896, when its status as a mission was terminated with the appointment of a resident pastor. In 1968, a new and larger church was completed. The parish school opened in 1921 with the Sisters of Mercy forming the faculty for it. The school building had long been a combination school-convent.

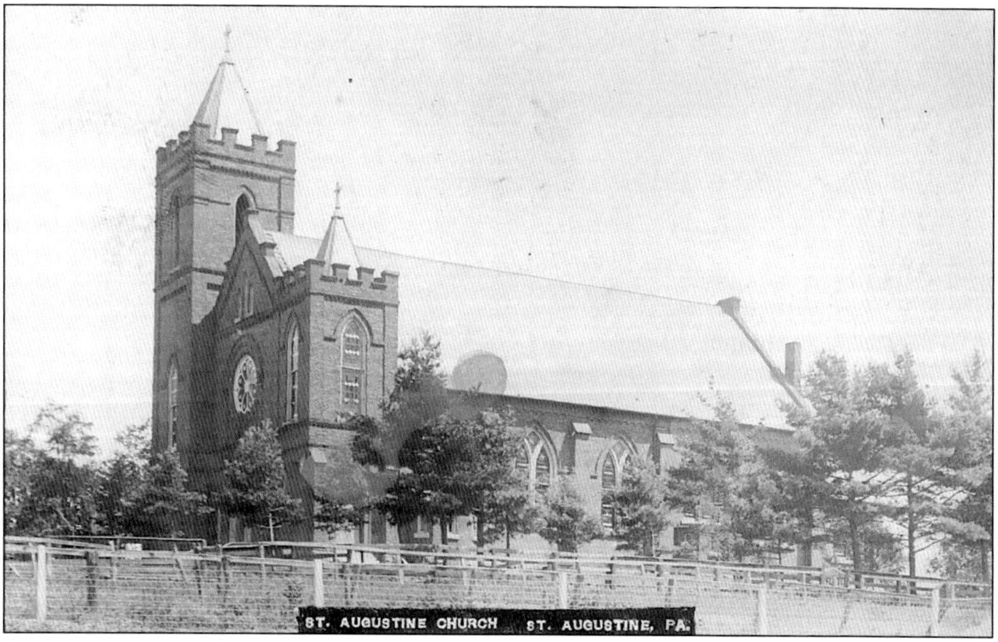

St. Augustine's Parish was established in 1848. The parish territory initially included Ashville, Frugality, and Chest Springs with 500 parishioners. Situated on the highest point in the village of St. Augustine, there is strong evidence this land was once a Native American reservation. Many Native American artifacts were found in the area. Work began on a small frame church in 1849. The present church was built in 1894. The rectory was a 14-room, two-story, brick-encased edifice.

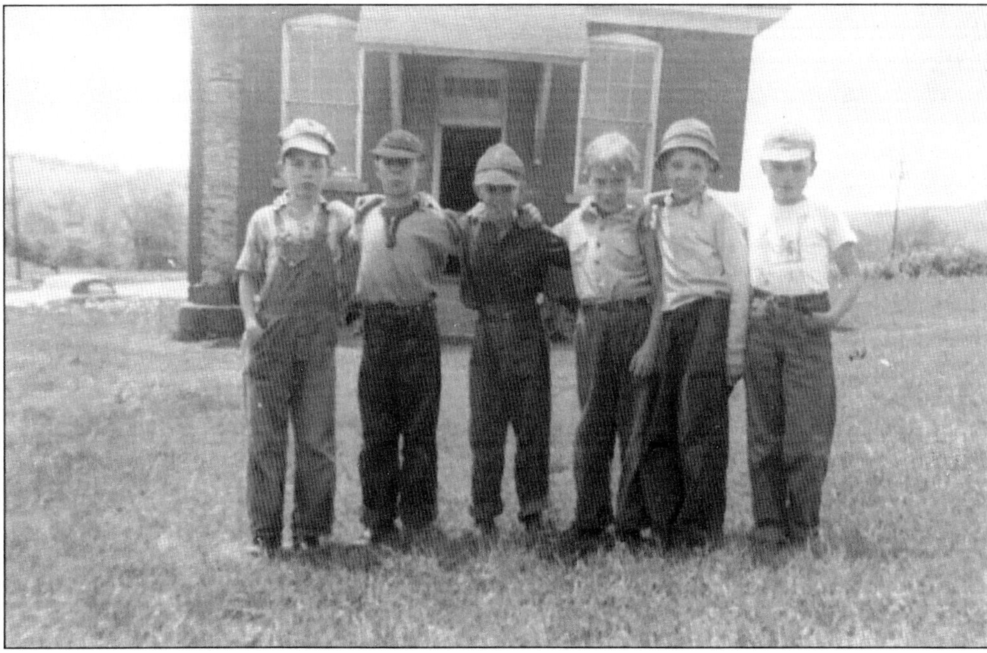

A group of youngsters gather outside the Beaver Valley Schoolhouse during the tenure of Ferdinand Nagle and George Adams. This was one of many one-room schoolhouses that served outlying districts early in the 20th century. These were often family-owned. Many of the students went on to enter major professions, such as medicine, law, and teaching. Classes were approximately 30 students and ranged from the first through the eighth grades.

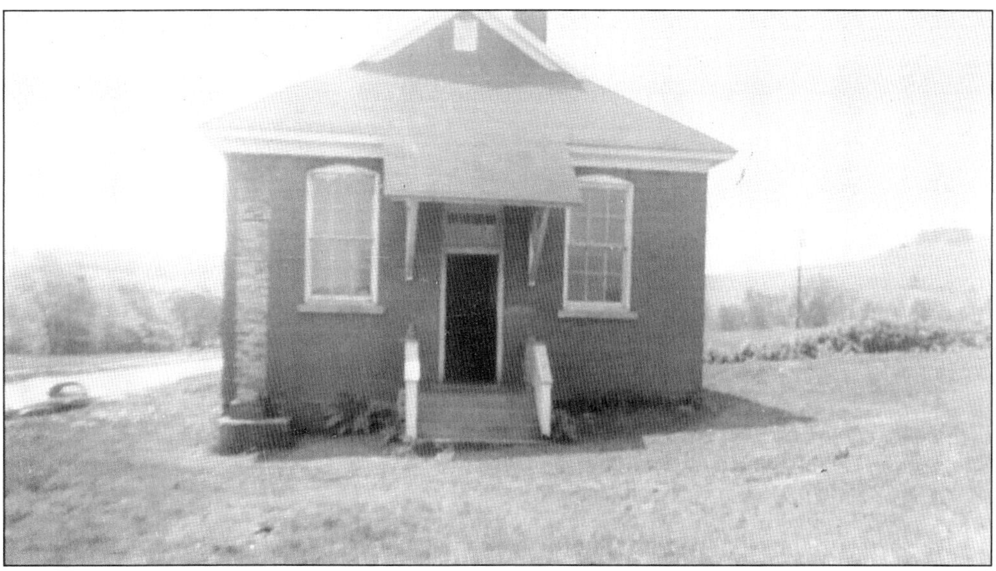

In 1887, there were 39 district one-room schoolhouses. In 1959, the Prince Gallitzin school district closed all one-room schools. The emergence of a modern educational trend brought about their decline. Quality education was often offered in these small schools; however, new technology, equipment, and opportunities emerged. Some of the last vestiges of one-room schools included Clark, Brown, Moyer, and St. Augustine schools. An era had phased into history.

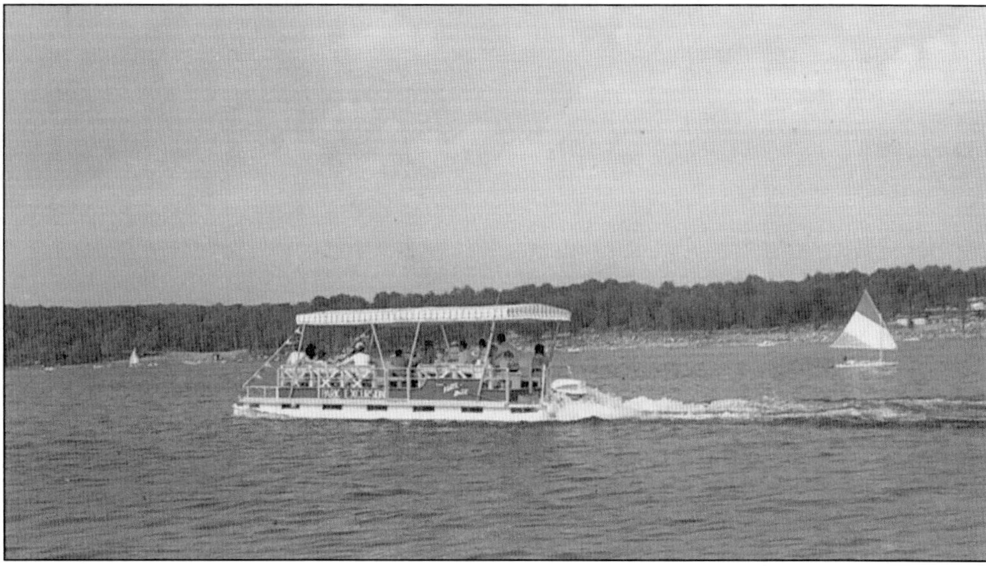

Excursion boats gently glide across the rippling waters of Glendale Lake in Prince Gallitzin State Park. This picturesque mountain lake came into existence during the mid-20th century. The idea of a park was conceived by the Patton Chamber of Commerce and the Sportsman's Club in 1955. A year later, the site was chosen. Much work went into the construction of this man-made lake. Excavation of the lake bed required the felling of timber, which was begun in 1958.

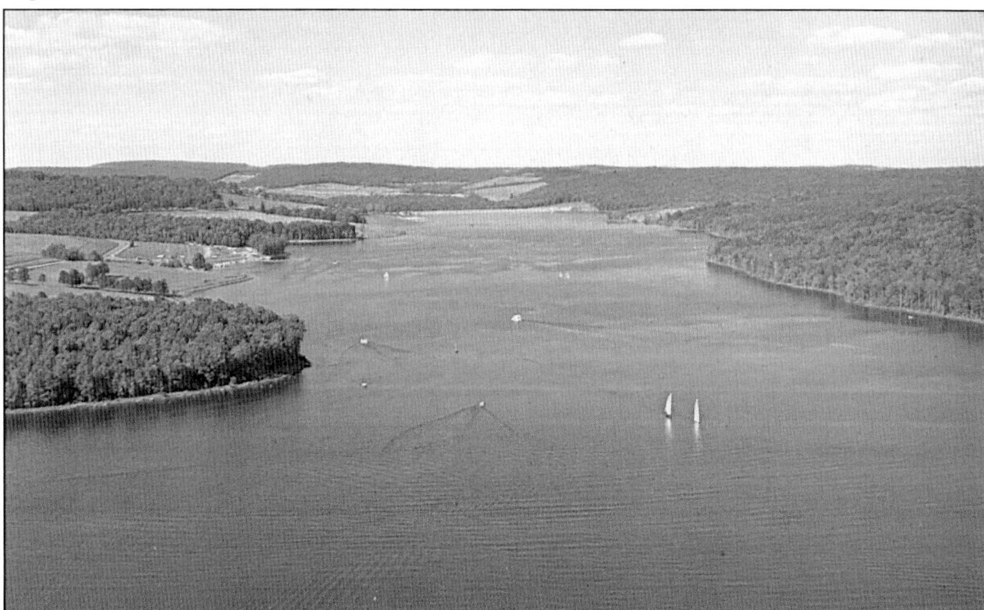

The 1,600-acre lake began to be filled in December of 1960 and was dedicated on May 29, 1961. This view from the Marina affords a glimpse of the Beaver Valley area across the water. The lake was opened for boating in July 1961. Sailboats are a common site on the lake. Prince Gallitzin State Park is one of the largest in the state. The Paradise Point Corporation developed the cabin area. By 1959, they revealed plans for 116 cabin sites. One hundred and fifty thousand seedling trees were planted in the park.

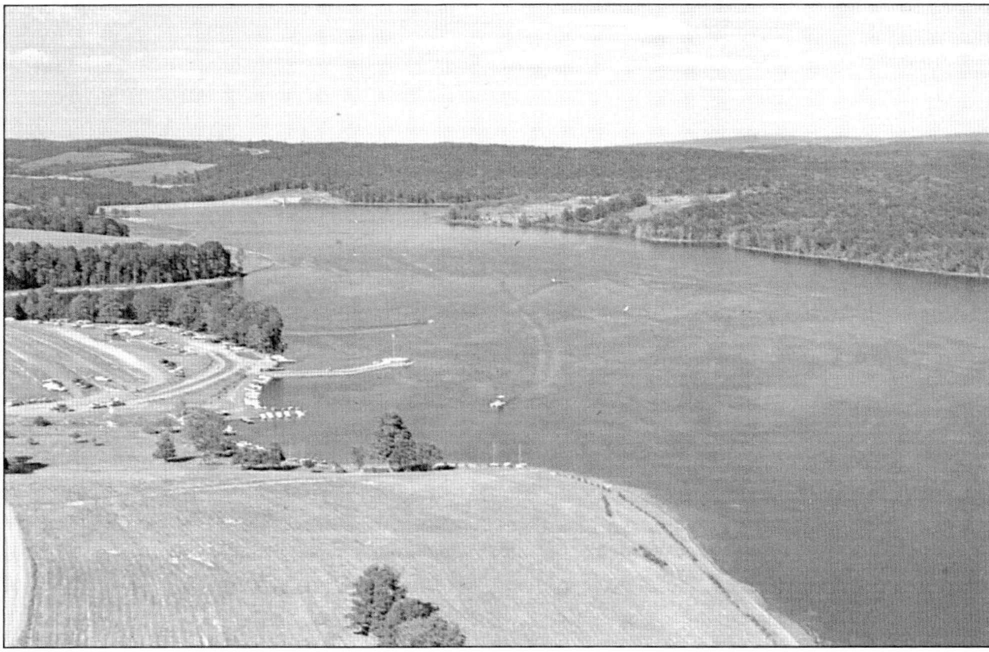

This aerial view focuses on the marina. The park provides facilities for boating, fishing, swimming, camping, picnicking, and other outdoor recreation. The Pennsylvania State Park Service cleared 1,500 acres of timber. The park includes nature trails, picnic areas, beaches, campgrounds, and a marina. Much of the salvaged timber was used in the construction of 1,300 picnic tables around the park.

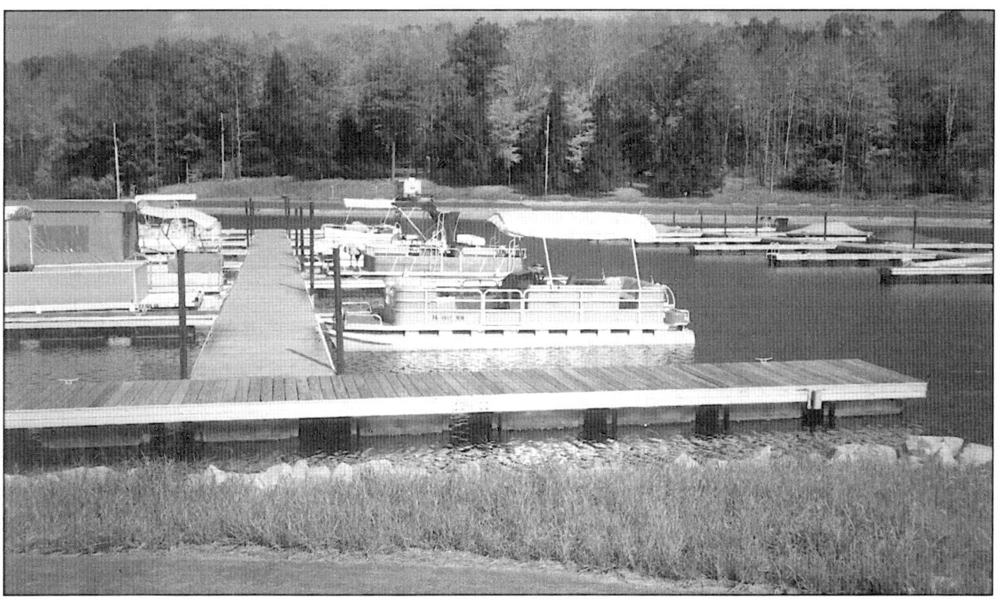

Pontoons and sailboats are a common sight at the park. Pontoons are recreational flat-bottomed vessels. They are great for sightseeing, as they accommodate many people, are easy to handle, and are quite comfortable, but not very fast. Boats with more than 10 horsepower are not permitted on the lake. Pontoons may be rented at Prince Gallitzin Park.

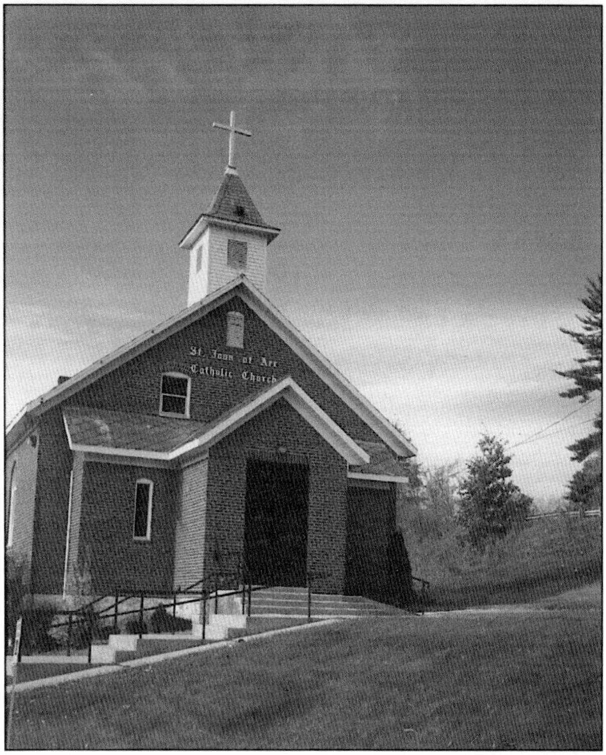

St. Mary Magdalene Church, now St. Joan of Arc frame church in Frugality was built in 1889. The hamlet already had a railroad station, a general store, and a five-story hotel called the Atlington. Frugality was a mission from Ashville. It has recently joined with St. Thomas in Ashville to form St. Joan of Arc. Early parishioners created a "brush road", now Route 53, so the priest could get to Frugality on horseback. The parish was later to serve Prince Gallitzin State Park.

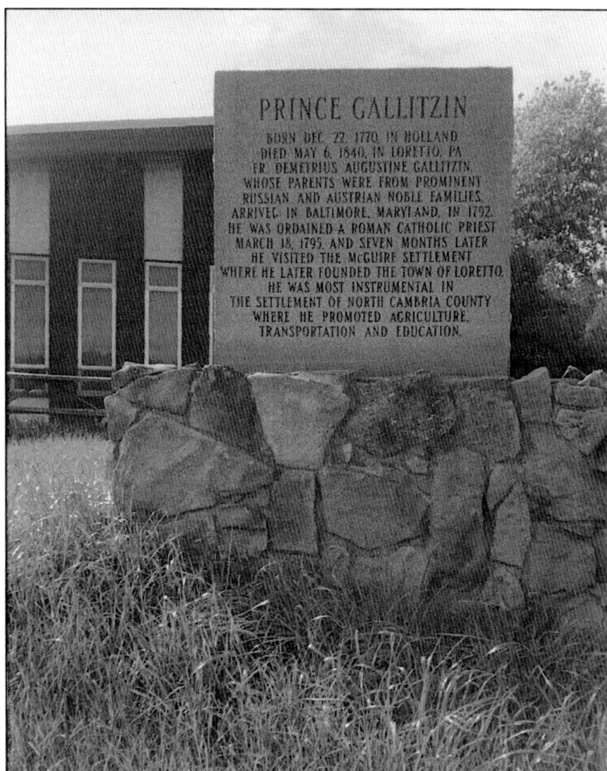

In the bicentennial year of 1976, two markers were dedicated to Prince Galltzin, the apostle of the Alleghenies. In May 1958, ground breaking was held with Governor Leader and 2,500 people present. A visitor center and Crooked Run Campground were opened. By 1962, the public docks got underway. The lake is V-shaped. In 1966, the park housed the National Campers and Hikers Association Convention. A guarded swimming beach with modern bath houses and dressing stockades are opened in summer.

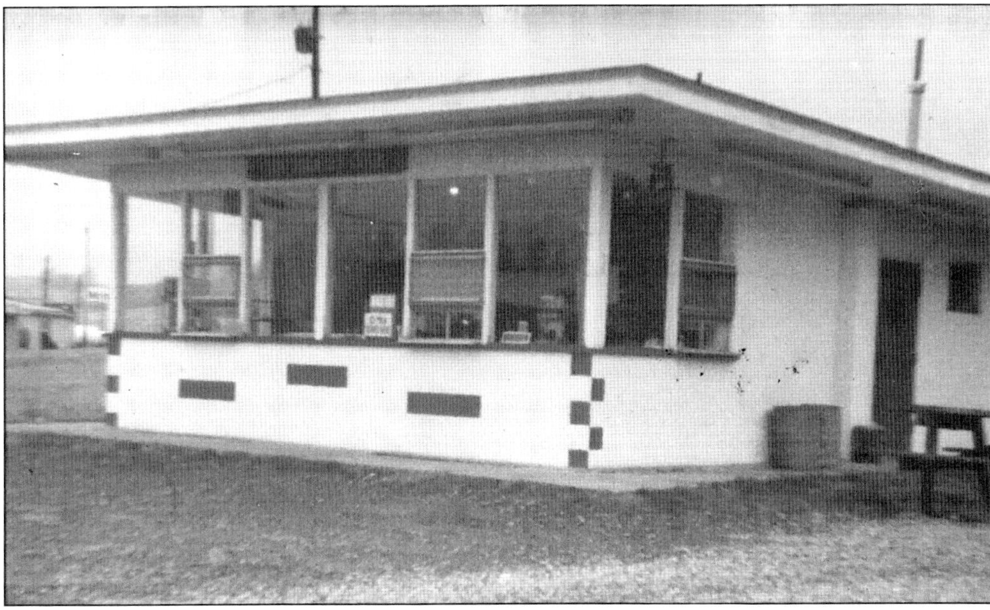

For many years, Greg's Pub and Grill was known as Pirate's Cove. Located along the picturesque lake, it was operated as a restaurant for over two decades by Richard and Marianne Caracciolo. In 1999, Greg Hoover bought the business and renamed it. He advertises an open-air patio. Other eateries around the park include Aunt Rose, Zimms, Noel's, and Ripper's. The mobile park is known as "Captain's Quarter's." The store was called the "Crow's Nest."

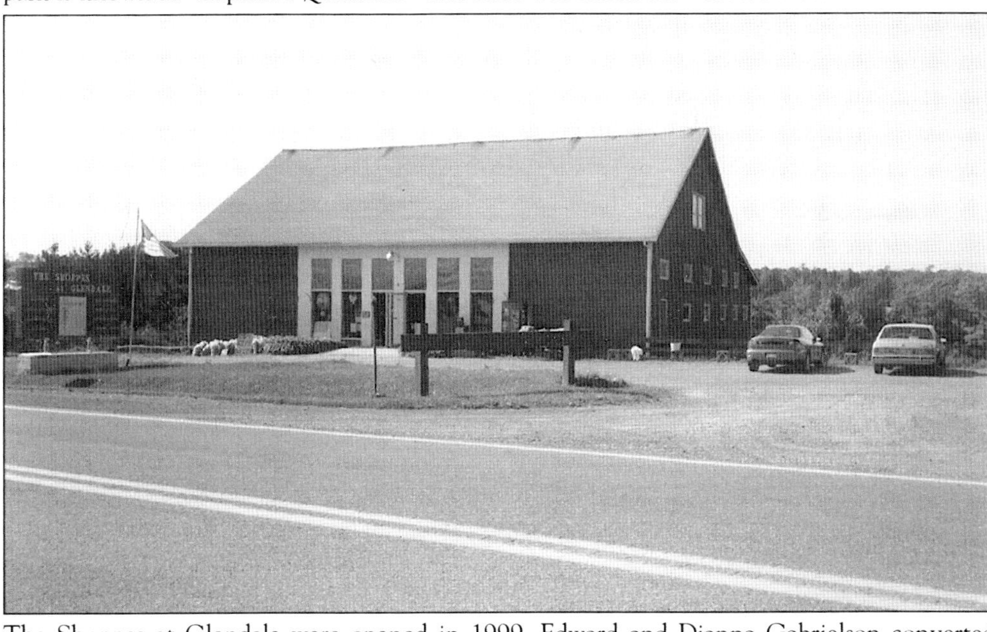

The Shoppes at Glendale were opened in 1999. Edward and Dianna Gabrielson converted the former "Crow's Nest" into an emporium-style retail trade that provides browsing and shopping for everyone. Miss Pinkerton's is an anchor for the new enterprise. Ample space is provided for local vendors. A farmer's market and camp store are included. Artists are invited to demonstrate their talents in the front foyer. The parking lot contains 70,000 Patton Paver bricks. Barbara Burkhart manages the Shoppes at Glendale.

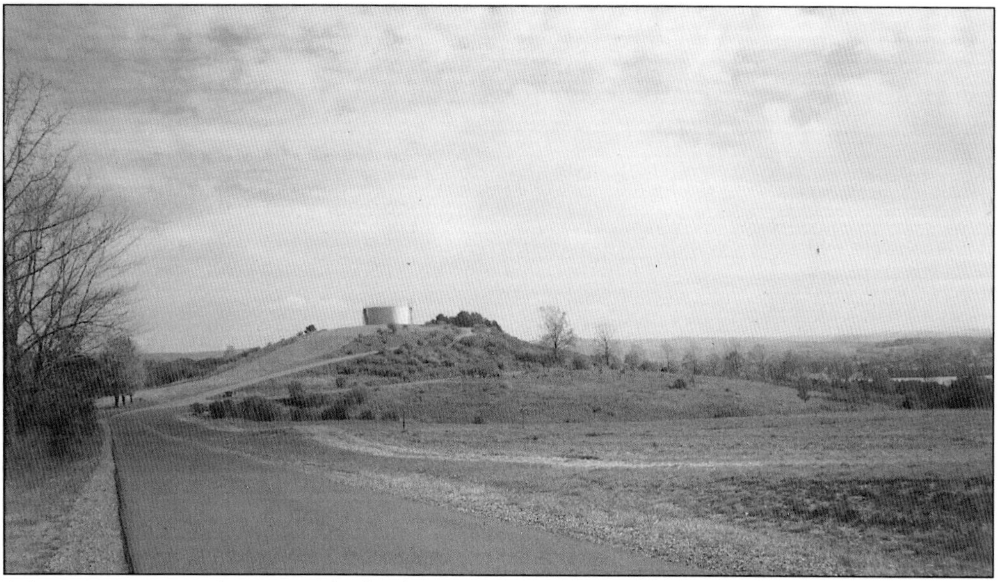

A huge water tower dominates the landscape atop Headache Hill at Prince Gallitzin State Park. While serving a practical purpose, it adds to the picturesque hilltop overlooking the lake. The massive tower assures an ample supply of water to campgrounds, marinas, food concessions, and other recreational facilities in the park. The Prince Gallitzin State Park offers the mooring, rental, and sale of boats. There are exercise areas for fitness enthusiasts and miles of trails.

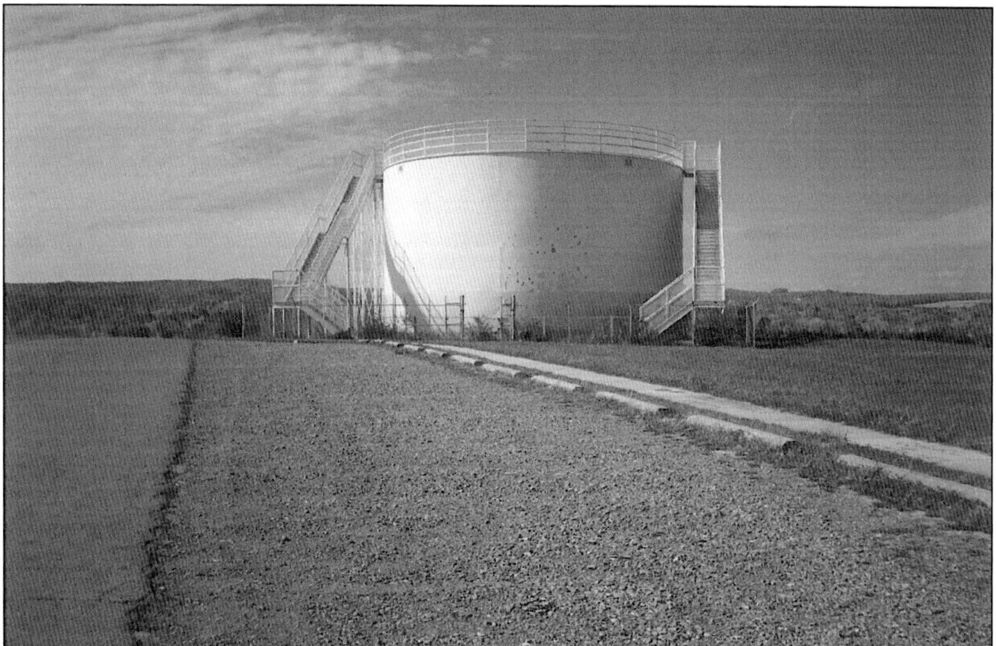

In 1967, this massive 400,000-gallon reservoir was constructed high on Headache Hill overlooking the lake. This vantage point affords a magnificent panorama of the mountain lake and surrounding hills. The steps lead one to an extraordinary scenic overlook, which affords a distant view to the opposite side of the lake.

Six

When Coal Was King

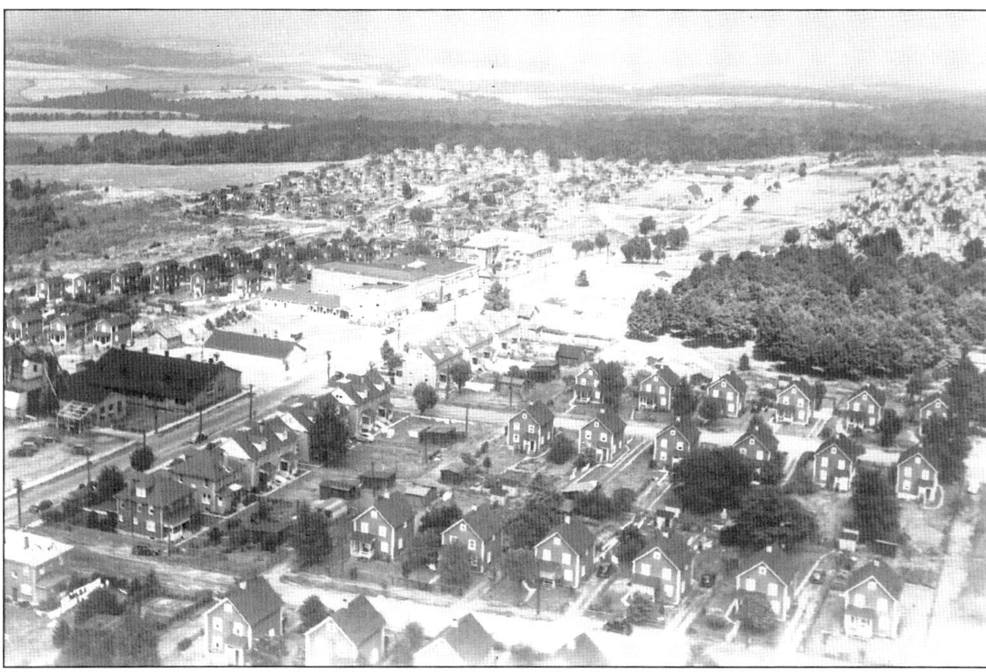

The little town of Colver, with only one access road, is a charming mountain village of 800 inhabitants. A cluster of trees shade Colver Park. Looking along Reese Avenue, the Commercial Hotel apartments, the company store, the soda grille, the fire hall, and the old wash-house are detectable. Note the striking similarity of the houses. The brick houses across the road were homes of the Cambria and Indiana Railroad employees.

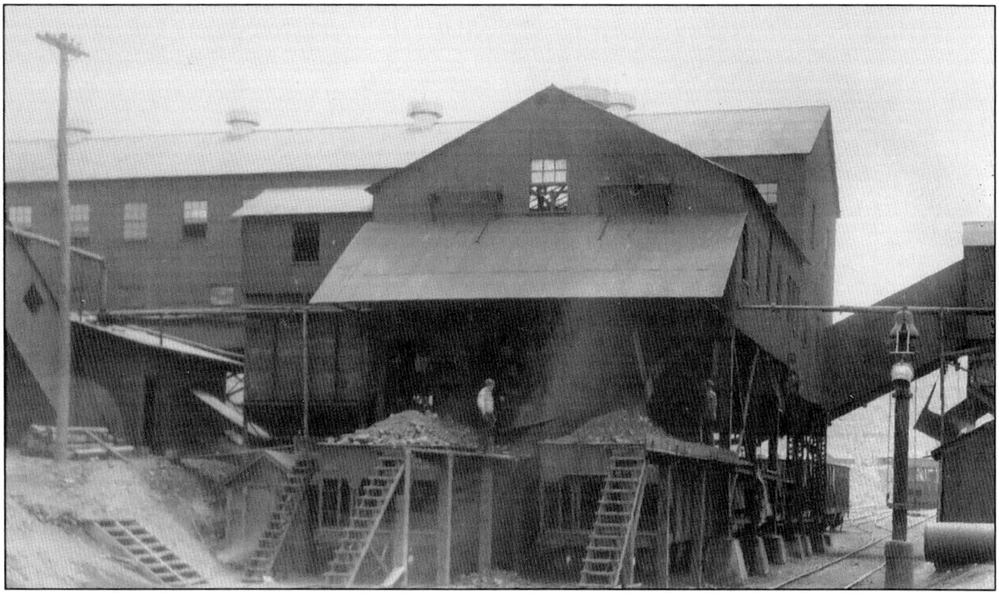

The Colver Coalmine opened in 1909 as part of the Ebensburg Coal Company. Rich veins of coal were discovered beneath the farmlands of Colver. The railroads and coalmines were the investment of two men: John Weaver of Williamsport and Dawson Colman of Philadelphia. The name Colver commemorates their joint enterprise with the first syllable of Colman and the last of Weaver. In its early years, the mine produced metallurgical coal that was in demand by the steel industry.

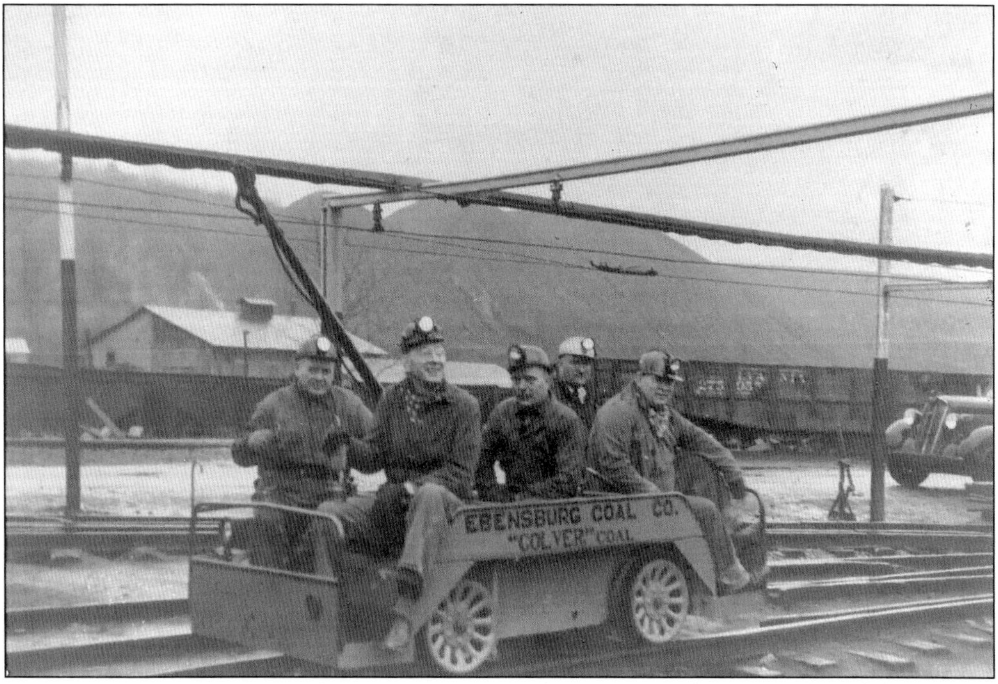

Fire inspectors are entering the mine to inspect for gas. Seen here are, from left to right, Dan Sullivan, unidentified, Waler Angert, Tom Aiken, and the mine inspector. Note the huge slag mounds in the background. These would be part of the landscape for many years.

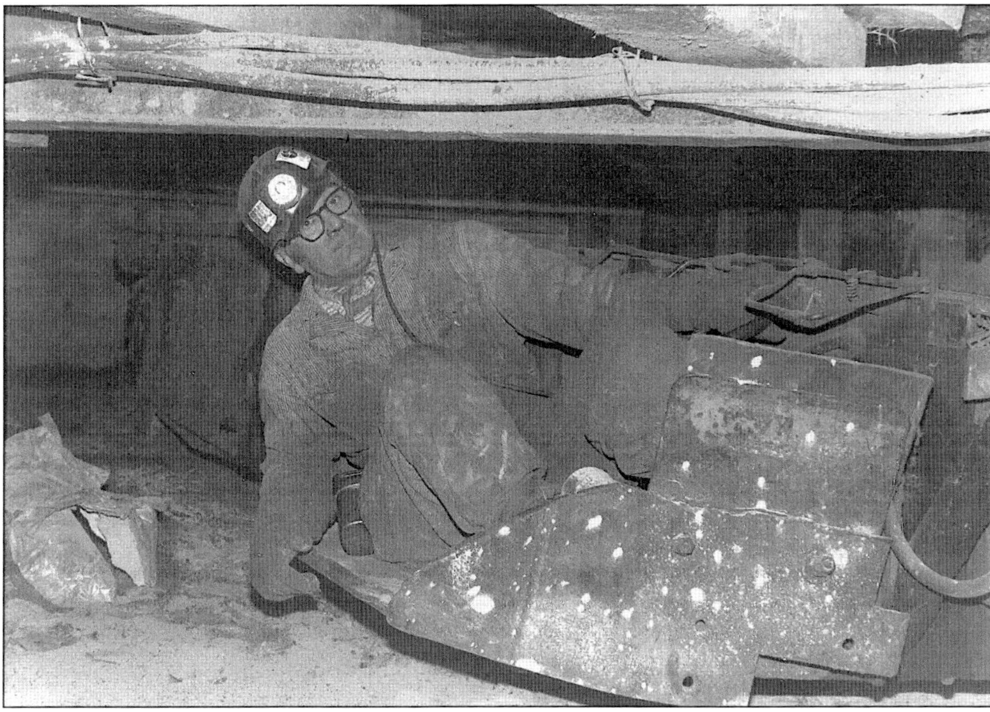

George Stoyka sits in a shuttle car, loading coal in July 1976. The mine employed over 1,200 employees at a time. Colver coal was shipped overseas, much of it going to Japan. The mine had been worked out, the quality of coal declining, when it closed on April 3, 1978. The 134 employees who were laid off were offered positions in other eastern bituminous mines. George Stoyka was the last miner to leave the mine.

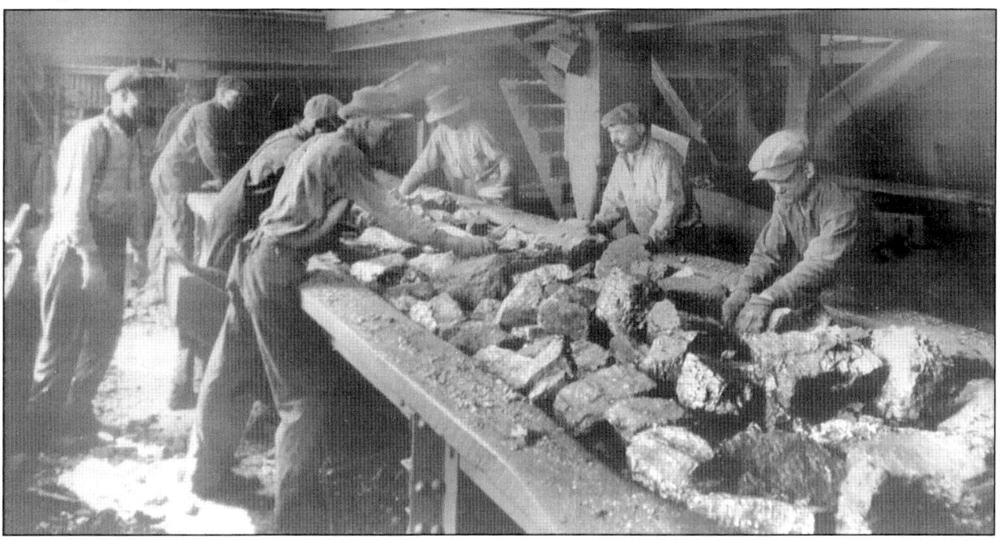

Rich bituminous coal was obtained from the Colver mine. Mines also produced dust, soot, and smoke. The miner had to remove inferior and unsaleable coal along with foreign particles such as rocks. When these elements are discarded, they form the many slag piles that are still visible. Coal dust saturates the air. The co-generation plant now takes care of these discarded piles that grew to massive proportions.

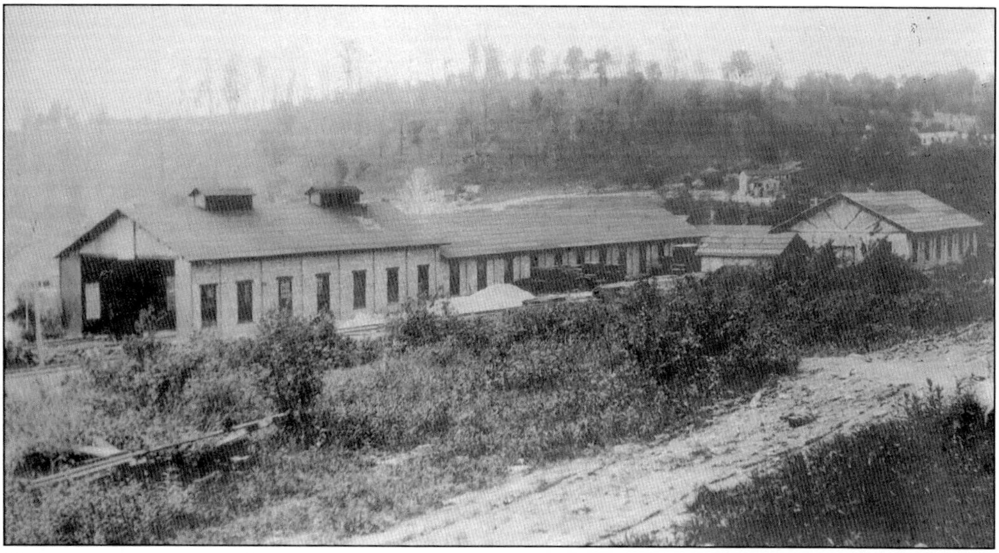

Coal company repair shops were necessary to keep equipment in smooth operation. Repair shops were a vital part of every mine. Each mine had its own repair shops.

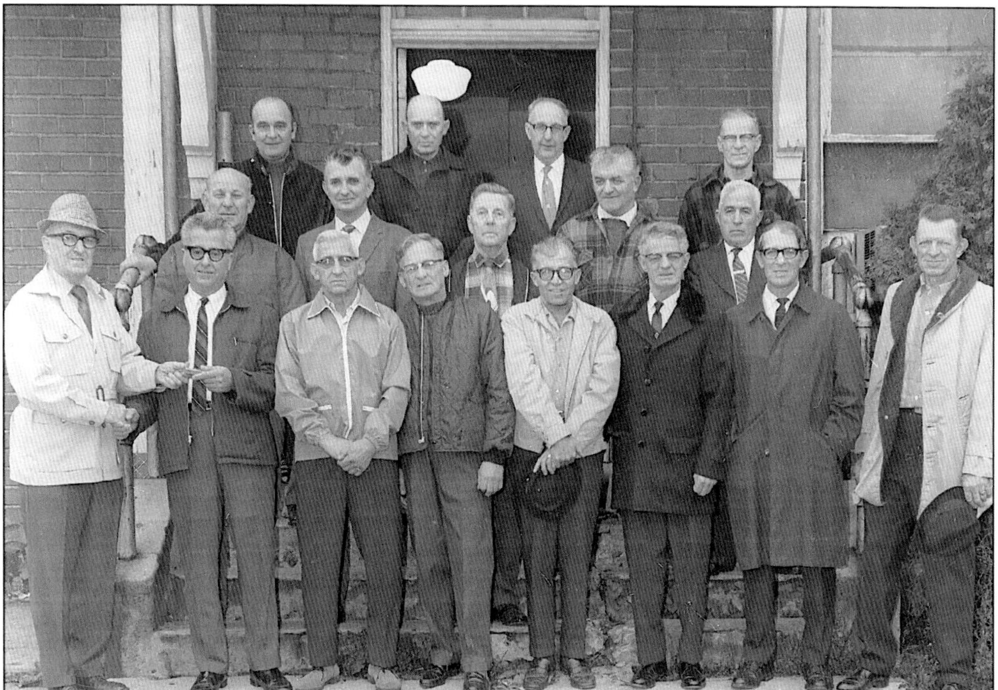

Superintendent Griffith Jones distributes service awards to miners. Seen here, from left to right, are the following: (first row) Joe Bartoccio, Joe Tononi, Alex Hudak, Francis Russick, George Hughes, Max Vassanelli, John Olinski; (second row) Mike Finch, George Mihalik, Bernard Shero, George Vay, Carmelo Palumbo; (third row) George Stoyka, John Visko, Raymond Miller, Maurice Burkey, Arnold Dotts, Andrew Hudak, John Zendzik, Clarence Conrad, Guido Mastrine, Frank Putsakulish, Sam A. Belin, William Metshula, Bob and Dave, Charles Mikula, Nicholas Bobby, John Bartock, Jules Becquet, Norbert Kirsch, and Howard A Ramsey.

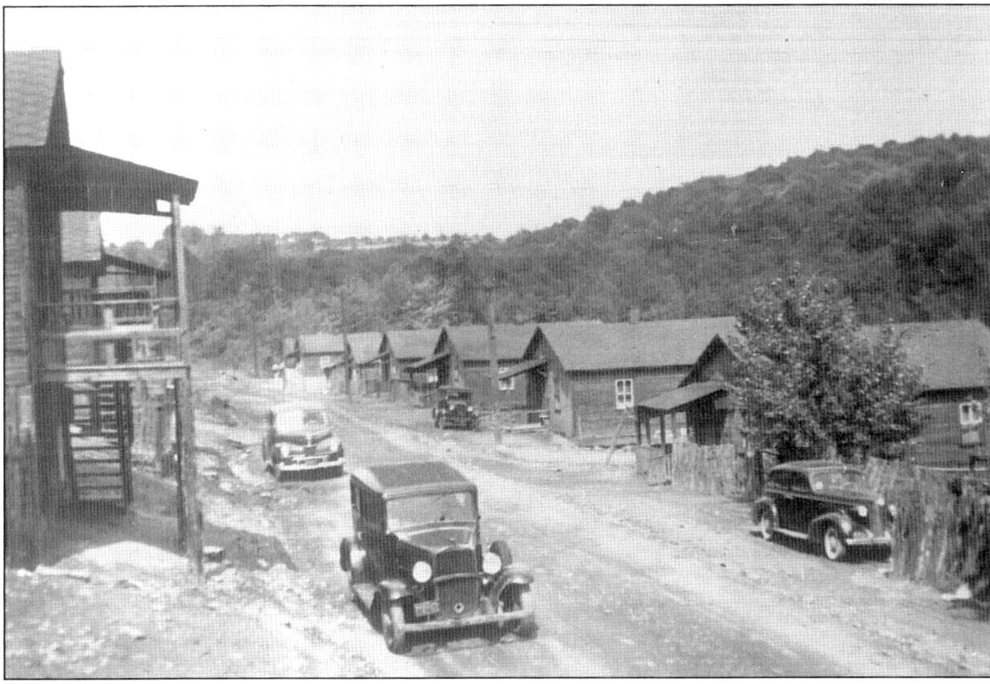

Colver is situated on a gently sloped hillside overlooking miles of scenic farmland. It was secluded when the rich coalfields were discovered. Company houses were built by the Ebensburg Coal Company in 1912. At one time, there were 1,200 employees working in the Colver Mine. Colver's main street is Reese Avenue. Shantytown, a suburb of Colver, now houses the co-generation plant. Other suburbs of Colver include Twenty Row, Nine Row, and Jewtown.

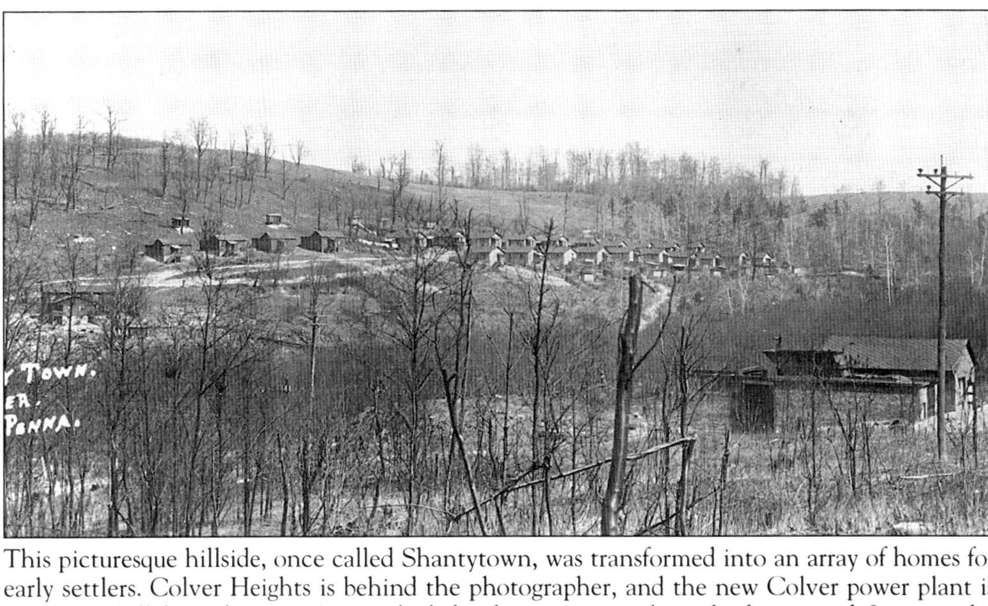

This picturesque hillside, once called Shantytown, was transformed into an array of homes for early settlers. Colver Heights is behind the photographer, and the new Colver power plant is across the hill from this site. An air shaft for the mine is in the right foreground. In time, the mountainous piles of discarded coal will disappear. A co-generation plant, which burns such debris has been added to the Colver landscape.

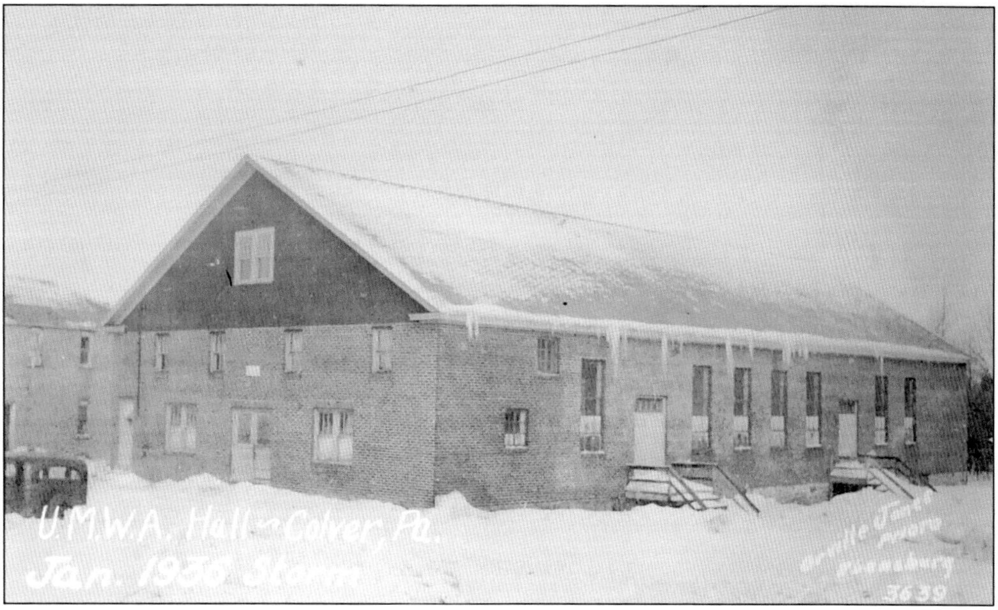

The United Mine Workers building was completed in 1936. April 1 was John Mitchell Day. Union mines were closed in honor of Mitchell, who served as president from 1898 to 1908. He is the father of the eight-hour work day in industry. He is also known for uniting 150,000 immigrant miners during a hard coal strike in 1902 to win better wages. On this day, Colver remembers 46 miners, whose names are listed on the Miners Memorial.

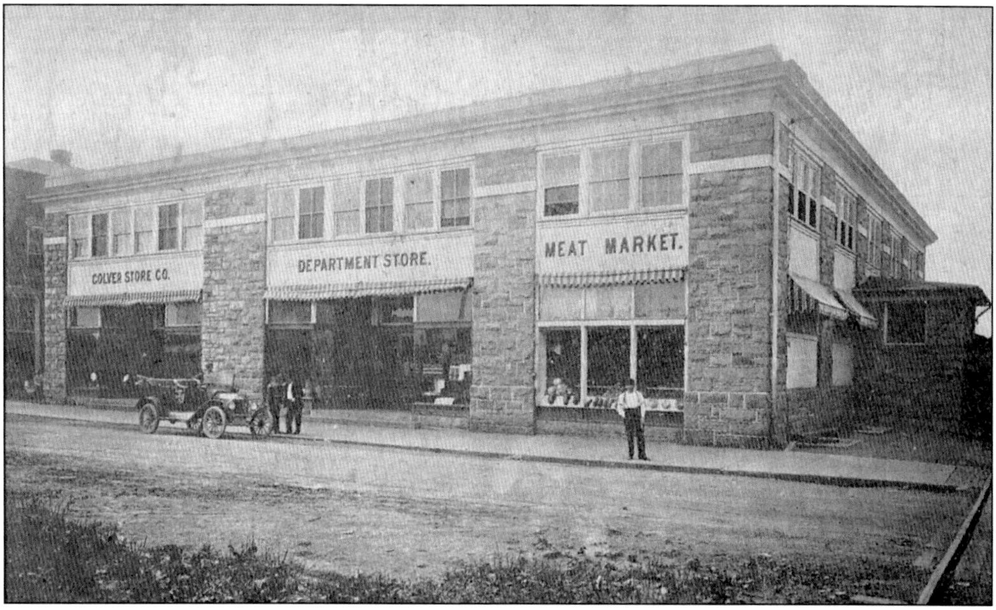

The company store was built in 1911 on Reese Avenue. It was constructed of stone blocks taken from the Colver quarry. In 1914, an addition was added to the western side. It covers 28,000 square feet and may be considered the department store of 1911. There were departments for food, clothes, housewares, linens, toys, sporting goods, stationery, and hardware. The store continued to provide similar goods through the long tenure of John Smylniky, which lasted almost to the millennium. Note the tracks beside the store.

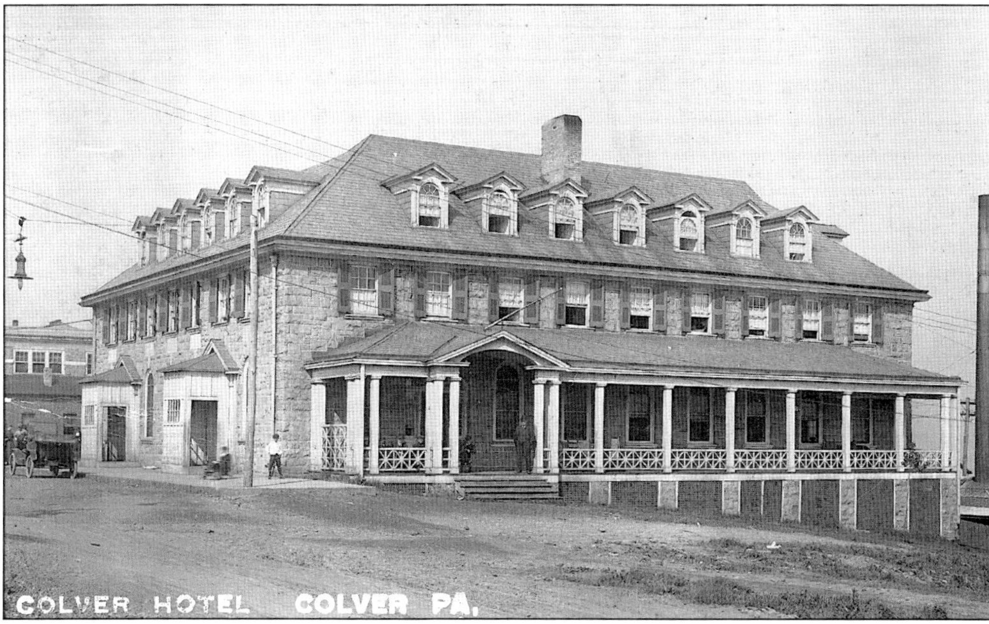

The Colver Hotel was established in 1911 by the coal company. It utilized the same stone as other prominent buildings and was designed in a Georgian Revival style of architecture. The hotel played host to salesmen and company officials. Lodging for single employees as well as families was available. The hotel dining room was the only restaurant in town. A need for housing prompted the hotel to rent to single employees. In later years, Fr. Carl Spishak was instrumental in converting the building into senior citizen housing through the Housing and Urban Development (HUD) program.

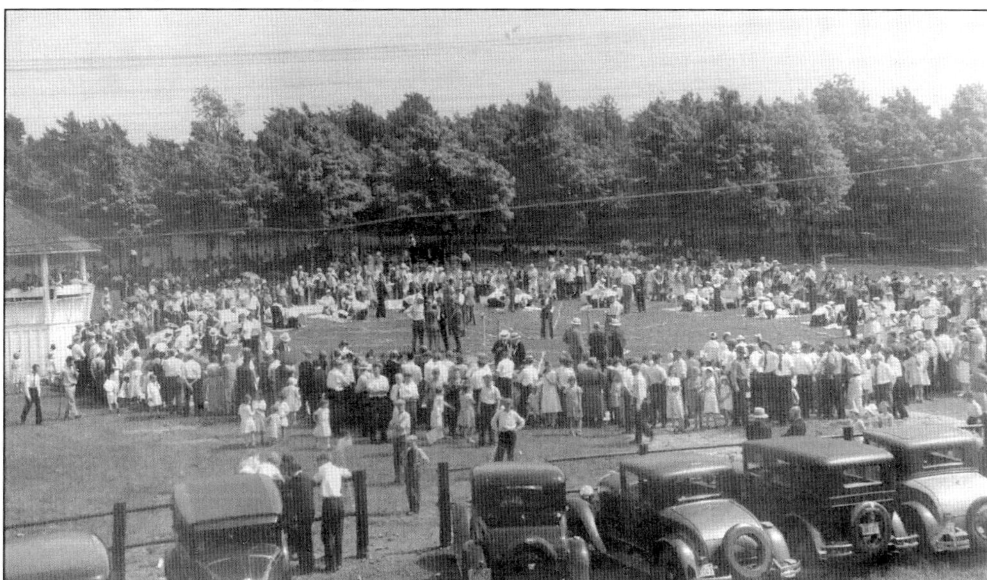

A park was established across from the company store early in the 20th century to provide recreation for the youngsters. The school was across the road. A hoist or shaft house was on the corner of Reese Avenue and Third Street. Miners gathered here and were transported to their places of work in the mine.

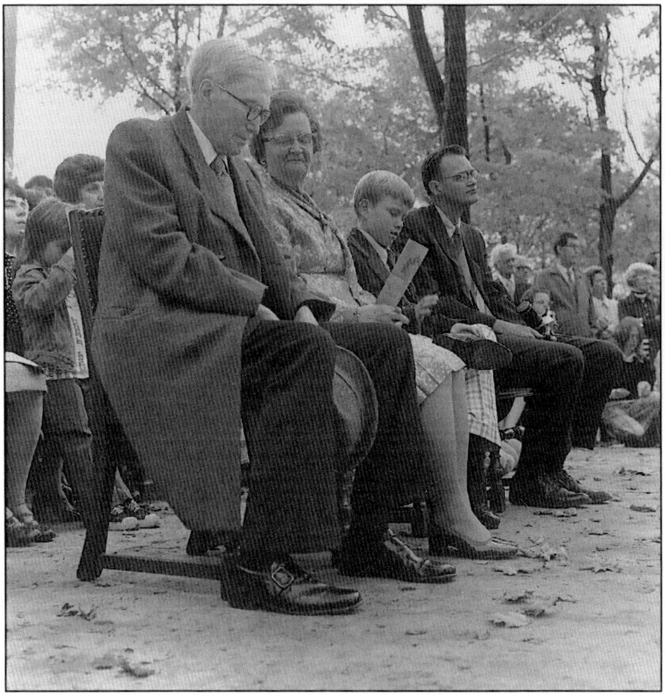

Dr. Alexander Douglas Martin, a native of Canada, responded to an advertisement in a 1924 requesting a physician for Colver Hospital. Martin became the hospital's administrator, general practitioner, and the sole staff physician, serving in that capacity from 1924 to 1973. He retired, but returned on a scaled down nine-hour workday. Dr. Martin, his wife, Eva, and son Dr. Douglas Martin attended the dedication of the park (see below). Their other children include James and Evelyn, who was a nurse in the U.S. Air Force.

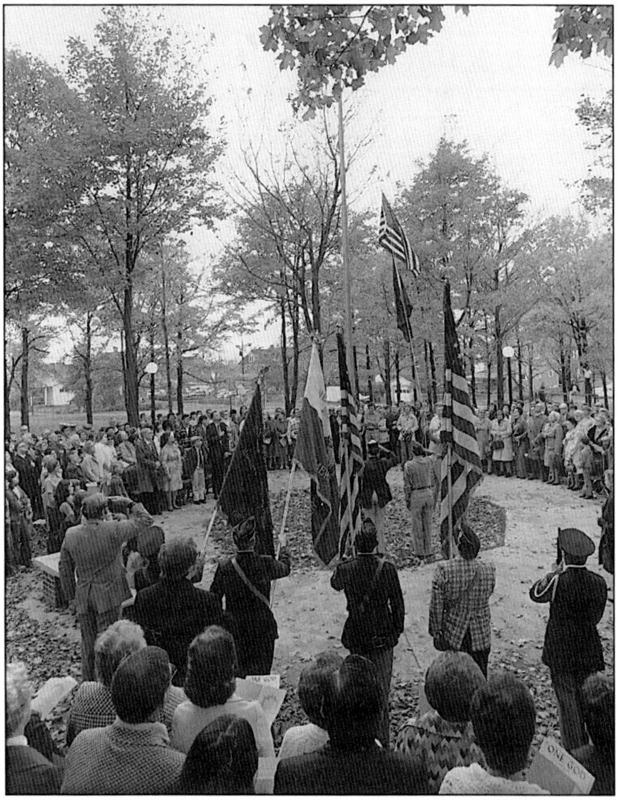

In October 1974, a refurbished park was dedicated to Dr. Martin with the unveiling of a plaque. Five hundred spectators witnessed the ceremony. Fr. Carl Spishak, pastor of Holy Family Church, was instrumental in promoting the park project. The park includes a monument, drinking fountains, and a lighted tennis court.

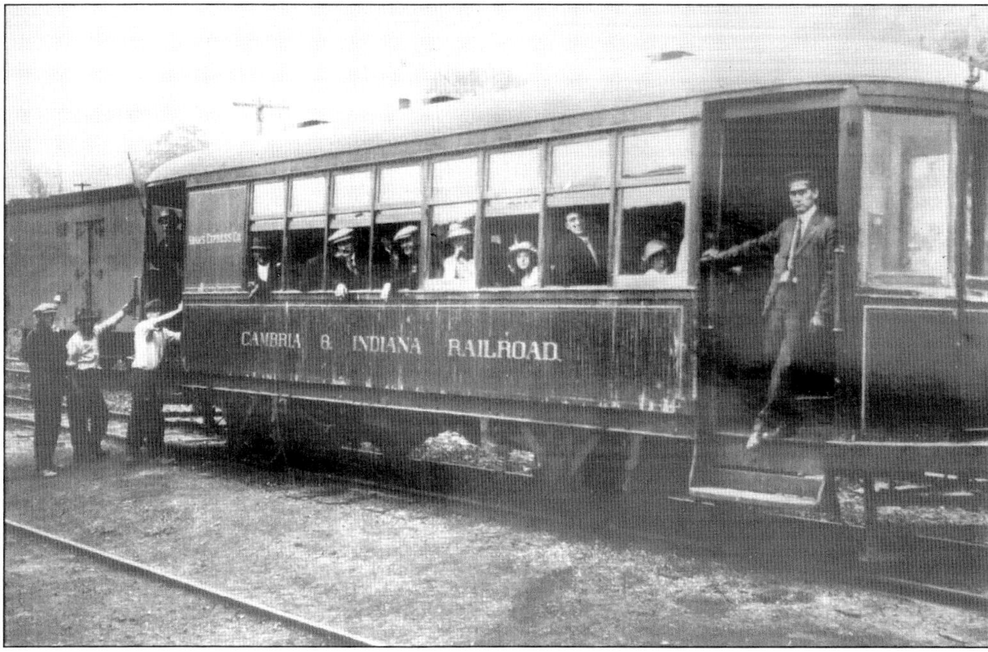

The town's fathers, Colman and Weaver, bought a small logging railroad, rechristening it the Cambria and Indiana Railroad (C&I) and extending it into Colver. It was constructed in such a way that tracks were laid beside the company store and went into the mines. Supplies were delivered and coal was transported. It was also used as a passenger train.

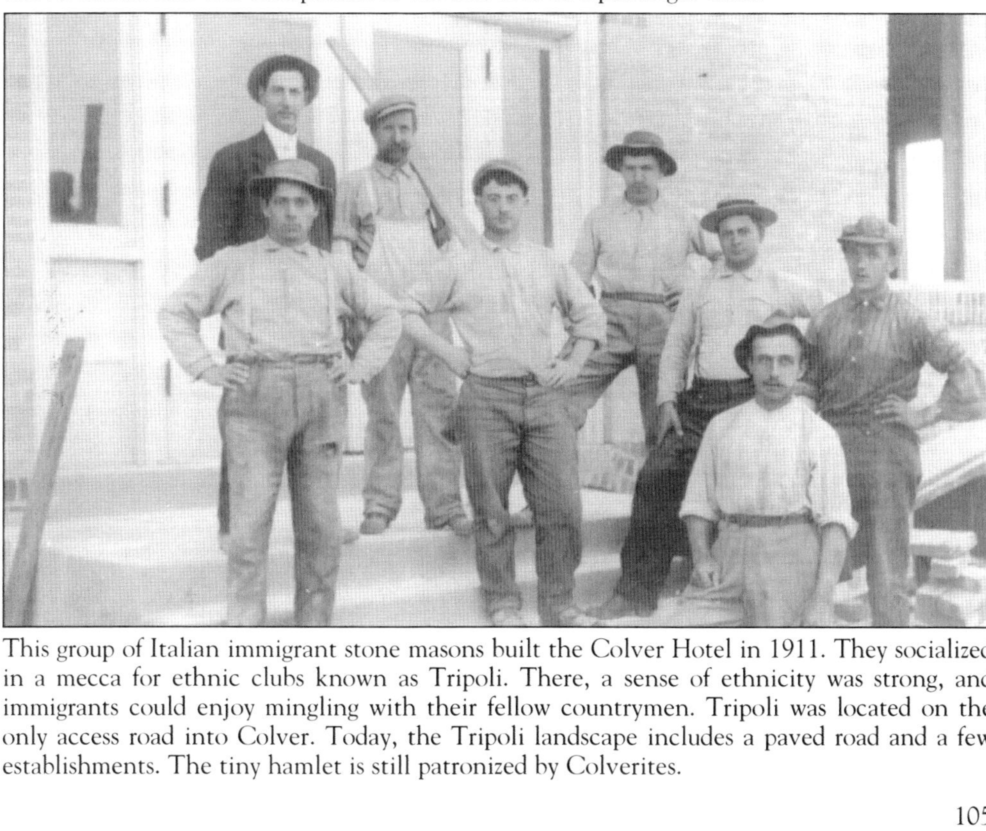

This group of Italian immigrant stone masons built the Colver Hotel in 1911. They socialized in a mecca for ethnic clubs known as Tripoli. There, a sense of ethnicity was strong, and immigrants could enjoy mingling with their fellow countrymen. Tripoli was located on the only access road into Colver. Today, the Tripoli landscape includes a paved road and a few establishments. The tiny hamlet is still patronized by Colverites.

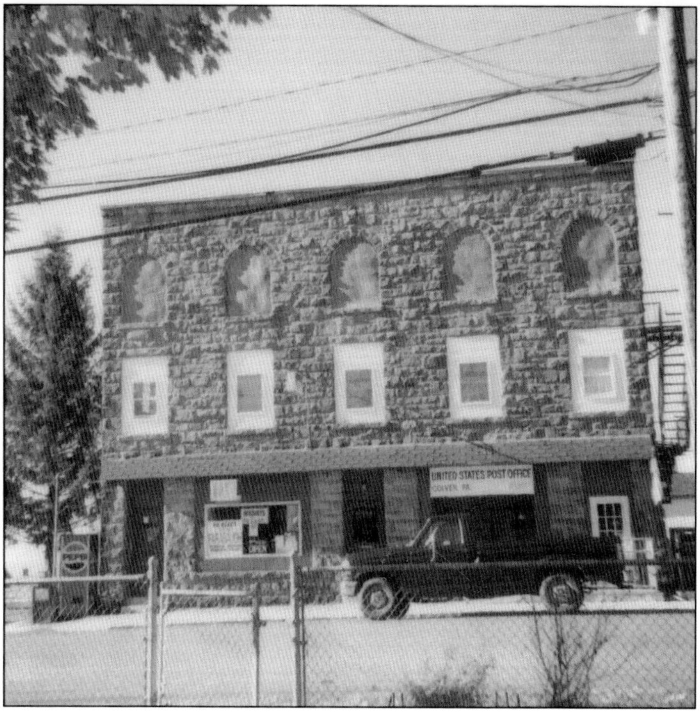

The administration building of the Colver Coal Company was constructed beside the theater in 1914. The street facade was built of stone to match the hotel and store. The main block of the building is three stories high with arched windows. The post office has always been on one side of this building and the Furnari store is on the other. Many of the company's structures north of Colver still stand, but have been abandoned.

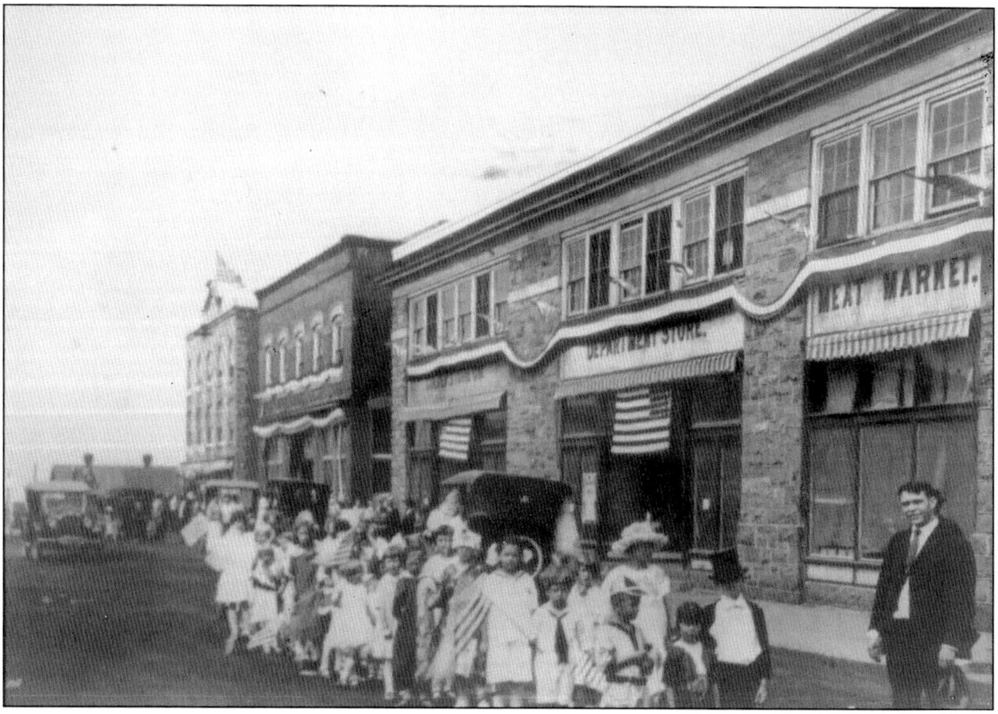

A small parade of children marches south on Reese Avenue in the 1930s. The administration building of the Colver Mines is in the background, followed by the amusement hall, which later became the Rivoli theater. The company store was a grocery store, a department store, and a meat market—what we might call a super store today.

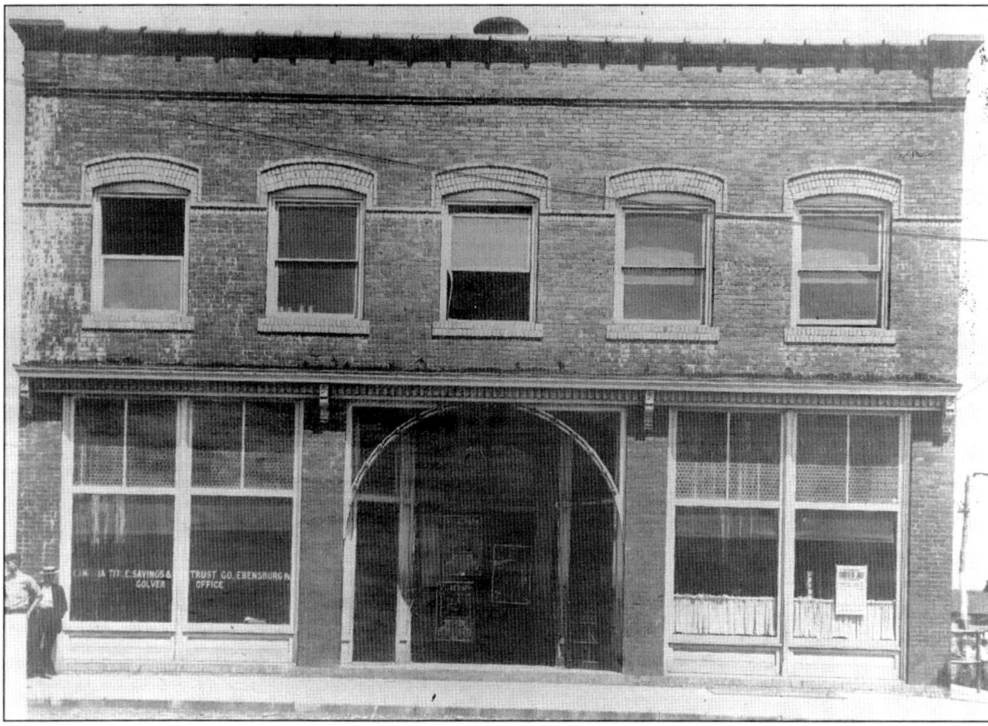

Colver always enjoyed entertainment. In 1912, a theater was opened on Reese Avenue. The residents planned all activities themselves until motion pictures came to town. The amusement building then became the Rivoli theater. A baseball team known as the "Colver Colts" was made up of miners and their families. A band was furnished for dances and recitals.

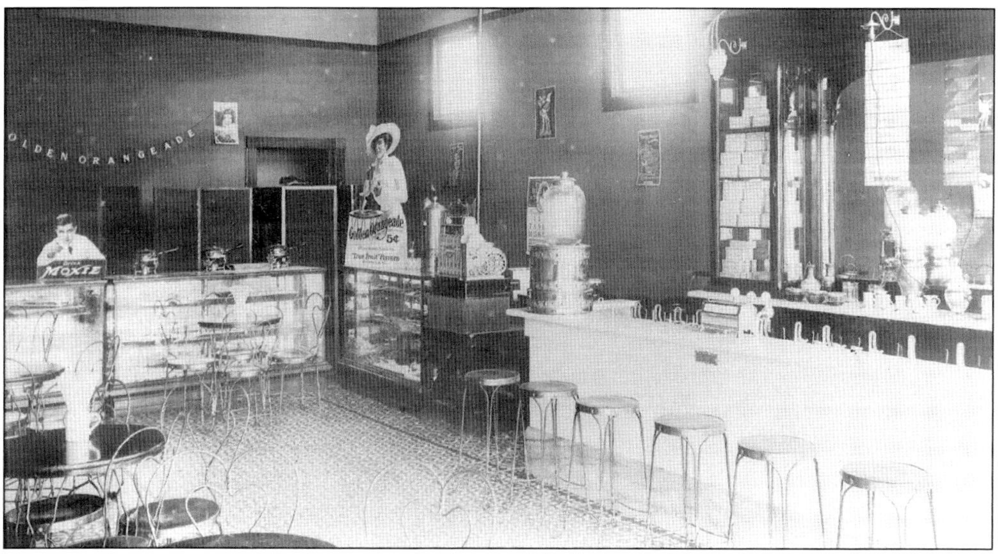

The interior of the ice cream parlor was a favorite gathering place for young and old alike. It was the only place in town where ice cream could be procured between Labor Day and Memorial Day. The ice cream parlor was located in the theater, where there was also a dance hall and offices. This is where townsfolk socialized, swapped stories, shared gossip, met new immigrants from abroad, and learned the latest news of the day.

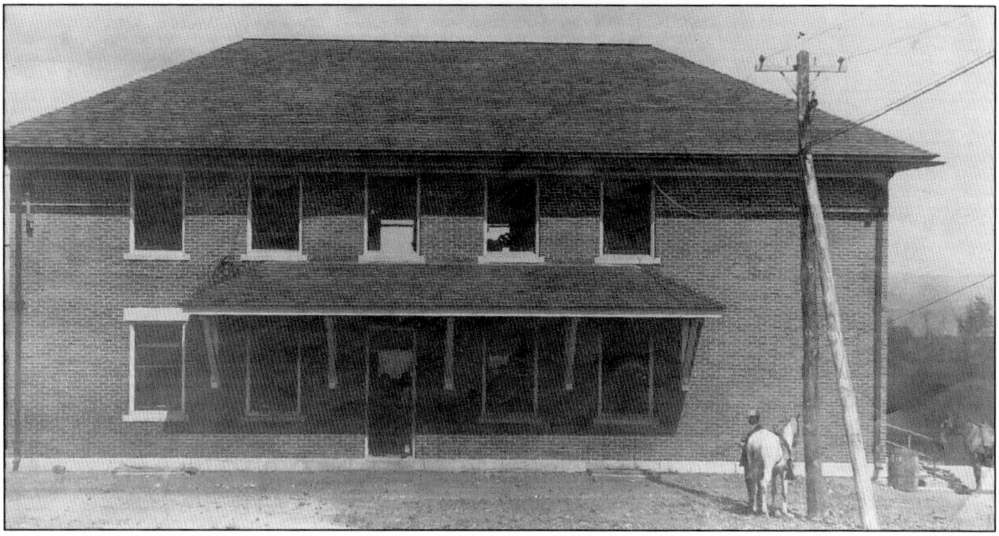

Colver Hospital was opened in 1912 as a 22-bed facility funded by the United Mine Workers and the Cambria and Indiana Railroad. Two houses were joined by a walkway on First Street. The hospital later moved into what was the office of the Ebensburg Coal Company. The reputation of Dr. Martin drew crowds. He worked at first with Dr. C.W. Johnston. In 1940, he bought the hospital building and donated it to the community two years later.

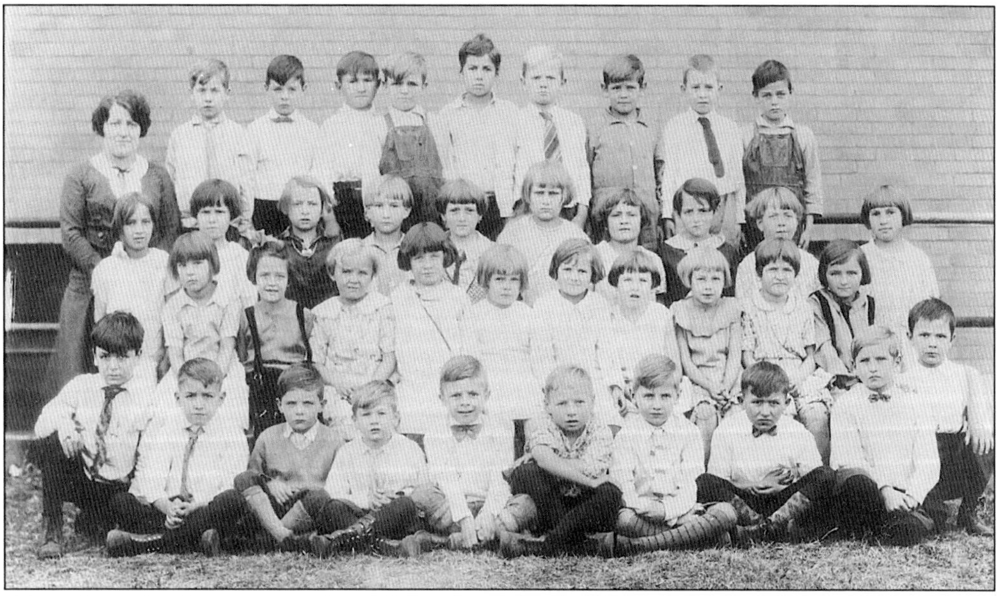

After this school was opened in 1912, the second school built became apartments. The children of Colver School gathered with their teacher, Miss Luther, *c.* 1928. Those seen, from left to right, are as follows: (first row) Badorf, Paul Magula, Charles Murdock, Jim Malone, Stanley Kozickie, Lloyd Cameron, John Gaboda, ? Bishop, George Stoyka; (second row) Saltgiver, Peggy Greizer, Ann Staruch, Nora Bonora, Mary Dilick, Helen Selko, Helen McCoy, Irene Machuta, Nina Humka, Mary Hazy; (third row) unidentified, Rosemary Yanosky, Mary Katona, unidentified, Teresa Cangroli, Verna Petak, Mary Kutsor, Ida Zampini; (fourth row) Robert Shannon, Tom Evans, Steve Pavuk, ? Badorf, Burnell Trantz, Leo Kozcki, Stanley Olinski, Harry Weakland, and John Todd.

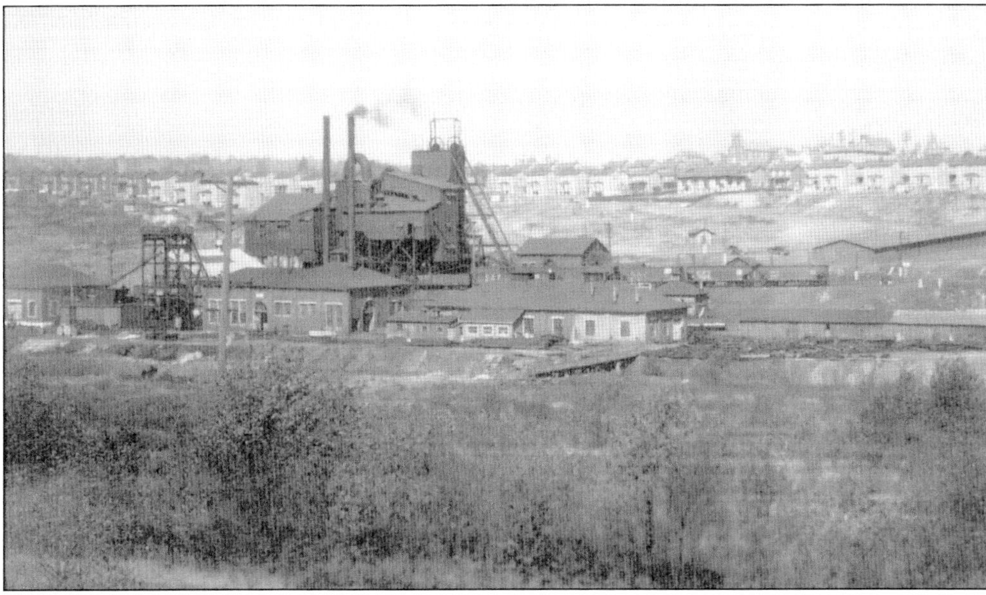

Revloc is a quaint, storybook hamlet nestled on a picturesque hillside of the Allegheny Mountains. Colman and Weaver excavated there for mines in 1917. The hamlet was administered by the Monroe Coal Company. In this photograph, the mine shaft dominates the landscape, and company houses dot the background. The Holy Redeemer Roman Catholic Church and the company store are on the right. The latter housed the post office, the UMWA hall, a school cafeteria, a social club, a pub, and a barbershop. It was an old-time mall.

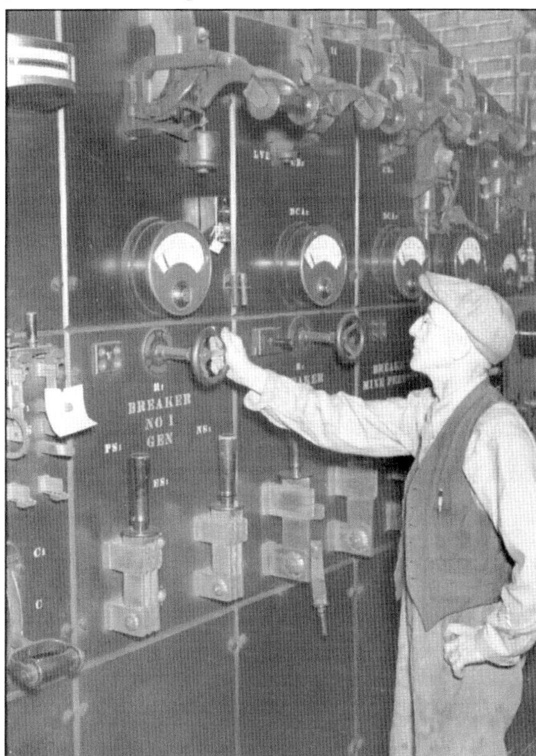

Mr. John Paul Sr. is regulating electricity at the substation. Electric power was used for hauling railroad cars in and out of the coal mines early in the 20th century. The generators were kept in operation 24 hours a day. Originally, mules had provided the power to haul coal from the mines. Revloc resulted from the holdings of Colman and Weaver, who prospered so well that the little village emerged. It was called Revloc, the reverse of Colver.

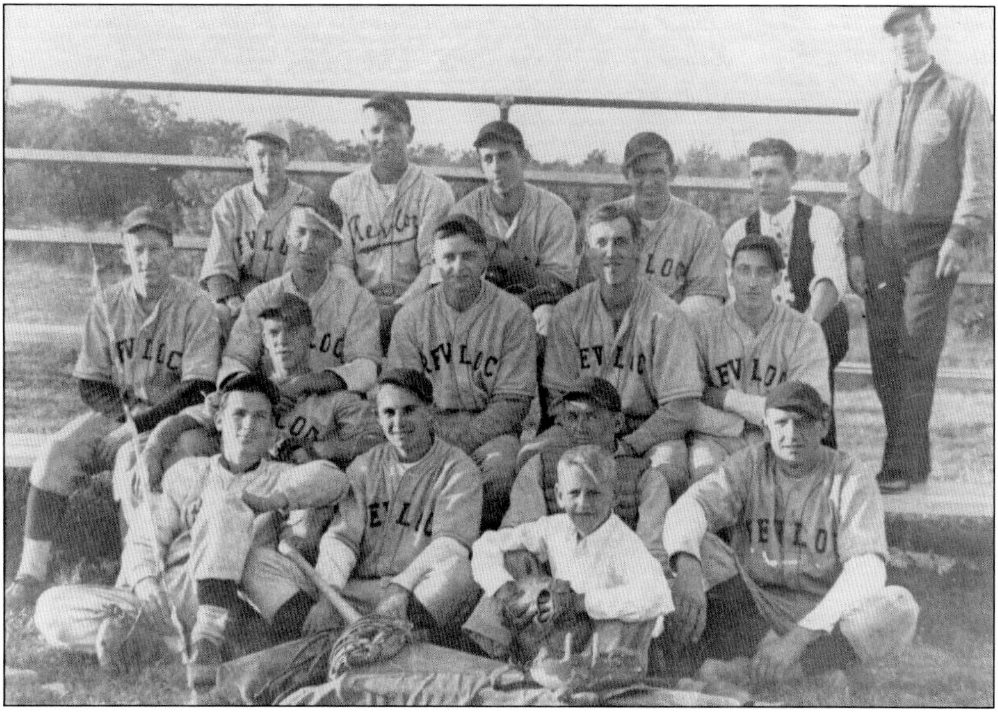

Shown is the Revloc baseball team in the 1930s. In front is Mike Urish. The team consisted of Metro Holowchuck, Walter Kielman, Charles Tishock, Joe Koval, Ray Nyland, Johnny Paul, Henry Haskowitz, Art Kozan, John Urish, Paul Spicher, Billy Paul, Buster Brown, Joe Urish, Mike Solonica, John Tishock, and manager John Urban.

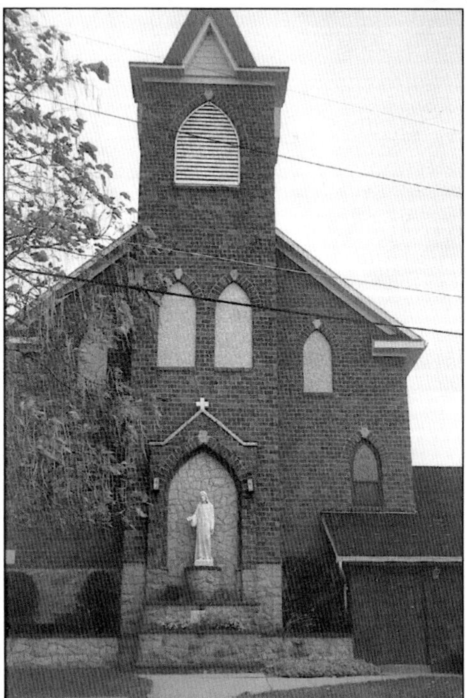

In 1918, the Most Holy Redeemer Catholic Church in Revloc began Sunday school classes in the public school. This evolved into the building of a brick church in 1924. It was dedicated a year later, and the rectory was built in 1960.

Seven

GATEWAY TO NORTHERN CAMBRIA

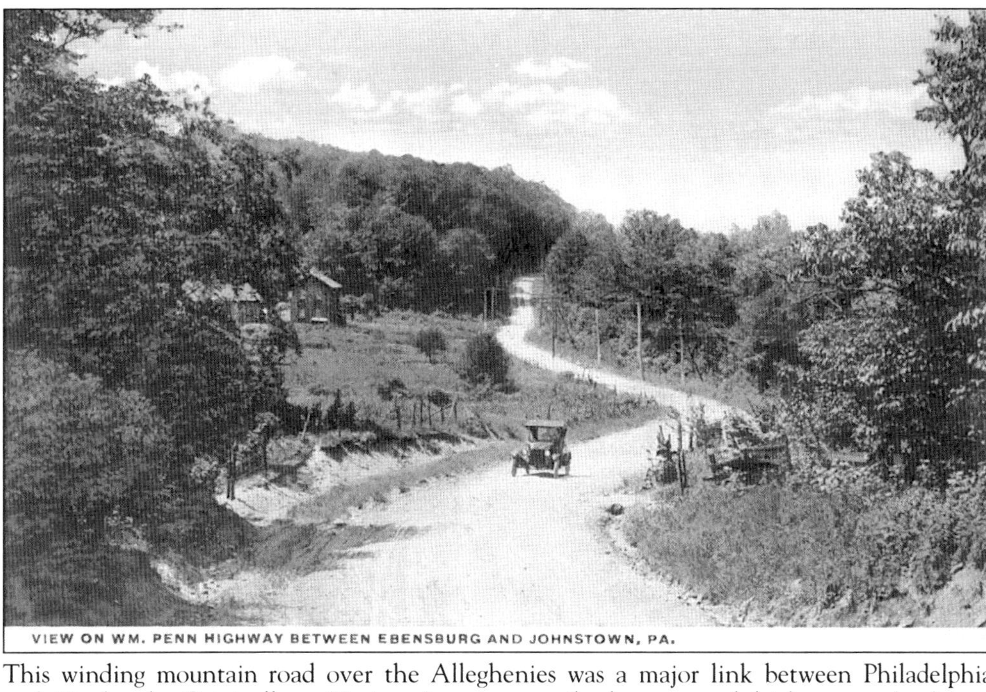

This winding mountain road over the Alleghenies was a major link between Philadelphia and Pittsburgh. Originally a Native American trail, the unpaved highway evolved into William Penn Highway, also known as old Route 22. In this photograph, a 1920s motorist makes his way westward from Ebensburg along the dusty mountain thoroughfare. Known as the Pike, this highway has been widened and paved.

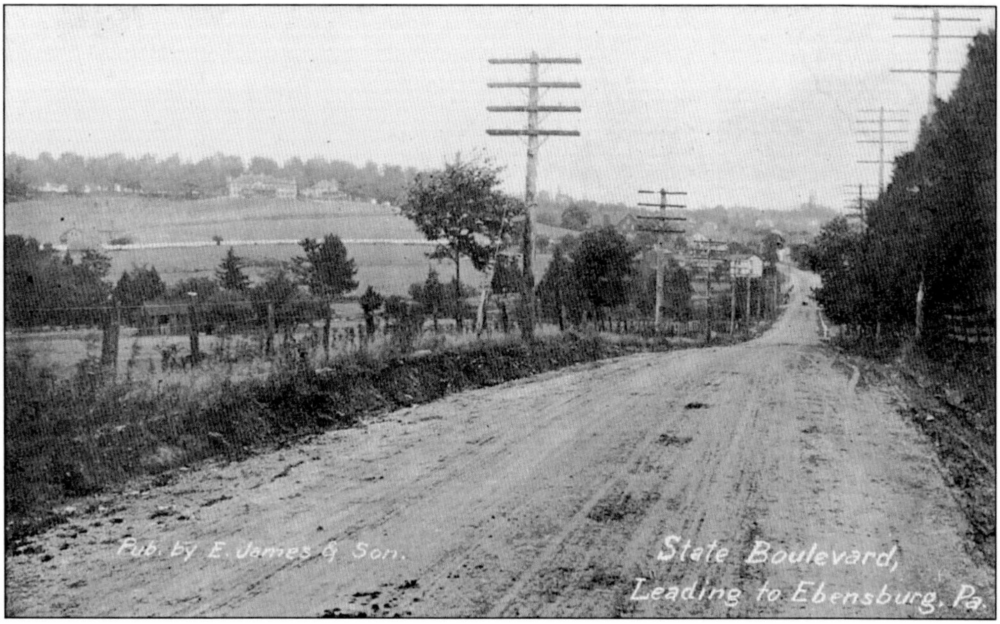

Traveling east, the state boulevard led into Ebensburg. This road is now Route 22. Note the Nellie Park Kelly summer home, now Aquinas Hall, and the Ebensburg Inn on the left hillside. The coachmen's house was at the foot of the hill. It is now the site of the Bishop Carroll High School. The courthouse tower is on the right. Unpaved highways were common in the area until the automobile became popular.

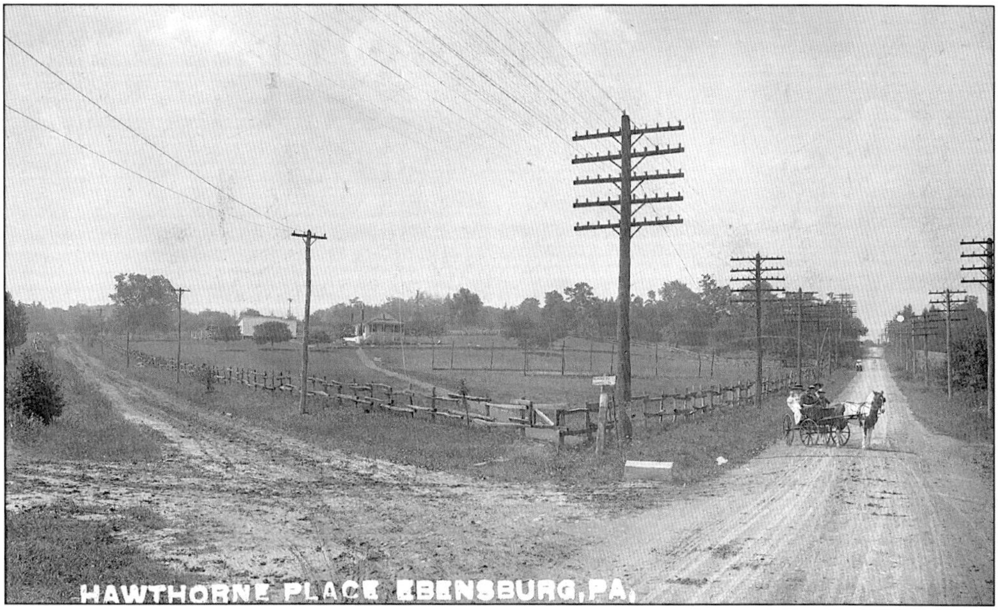

Hawthorne Place was located at the intersection of old Routes 22 and 160 in west Ebensburg. Early in the 20th century, it was the site of a cottage and recreational area owned by Dr. T.M. Richards. Note the deep wagon tracks. The wooden fence around the property, often necessary to protect cattle, is quite indicative of that era. The building on the right is the old Philadelphia–Pittsburgh turnpike tollhouse, c. 1910.

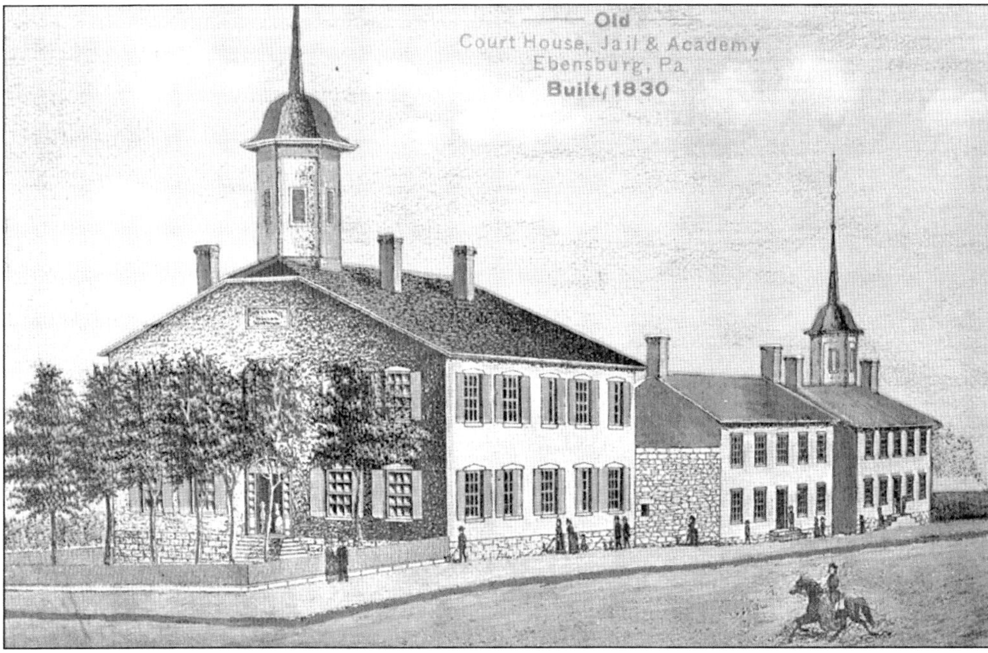

Built in 1804, the original Cambria County courthouse was a log structure on East Sample Street. It was constructed on the northwest corner of the courthouse grounds. The lower portion of the two-story log structure was the jail; the upper portion was the courthouse. A Congregational Church, the first courthouse, the school, and the jail were all one. In 1830, a brick structure was built near the courthouse with three classrooms as a school. A third building became the Cambria County jail.

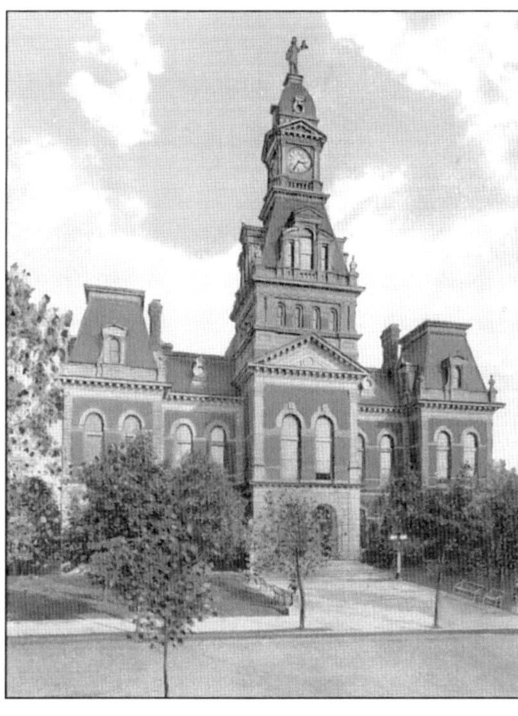

The construction of the new Cambria County courthouse was begun on July 9, 1880. John Schenk, the contractor, leased several acres of land to set up a brickyard and enough clay for one million bricks. The courthouse was finished in 1881, complete with metal sealing and roofing. The cornerstone was laid in December 1881. Gas fittings were installed and gas jets illumined the building. The first carload of furniture arrived in February 1882. The courthouse tower featured a statue of Justice and a four-sided clock.

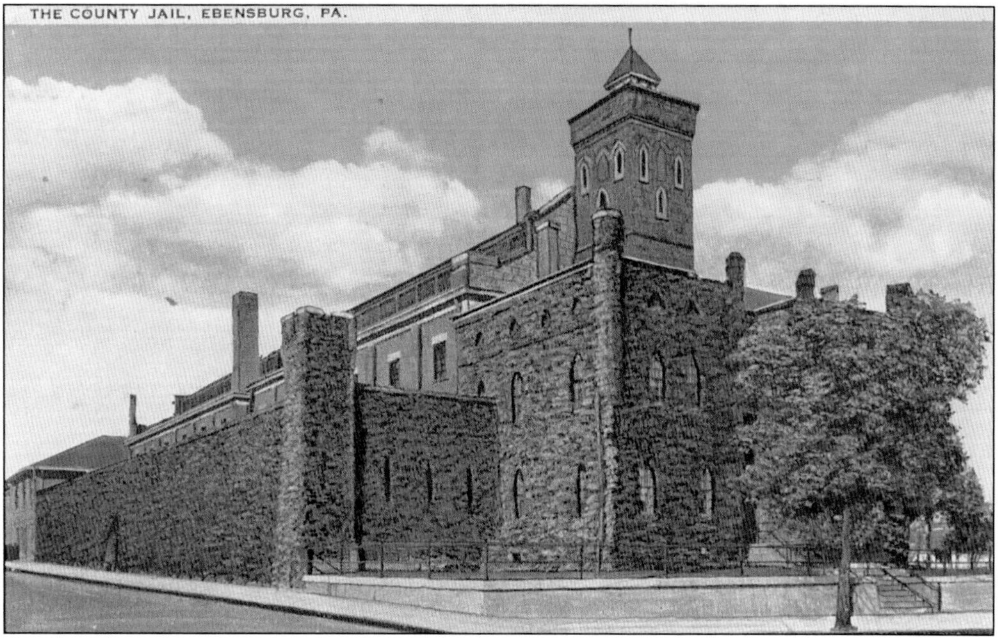

The new jail was completed on North Center and West Sample Streets in 1872. It was a massive edifice with an apartment for the sheriff in the front. There were 17 well-lighted and heated cells, each with a water closet and ventilation register. A horizontal window opened onto the jail grounds. The ventilating system was underlaid with iron plates, and the edifice was surrounded by a 22-foot stone wall. A new jail has been completed on Manor Drive and the old building has become a storehouse for records.

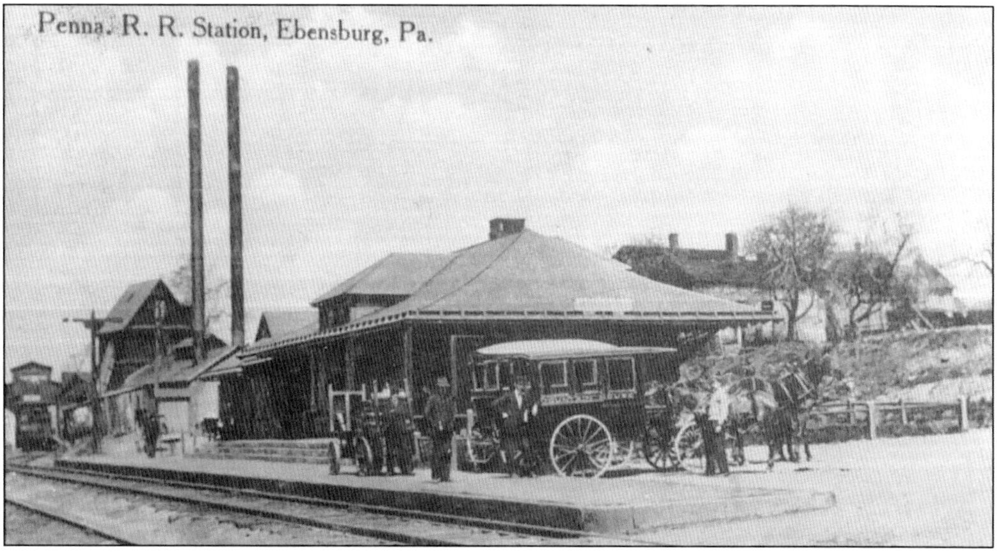

In 1862, the Ebensburg and Cresson Railroad Company built a branch line that was 11 miles from Cresson into Ebensburg. The county seat is not on the main line. It was constructed by the P&T Collins engineering firm. Until that time, towns along the main line offered rental horses and buggies to travelers bound for the county seat. In March 1902, a new railroad station was built on South Center Street. Ebensburg was the town at the end of the spur. The stacks in the background belong to Ebensburg's power plant.

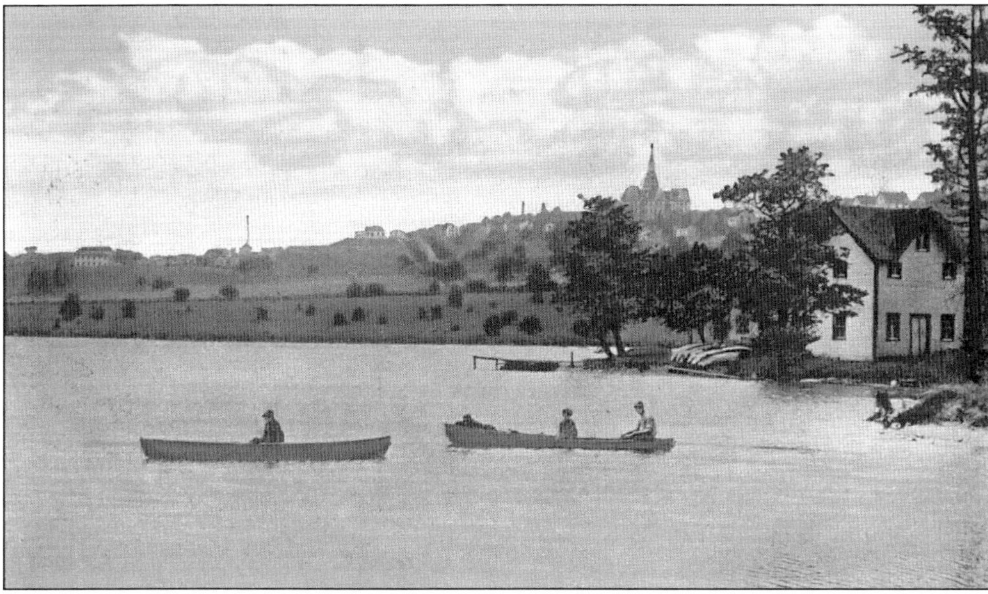

Lake Rowena is a 19-acre body of water located below and east of the county courthouse in Ebensburg. In 1935, an attempt was made to convert it into a bathing, boating, and fishing resort. In 1951, the lake was restored and formally turned over to Ebensburg Borough by the State of Pennsylvania. In August 1952, a recreational facility was added, and the boathouse was put into operation the following year. The original gatehouse, built in 1825, was destroyed by fire in 1943.

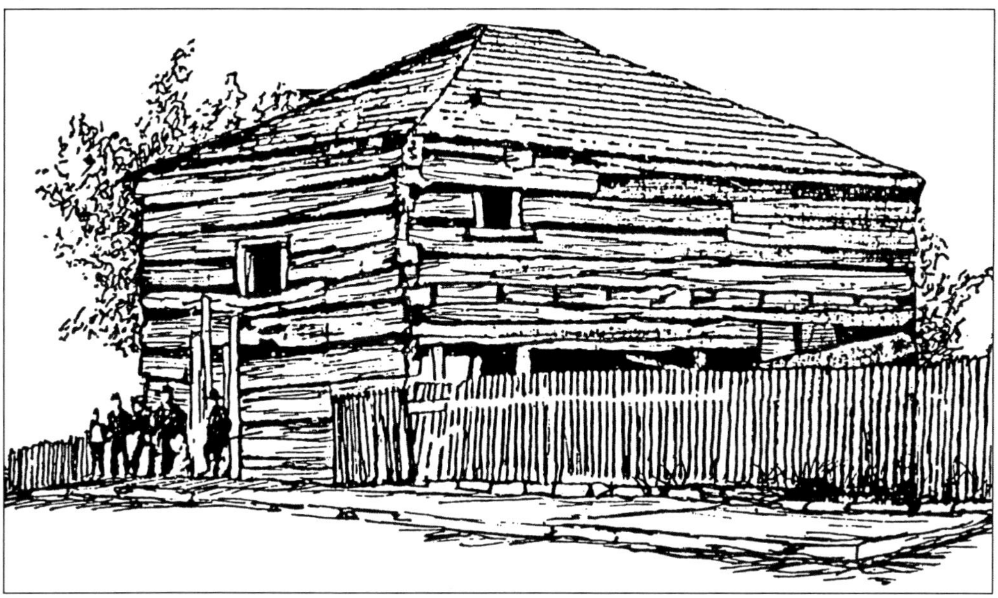

This log church was built on the northwest corner of Carolyn and High Streets in 1804. It was a Welsh Independent Church, but not the first house of worship built by Rev. Rees Lloyd. The Ebenezer Chapel was built in 1797. Lloyd's son was named Ebenezer. The name commemorates Ebenezer of biblical fame (1 Samuel 7:12). "Here I'll rest my Ebenezer" was a Welsh hymn sung by the early settlers. The term evolved into an appropriate name for the new county seat of Cambria County, Ebensburg.

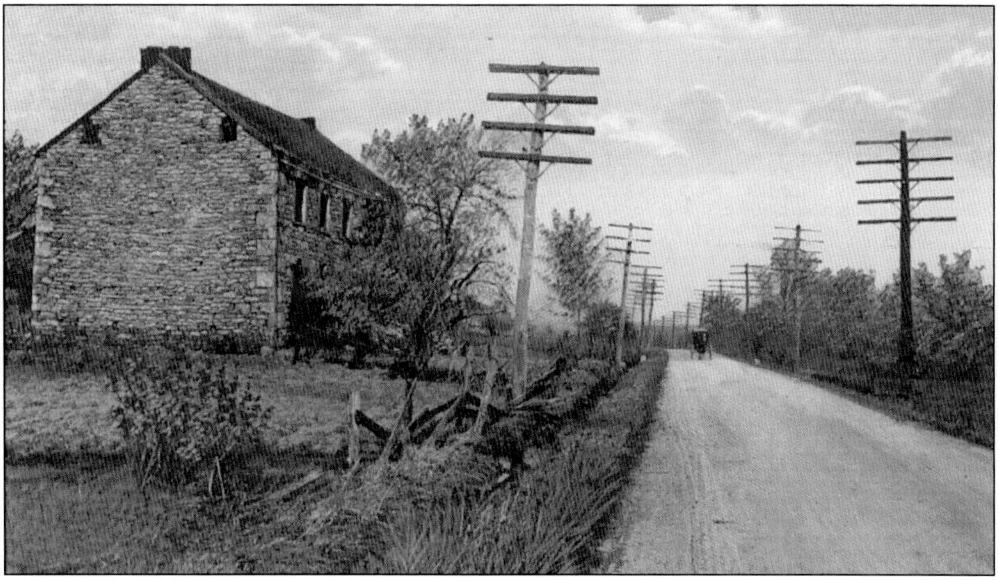

The old stone house was built by Rees Lloyd in 1805. Located in the second block of east High Street, it stood across from the oldest surviving log cabin in Cambria County. The venerable old log building of 1799 is now a private home. The old stone house served as a meetingplace for the county commissioners when they moved their offices into a rented room in 1809. James Meloy was the county commissioner. The stone house was eventually dismantled.

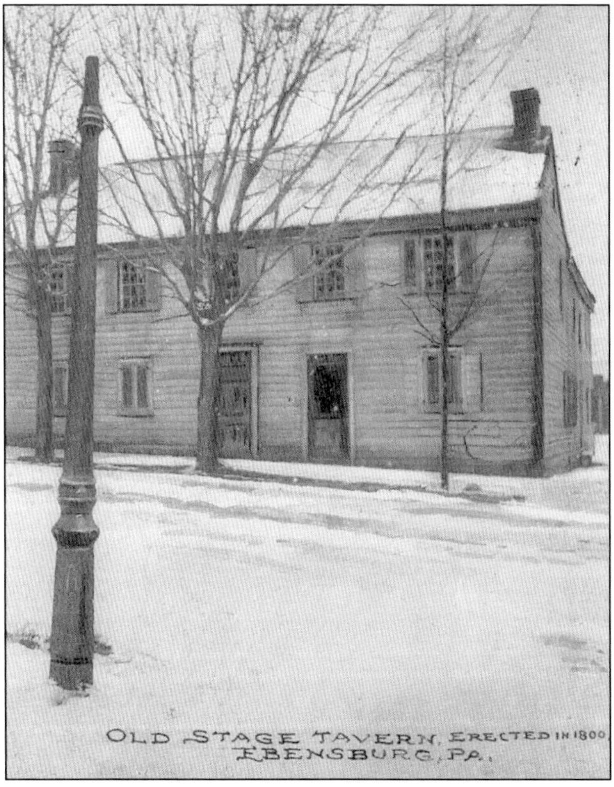

The Stage Tavern was a log structure on the northwest corner of High and Locust Streets. Built *c.* 1800, it houses the old Berry Hill Tavern. It became a stagecoach stop in 1820. Berry Hill was Abraham Barker's home during the era of the Underground Railroad. Barker, a friend of President Lincoln, was a staunch abolitionist who helped fugitives escape. Initially, he came to the area seeking a fortune in the lumbering industry.

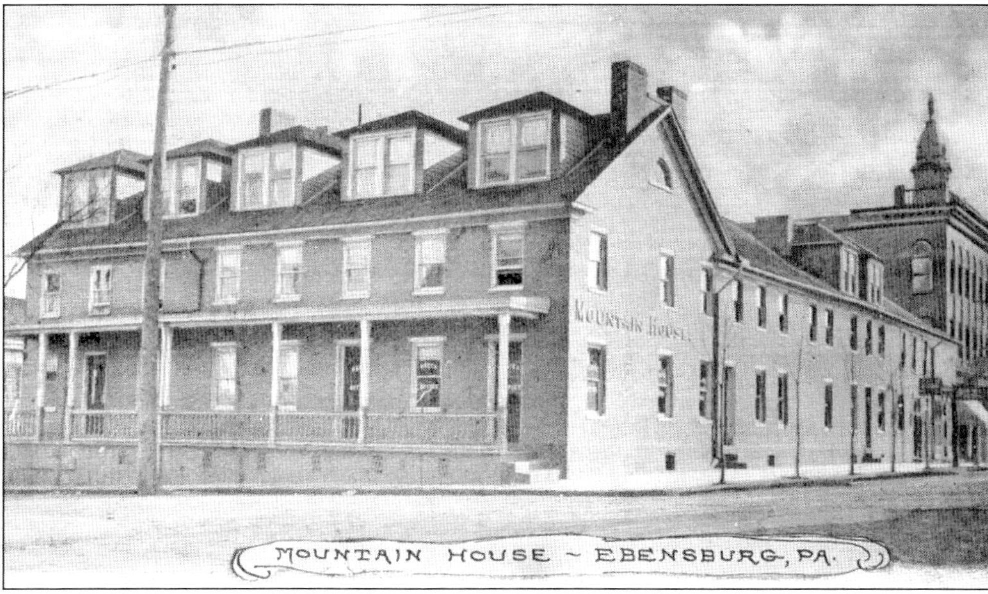

The Mountain House, the former Washington Hotel, was built on the southeast corner of Center and Highland Avenue in 1828. It was originally the home of the Rhey family. They envisioned the profitability of converting it into a hotel. It has been called the Washington Hotel, the original Exchange Hotel, and the Andrea Hotel with Andrew Rhey as proprietor. It was destroyed in the fire of 1915.

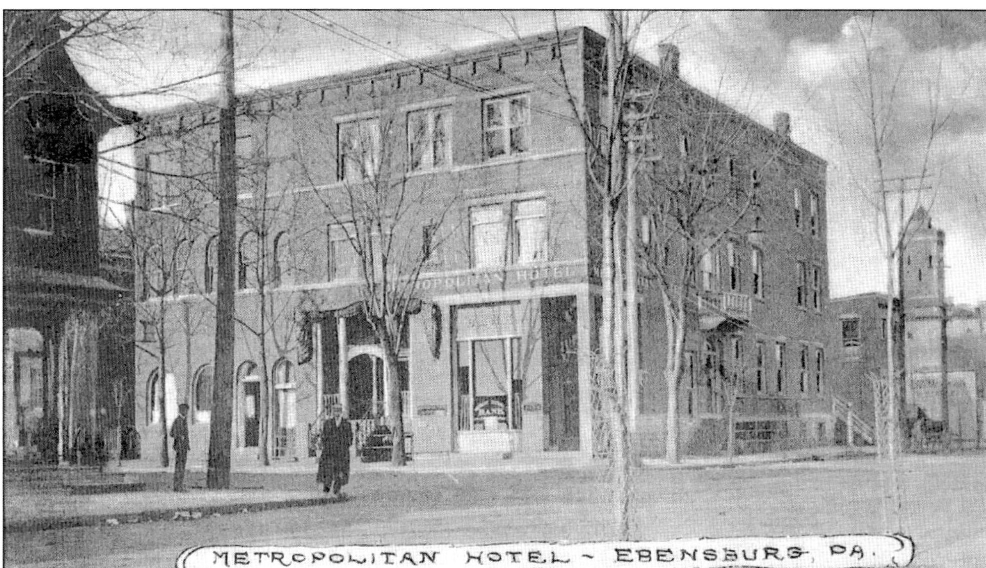

The Metropolitan Hotel was a huge three-story structure situated on the site of the Cambria House—the northwest corner of High and Center Streets. Built in 1890 by Capt. Thomas Davis and J.C. Lloyd, it was sold in 1902 to William Kimball, proprietor of the Central Hotel. In 1916, the American National bank bought a portion of the building. By 1919, the bank owned the building, but kept the hotel business in operation. Today, under a facade of red brick, the old Metropolitan still stands.

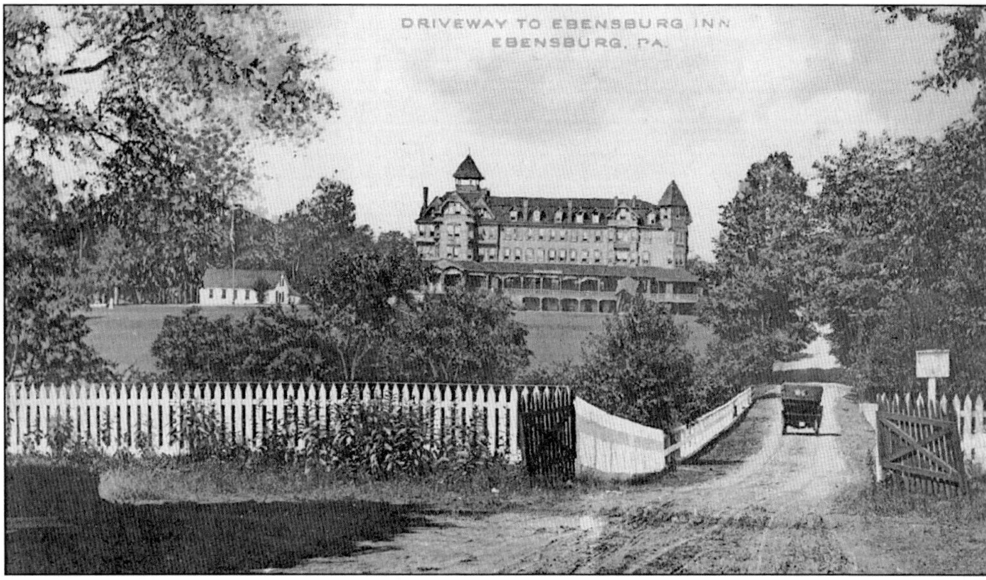

The Ebensburg Inn, originally Maple Springs, was built in 1883 by Thomas Heist. It accommodated 250 guests and had a dining room capacity of 800 people. It was the essence of modern conveniences. In 1900, the millionaire D.E. Park of Pittsburgh bought it and renamed it the Ebensburg Inn. His sister, Nelly Park Kelly, built her home beside his; the house is now known as Aquinas Hall. In 1917, the mansion closed and was dismantled. The lumber was used in building houses for a growing population.

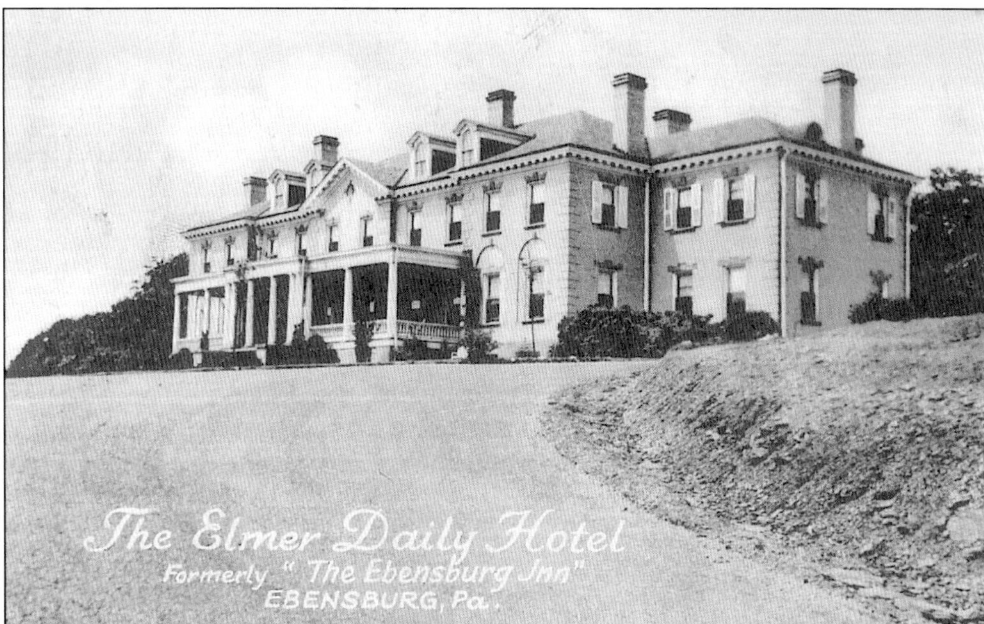

The Daily Inn came into existence in 1941, when Nelly Park's homestead was purchased by Elmer M. Daily and converted into an inn. The Daily Inn was popular during the first half of the 20th century. In 1959, it was sold to the Diocese of Altoona-Johnstown and became part of the Bishop Carroll High School complex. Elmer Daily donated $15 million to the diocese at the completion of the deed.

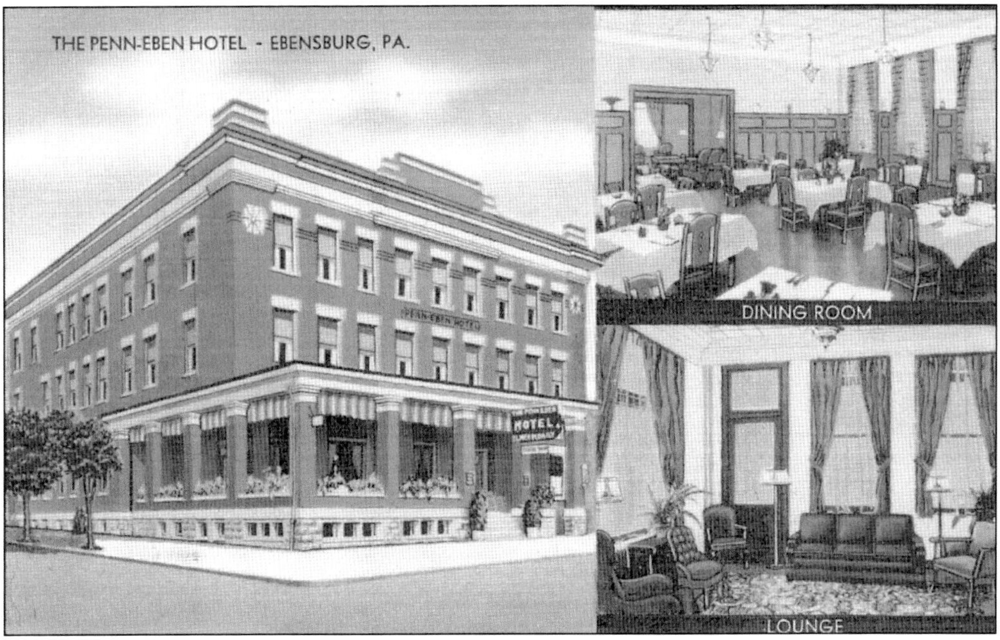

The Penn Eben Hotel was the Exchange Hotel. T.V. Hott converted the E. Roberts House on the northeast corner of High and Julian Streets in 1908. A fire demolished the building in 1913. Hott built a hotel of 37 rooms, the largest and most distinguished in town. It was sold in 1934 to Elmer M. Daily, who renamed it the Penn Eben Hotel. Daily was president of the Middle Atlantic Baseball League. The dining room accommodated 60 guests and played host to many dignitaries.

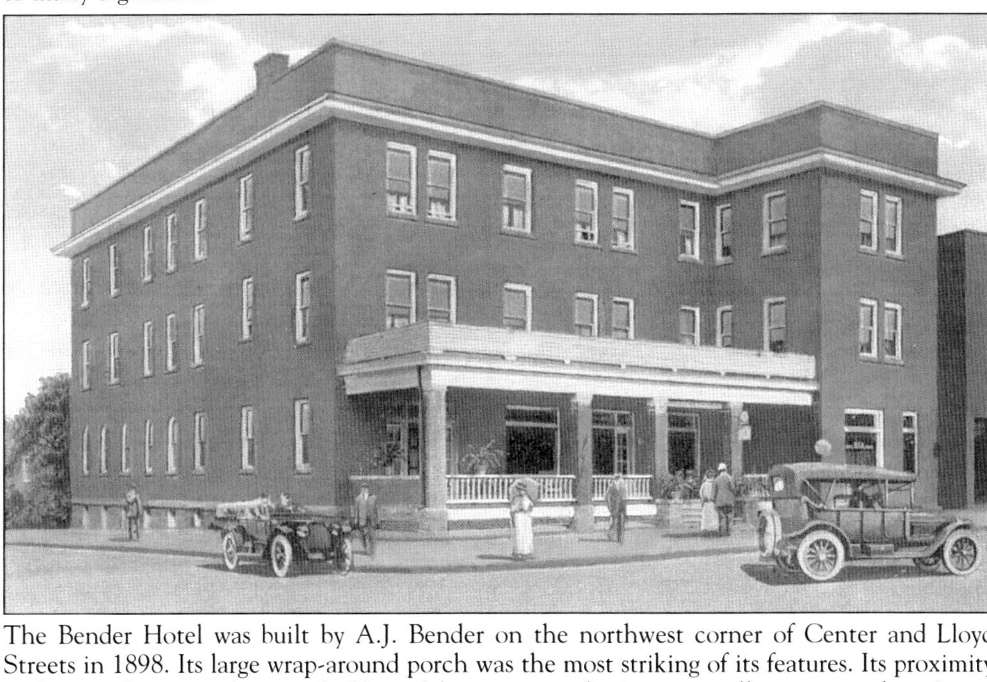

The Bender Hotel was built by A.J. Bender on the northwest corner of Center and Lloyd Streets in 1898. Its large wrap-around porch was the most striking of its features. Its proximity to the courthouse made it an ideal hostel for visitors on business, as well as resort seekers. It was very successful and eventually became the Knights of Columbus building.

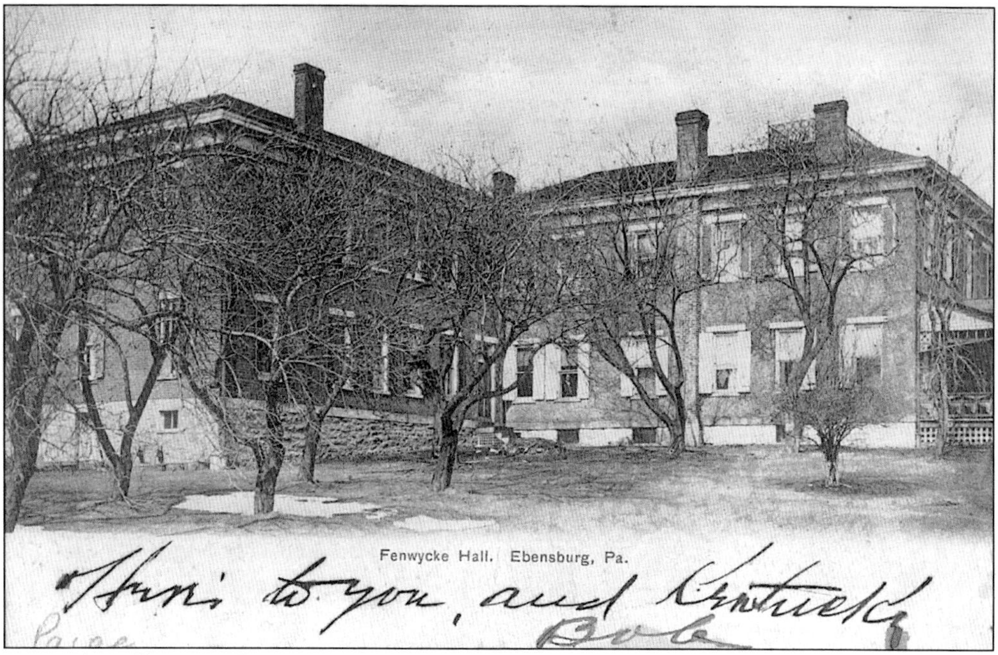

Fenwyck Hall, originally Moore House, was built by Johnston Moore on North Center Street before 1870. Moore had filed a plan in the courthouse, designating the property north of Horner Street into Moorestown. In 1887, it was purchased by Emma McNamara, who converted it into a guest house. It was designated for vacation seekers who wanted to avoid hotel dwelling. It served guests from out of town and locals alike. Many patrons were those who were in the process of building homes.

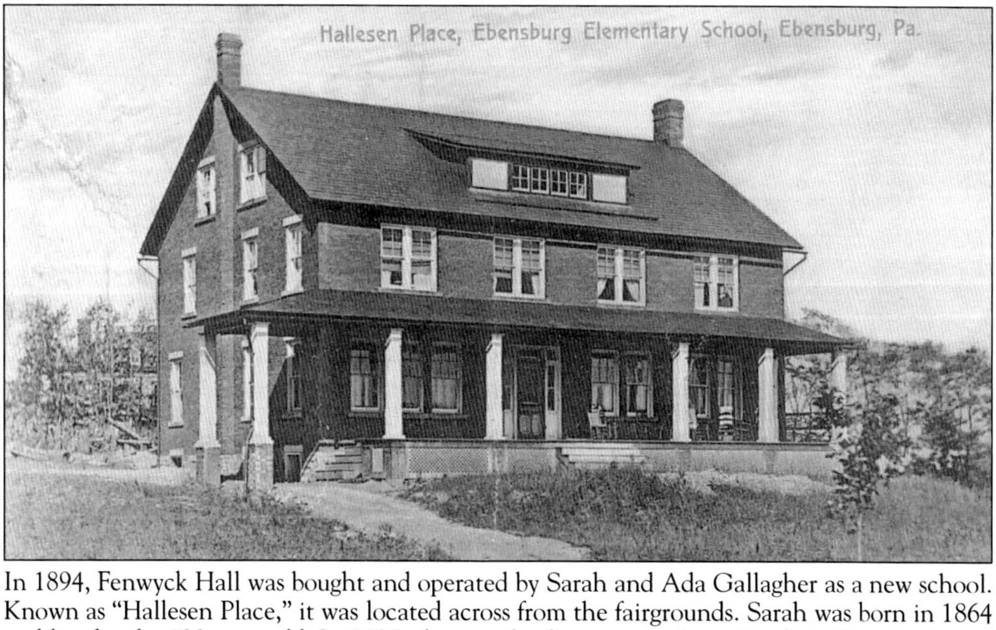

In 1894, Fenwyck Hall was bought and operated by Sarah and Ada Gallagher as a new school. Known as "Hallesen Place," it was located across from the fairgrounds. Sarah was born in 1864 and lived to be 100 years old. In 1935, she was the first woman from Cambria County elected to the Pennsylvania state legislature. She authored textbooks and was a co-founder of the Ebensburg Public Library. In 1910, the annex was removed and turned to face Center Street.

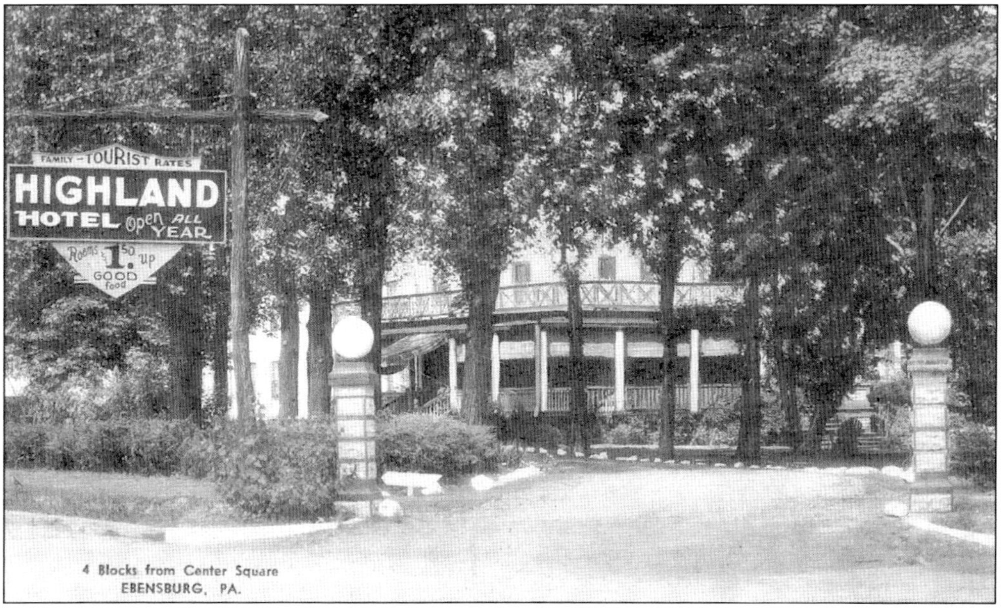

Highland Hotel was the converted Titan Coffee House on the northeast corner of Highland and Center Streets. It advertised that it had "all outside rooms, spacious, shady porches with an elevation of 2,500 feet above sea level in the heart of the Alleghenies." This was an attracting feature before the turn of the 20th century. It stood four blocks from the center of town and cost $1.50 per night.

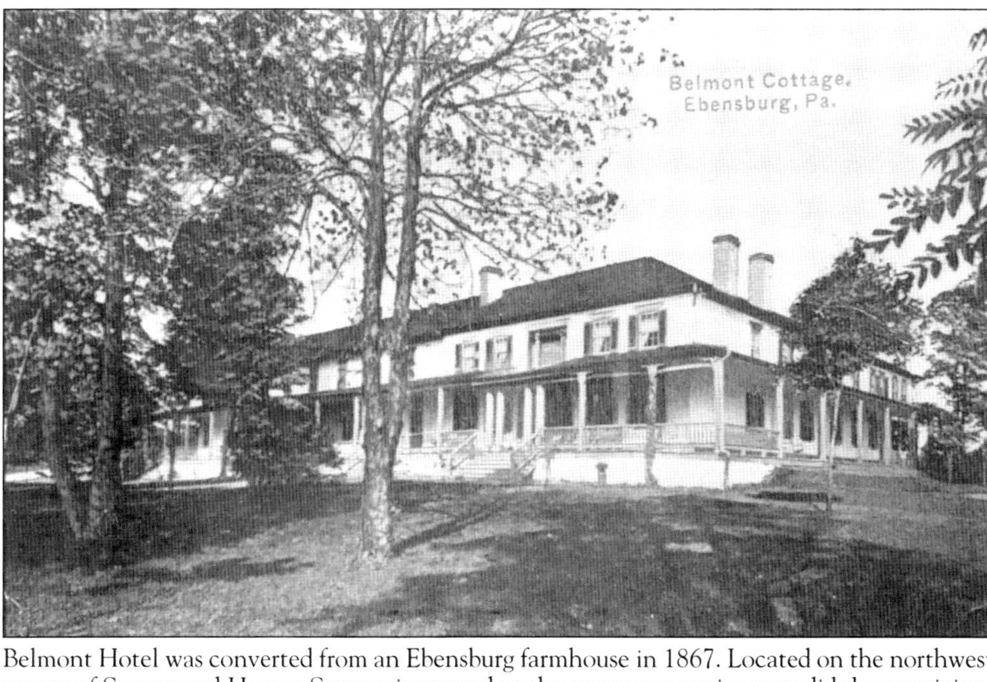

Belmont Hotel was converted from an Ebensburg farmhouse in 1867. Located on the northwest corner of Spruce and Horner Streets, it catered to the summer vacationer as did the prestigious Central Hotel, operated by Mrs Litingzer on southeast corner of High and Julian Streets. The Belmont was the first primarily resort hotel in town. It was owned by Mr. Shoemaker, who sold it along with a large stretch of land to C.H. Kemp in 1881.

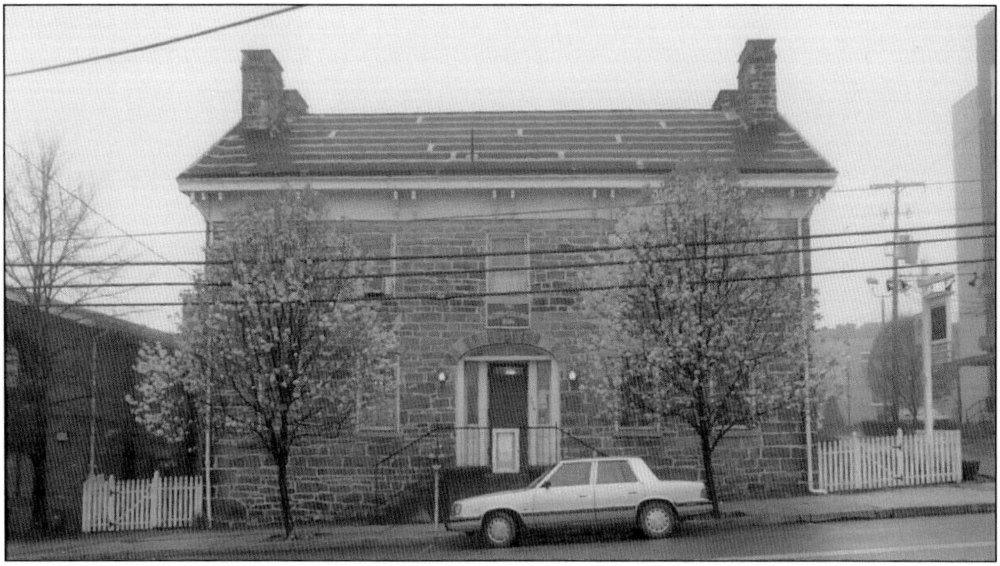

Philip Collins, an associate judge, built the stone mansion on High Street in 1832. His son-in-law, Philip Noon, changed the style of the house from Federal to mid-Victorian. Noon sold the inn to David Park, who added an auditorium and offered the property to the community. Atty. Lewis H. Ripley bought the historic building in 1983 and converted it into a country inn. In 1986, the Noon Collins Inn was added to the National Registry of Historic Places.

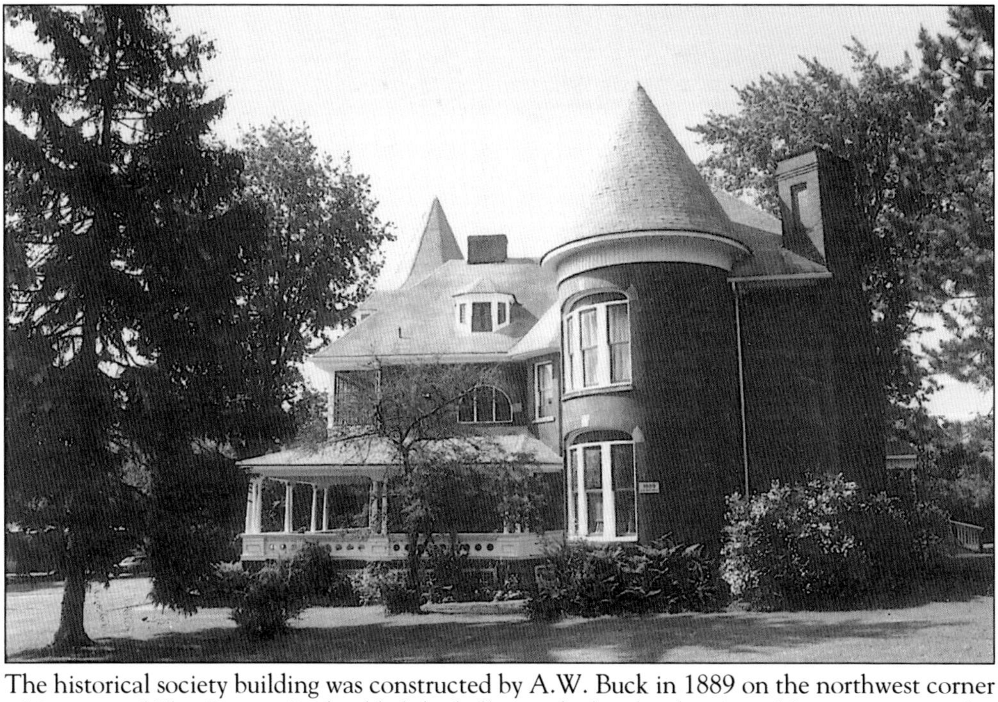

The historical society building was constructed by A.W. Buck in 1889 on the northwest corner of Center and Elm Streets. Buck added the ballroom for his daughter's wedding reception. This building became the chapel of the Sisters of St. Joseph when the building was sold to the Holy Name Parish. It served as a convent from 1924 to 1990, when it was bought by the historical society. The addition is now a library.

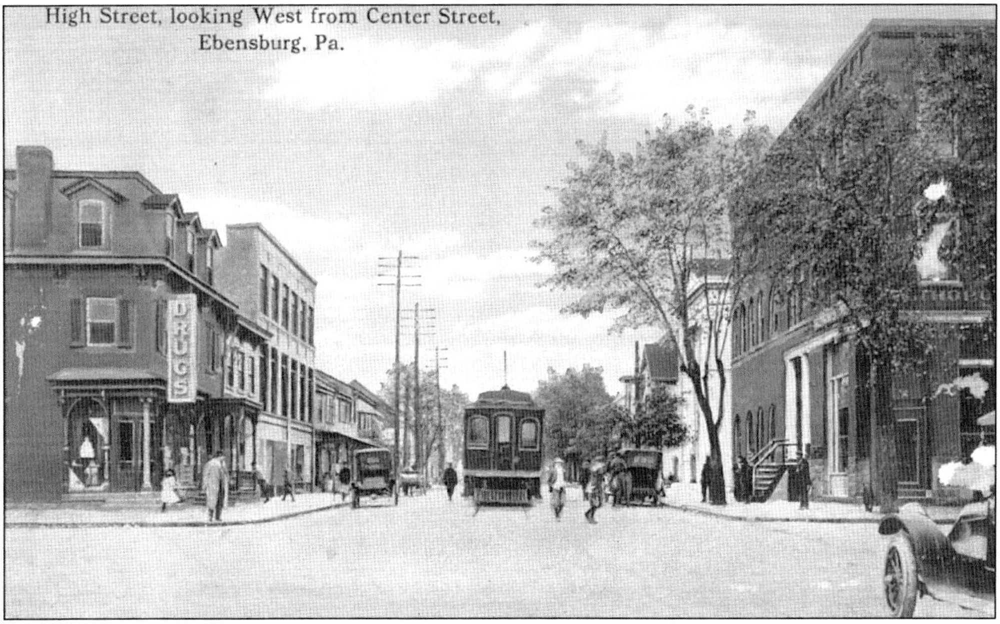

Ebensburg's High Street faces west from Center Street in this photograph. The Metropolitan Hotel is featured on the right. The white building is the new bank of 1912, which still functions in that capacity. The corner drugstore on the left is that of Harne Tibbott, who was originally employed as a bellhop at the Ebensburg Inn. Note the different modes of transportation: horse and buggy, trolley, and automobile.

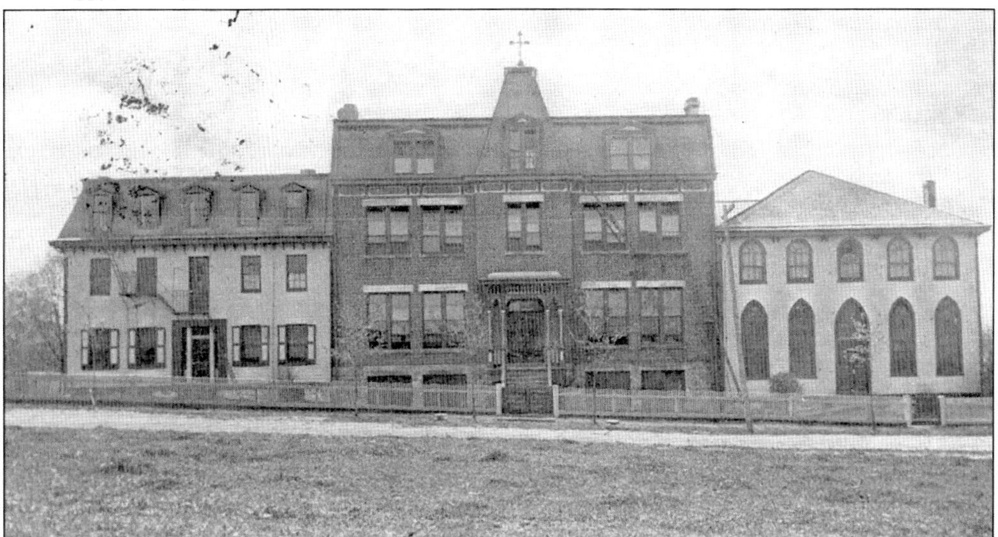

James McGuire built his home on the corner of Beech and west Horner Streets in 1855. It became the Mount Gallitzin Seminary in 1869. Staffed by the Sisters of St. Joseph of Baden, Pennsylvania, boys ages 4 to 12 were cared for and housed. Additions were added through the years. On January 11, 1921, Bishop McCort established an infant's home at the site. It remained in that capacity for many years. The building was considered for an academy for girls in 1960, a project that lasted only one year.

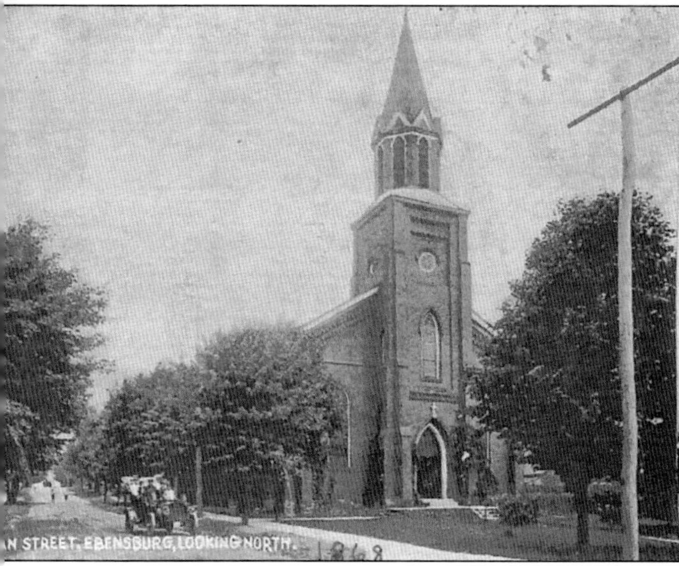

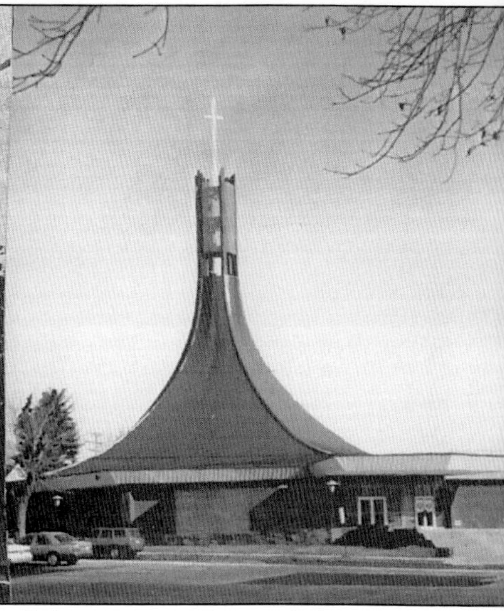

The Holy Name Parish, originally St. Patrick's, was founded in 1816. A few Catholics erected a frame church on the corner of Horner and Julian Streets. Twice, the congregation built a larger church and twice, they outgrew the edifice. With the building of the third church in 1867, the name was changed to Holy Name. In 1966, the sesquicentennial anniversary of the parish, Monseignor McCaa envisioned a new church, designed, and built it in accordance with Vatican II. It was dedicated by Bishop James Hogan on February 25, 1968.

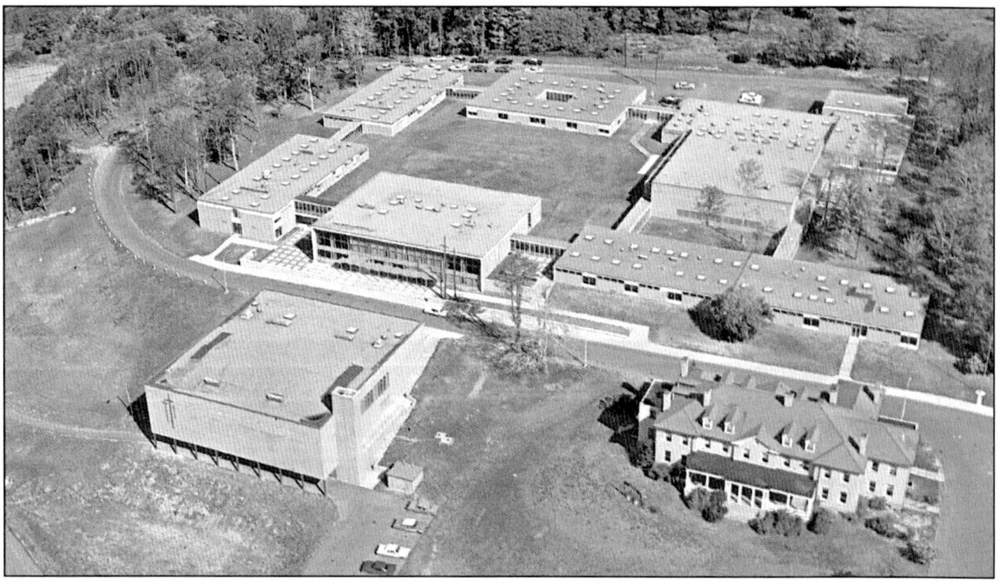

The Bishop Carroll High School came into existence when the Diocese of Altoona-Johnstown purchased the Ebensburg Inn on June 18, 1959 as a high school for boys. It was named Aquinas Hall. Girls would be schooled in the converted infant's home. This plan, however, was deemed impractical, and on March 9, 1961, ground was broken for Bishop Carroll High School. Named after Bishop Howard J. Carroll, who served the diocese from 1958 until his untimely death in 1960, the school opened in 1962 with an enrollment of 300 students. Fr. Faber Molloy was its first principal.

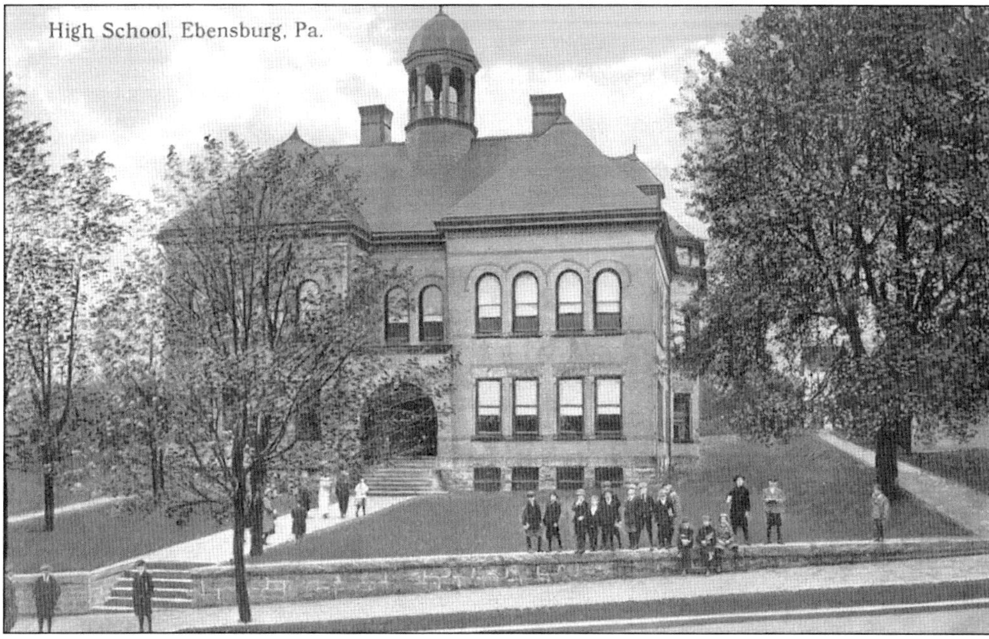

The original Ebensburg High School dates to the 1880s. The first graduation was held in 1890 in the Opera House with a class of nine students. The new Ebensburg Cambria High School opened on the northwest corner of Horner and Center Streets on September 9, 1929 with 320 students enrolled. It was initiated when 32 students received diplomas in commencement exercises that June. The last class graduated from Ebensburg Cambria High School in 1958.

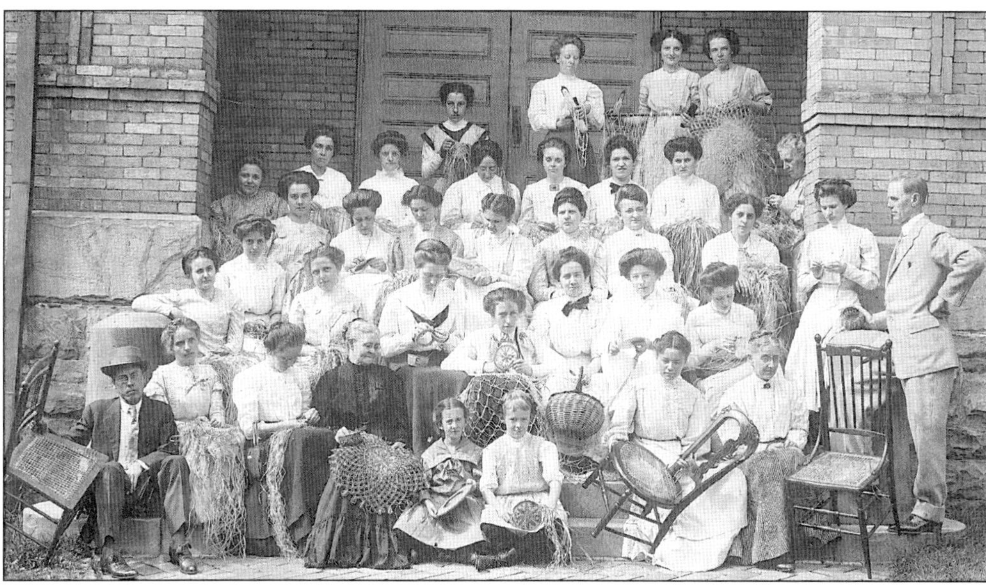

Industrial art classes were held in Ebensburg in 1910. The scene could well be the forerunner of today's vocational technical school that offers industrial arts. The classes brought people together when education for adults was in its early stages. Basket- and mat-weaving (along with repairing cane-seated chairs) was the order of the day. The gentleman standing on the right is the instructor, Mr. Karlson.

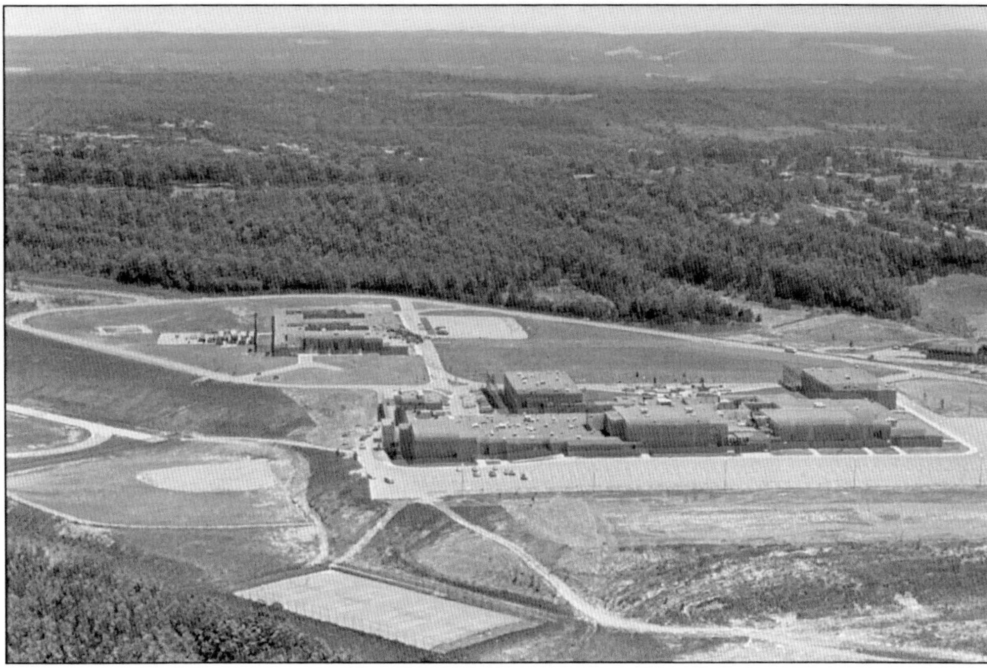

The Central Cambria school district broke ground for a new education complex on June 10, 1971. It included a $2.2 million elementary school, a $7.5 million high school, and a $4.2 million Admiral Perry Vocational Technological High School. In November 1972, 800 students and 750 adults were enrolled. The chief administrator was Dr. F.K. Shields. The anchor is from the third ship christened *Wasp*. The first *Wasp* was commanded by Admiral Perry in his discovery of the North Pole. Peary was born in nearby Cresson, Cambria County.

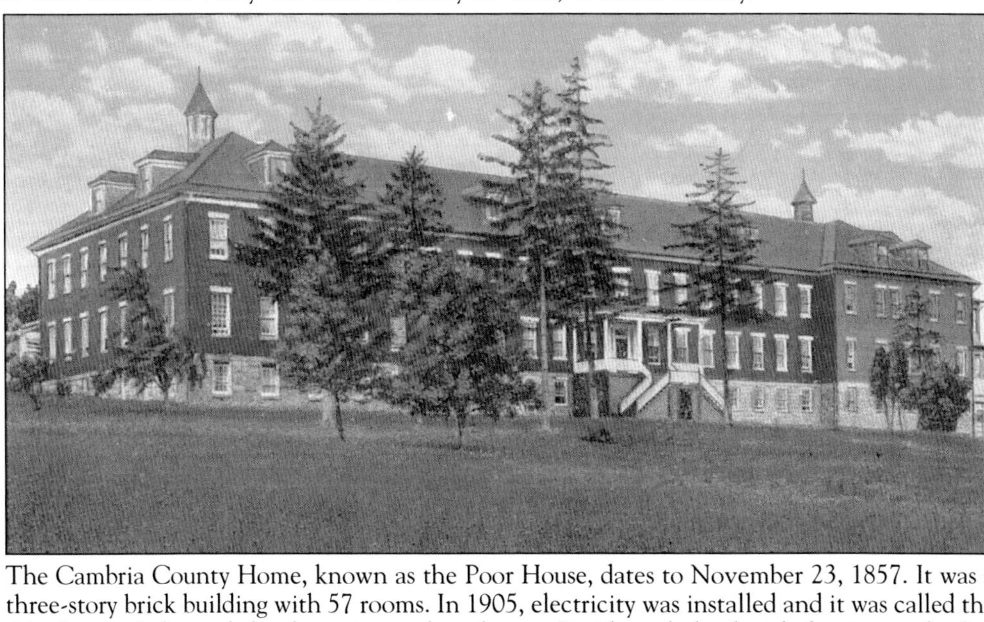

The Cambria County Home, known as the Poor House, dates to November 23, 1857. It was a three-story brick building with 57 rooms. In 1905, electricity was installed and it was called the Almshouse. It housed the decrepit, aged, and poor. Residents helped with farming and other chores. In 1911, two wings completed the building until 1928, when a hospital unit was added. It was slowly evolving into a nursing home.

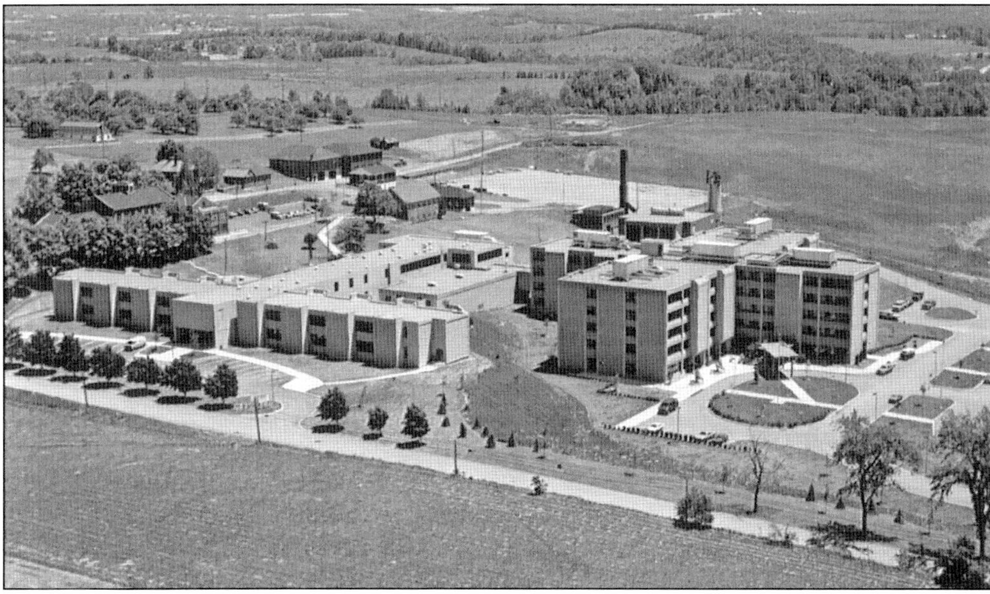

The Laurel Crest Manor Rehabilitation Center emerged from the County Home. The five-story building that would become a nursing home was completed in 1976. The 1955 building was renovated, giving the facility a capacity of 705 residents. Currently, Laurel Crest offers physical and occupational therapy, audiology, speech and psychological services, and specialty health care. It is a leader in advanced health care, providing both in- and out-patient services. Laurel Crest is located in the heart of the picturesque Laurel Highlands of the Allegheny Mountains.

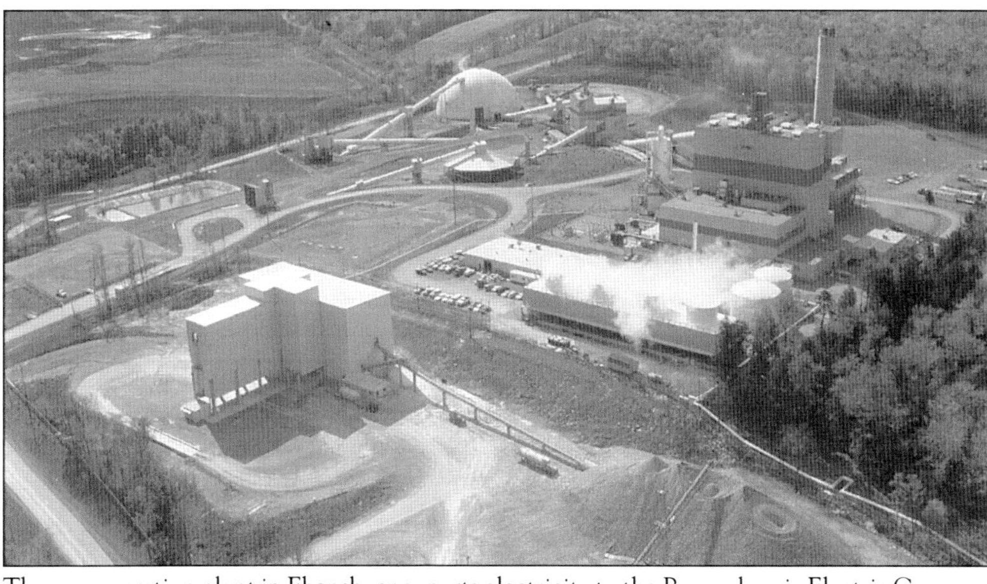

The co-generation plant in Ebensburg exports electricity to the Pennsylvania Electric Company and steam to the Laurel Crest Rehabilitation Center. The 77-acre site is a refuse-fired facility. Designed, constructed, and operated by Air Products, it began operation in March 1991. This facility is the first to use bituminous waste coal as a fuel supply. Millions of tons of acidic waste coal, discarded by abandoned mines, were unsightly blights on an otherwise picturesque landscape. The plant brought about fresh new ideas and new technology.

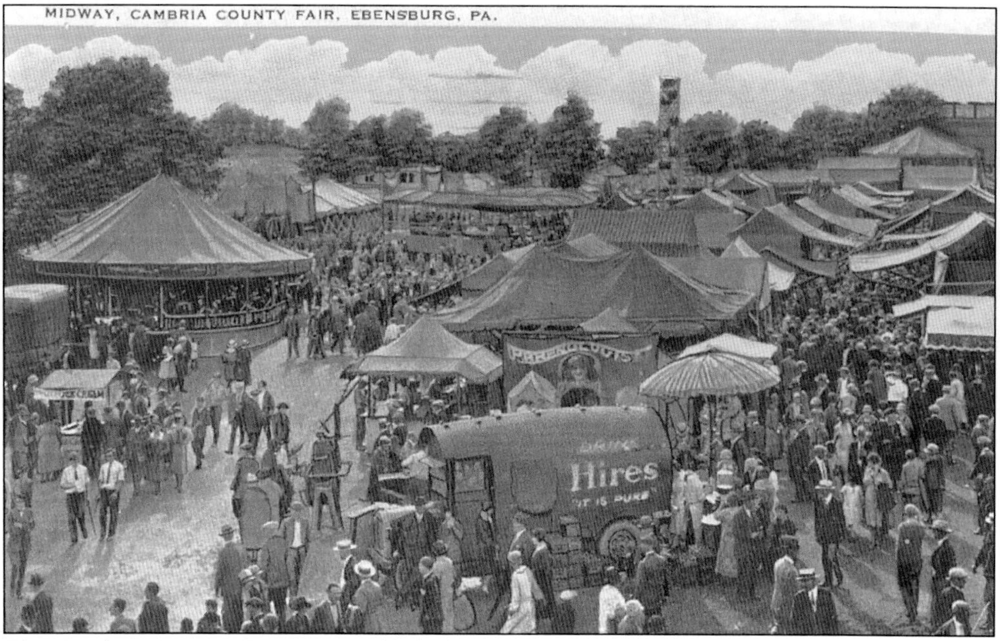

The Cambria County Fair was established on Jane Jones Farm in 1924. Fairs had long been an attraction in the area. In that year, with the help of Charles Schwab, the fairgrounds were established. It was described as the greatest united community event, a wonder city created overnight. Agricultural, horticultural, livestock, poultry displays, and competitions along with a huge racetrack continue to draw crowds. Each September, educational and entertaining events attract young and old alike.

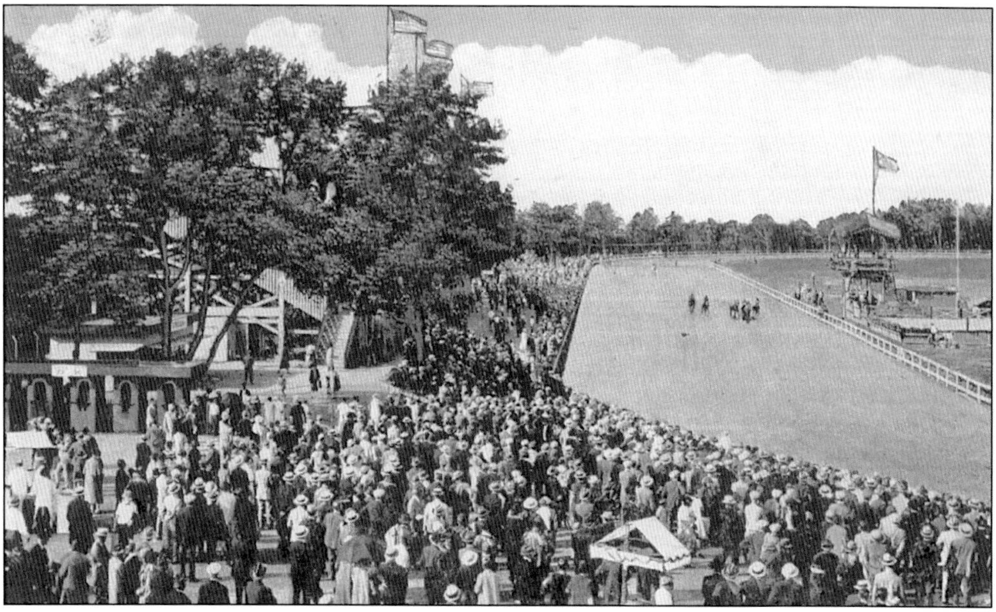

The racetrack at the fairgrounds continues to draw crowds. Horse racing was introduced at the fair from its inception. Fairs had been held in Ebensburg by the Interstate Fair Association. Carrolltown had a fairgrounds and Johnstown had Luna Park. The 1920s was a decade of change; Ebensburg was no longer a point of destination as a resort town.